# 'AS' Level
# ICT

## 3rd edition

# P.M.Heathcote B.Sc.(Hons), M.Sc.

*Published by*
Payne-Gallway Publishers Ltd
26-28 Northgate Street
Ipswich IP1 3DB
Tel   01473 251097
Fax  01473 232758
E-mail  info@payne-gallway.co.uk
Web site  www.payne-gallway.co.uk

2003

# Acknowledgements

I would like to thank the many colleagues and friends who have contributed to this book, and I am grateful to the following Examination Boards for permission to use questions from past examination papers:

The Assessment and Qualifications Alliance (AQA), Edexcel Foundation (Edexcel), Northern Ireland Council for the Curriculum, Examinations and Assessment (NICCEA), Scottish Qualifications Authority (SQA).

The answers in the text and in the teacher's supplement are the sole responsibility of the author and have neither been provided nor approved by the examination boards.

I would also like to thank the following organisations for permission to reproduce copyright material in the form of articles, photographs and artwork:

*Armstrong Healthcare (Figure 4.1)*

*Polartechnics Limited*

*Canon (Figure 28.2)*

*Scanner Technologies Limited (Figure 15.5)*

*Formic Limited*

*The Economist, London*

*Hewlett Packard Company (Figure 28.3)*

*The Guardian*

*Machinery*

*Times Newspapers Limited*

*Network Associates (Figure 8.1)*

Graphics editor and designer: Flora Heathcote
Cover picture © "Valley Deep" reproduced with the kind permission of Neil Canning
Cover photography © Mike Kwasniak, 160 Sidegate Lane, Ipswich
Cover design by Tony Burton

*First edition 2000. Reprinted 2001, 2002.*
*There is no second edition. To avoid confusion, as this is half of 'A' Level ICT 3$^{rd}$ edition, this is the Third edition 2003. Reprinted 2003, 2004.*
10 9 8 7 6 5 4 3
*A catalogue entry for this book is available from the British Library.*

*ISBN 1 904467 14 8*

*Copyright © P.M.Heathcote 2003*

Printed in Malta by
Gutenburg Press Ltd

# Preface

The aim of this book is to provide a comprehensive yet concise textbook covering all the topics studied for the AQA AS Level course in Information and Communications Technology.

The book is divided into 3 sections covering all the material for each paper in a modular scheme such as that offered by the Assessment and Qualifications Alliance (AQA). Within a section, each chapter covers material that can comfortably be taught in one or two lessons, and the chapters are sequenced in such a way that practical sessions can be based around the theory covered in the classroom.

Section 3 contains topics that need to be covered in order for the student to tackle project work. Sections 1 to 3 together cover all the requirements of the AQA AS specification.

Sample examination questions and answers are included at the end of Sections 1 and 2 to show students the type of answers that are likely to score well in the examinations.

Throughout the book, case studies are used to illustrate the points made. Each chapter contains exercises and questions from past examination papers, so that the student can gain plenty of experience in 'exam technique'. Answers to all the questions are available, to teachers only, in a separate Teacher's Supplement which can be downloaded from our web site www.payne-gallway.co.uk

# Contents

# Table of Contents

## SECTION 1

# SECTION 2

# Section 1

## Information: Nature, Role and Context

# Chapter 1 – The Role of ICT

## Computing – a look backwards

Within half a century, computers and information technology have changed the world and affected millions of lives in ways that no one could have foreseen. Here are some of the things that people have said about computers:

"I think there's a world market for maybe five computers." *(Thomas Watson, the chairman of IBM, in 1940)*

"I have travelled the length and breadth of this country and talked with the best people, and I can assure you that data processing is a fad that won't last out the year." *(The editor in charge of business books for Prentice Hall, in 1957)*

"There is no reason why anyone would want to have a computer in their home." *(President of Digital Equipment Corporation, in 1977)*

Contrary to these predictions, computers are transforming the ways in which we learn, communicate, do business, enjoy our leisure and live our everyday lives. Whatever career you pursue in the future, a knowledge of computer skills and concepts is likely to be beneficial or even essential. This course aims to make you competent and confident in the use of computers and to give you an understanding of the uses and impact of computers in society today.

In this chapter we'll look at some of the ways that information technology has changed patterns of work.

## Computers and employment

Ever since the industrial revolution, people have feared that machinery will displace workers, and information technology is no exception.

In spite of dire predictions, however, there is no evidence that the introduction of computers has led to mass unemployment – in fact, overall more jobs have been created by computers than have been displaced by them. Nevertheless, in some areas computers have substantially replaced the workforce. In the 1980s, thousands of factory workers were made redundant by the introduction of robots on the factory floor making everything from biscuits to cars. In the 1990s, thousands of clerical and white-collar workers saw their jobs disappear with the introduction of company databases, desktop publishing, computerised accounting systems and increased automation in banks, building societies and organisations of all kinds, large and small.

## The changing nature of employment

Today, most people no longer work in farms or factories but are found instead in sales, education, health care, banks, insurance firms and law firms. They provide services such as catering, writing computer software, or advertising and delivering goods. These jobs primarily involve working with, creating or distributing new knowledge or information. Knowledge and information work account for about 70% of the labour force in Britain and the US.

Computers have taken over many of the tedious tasks that humans once performed. Consider that only a generation or so ago:

- Taking cash out from your bank account involved queuing at the bank's counter, having the cashier give you the money and manually note the transaction in a book;

- Putting a newspaper together involved picking up individual letters made out of lead and placing them manually in position, with correct spacing achieved by placing a strip of lead ('leading') between lines;

- All long distance calls had to go through an operator who manually made the connection.

The introduction of computers has in many instances led to a change in the types of job available. Many publishing firms feared that desktop publishing would result in fewer jobs in the publishing and printing industries. In fact thousands of new publishing and printing companies have been created in the last decade – a quick flip through the yellow pages under 'Printing' will verify this!

In many cases, workers displaced by computers are retrained to perform computer-related jobs that may be more satisfying than their original jobs.

- A secretary may find it more satisfying to use a word processor to produce high quality output which can be saved and amended, rather than having to retype whole pages because a minor error was made;

- An engineer or draughtsman may find it more satisfying to create designs using a computer-aided design system with complete accuracy, than drawing by hand;

- An accounts clerk may prefer to use an Accounts software package rather than to do the accounts manually.

> ➤ **Discussion: Computerisation often leads to a change in the tasks that a worker has to perform. In some cases the new tasks may be more satisfying, and in other cases, less satisfying. Think of some examples where computerisation has one of these two outcomes.**

## What is Information and Communications Technology?

ICT means using a computer to:

- **Input data** by using an input device such as a keyboard, a bar code reader, voice recognition or magnetic card reader, for example

- **Store the data**, for example on a hard disk, for further processing or for recalling later

- **Process the data** by sorting it, adding it to a total or changing it in some way

- **Output information** in the form of a report, a chart or an answer to a query

- **Communicate information** to someone else by means of the Internet, an e-mail, or a shared network of computers.

An example of this process is the ICT system used in a supermarket. The data about which items are bought is *input* by using a scanner to scan the barcode which identifies an item. The price is *looked up* from the computer's hard disk, where it has previously been *stored*. The receipt is *printed out* and given to the customer. If a customer has bought one packet of Cheerios, then the total quantity in stock is *reduced* by one. A report ordering replacement supplies, if stock is low, is generated at the end of the day and *transmitted* electronically to the supplier.

*Figure 1.1*

---

**Discussion: Think of several other examples of data in an ICT system being input, processed and output.**

---

## Personal qualities for ICT professionals

To rise to the top as an ICT professional, you will need more than technical knowledge and the right qualifications. A browse through a single day's advertisements for jobs in ICT will soon throw up commonly required characteristics in prospective employees. Look at the extracts shown in Figure 1.2 and see what you can pick out.

### Software Installation and Support Engineer

AutoRite develops and distributes software for use in television newsrooms and studios across the world.

We need a young, enthusiastic science or engineering graduate to join our existing technical team. The post will include installing software at sites around the world, providing support for existing clients and assisting with the testing and documentation of software currently under development.

You will need a good knowledge of Novell, Windows and DOS, and some experience with PC hardware. Previous exposure to the television environment is desirable but not essential. More important is the ability to use your own initiative, to be able to cope under pressure, and to be flexible. You must be willing to travel, sometimes long...

...responsibility must be taken for ensuring consistency of data. T... fulfil these requirements a keen and conscientious approach to detail is essential, to ensure

### INFORMIX DATABASE ADMINISTRATOR

You will be responsible for the routine administration, tuning and upkeep of the entire Informix database as well as working closely with the development team.

### BMS
#### Computer Operations Supervisor

Based within a department provid... computer systems in a network environment, the postholder will ... responsibility for the maintenanc... the network and the installation o... hardware and software.

The successful candidate will ha... least two years' proven experienc... PC and network environment, wit... good all-round understanding of ... databases, word processing and spreadsheets. Ideally with formal computer qualifications, s/he will additionally have well-developed interpersonal and negotiation ski... with a customer-focused, flexible approach.

Requirements include an ability to communicate well with a wide range of people, good organisational skills and a

### MICROTEC POST-SALES SUPPORT CONSULTANT

Package up to £22k

MicroTec, based in Bristol, is the market leader in the supply of Management Information Systems to Colleges and Universities. We are looking for a post-sales support consultant to join our successful team which provides application and technical support to our customers. The ideal person will have a background in either Higher or Further Education administration procedures along with excellent communication skills and a real desire to provide a first class service

*Figure 1.2: Careers in ICT*

The particular personal skills required will depend on the type of job being advertised. Skills required for a systems analyst or someone working in user support may differ from those required for a project leader. Typical skills required may include some of the following:

- **Oral communication skills.** Many jobs such as those of a technical support engineer or systems analyst involve working with non-technical end-users. The ability to listen carefully and understand a user's problem or requirements is one of the most important skills required for a systems analyst. You have to act as a liaison between non-technical users and managers on one hand, and technical people on the other. You must be sensitive to the concerns of managers, programmers, end-users and employees.

- **Written communication skills.** You must also be able to communicate the information and proposals in clear English in written reports, and give oral presentations when required. In some jobs you may be required to write clear instructions or user manuals.

- **Patience and understanding.** If you are investigating user requirements you need to be calm and patient in order to prevent users from becoming flustered or stressed.

- **Approachability.** If you are working in user support, for example, it is important that people feel comfortable asking you what may appear to them to be 'stupid questions'.

- **Good analytical skills.** A systems analyst will need to be able to analyse users' requirements even though they are not clearly explained.

- **Problem-solving abilities.** Anyone involved with user support, after-sales service or programming will need well-developed problem-solving abilities.

- **Design skills.** A systems analyst, for example, requires creative and critical thinking as well as the technical knowledge to design new systems.

- **Ability to take the initiative.** This is one of the most highly-rated skills for ICT professionals, according to a recent survey.

- **Management skills.** Project leaders, systems analysts, network administrators or database administrators, among others, need to be able to manage schedules, resources and people. They also need to be able to motivate the people working for them and may need to manage change within an organisation.

**Exam Tip:** **If you are asked to state personal qualities needed by an IT professional working in a certain capacity, you must first state the quality, then explain why it is needed for this particular job.**

## Exercises

1.  Explain what is meant by Information and Communications Technology. (3)
    *AQA ICT1 Qu 1 May 2001*

2.  Three components of an Information Processing System are *input*, *processing* and *output*. State what is meant by:
    > input
    > processing
    > output
    and give an example of each. (6)
    *AQA ICT1 Qu 3 January 2001*

3.  An advertisement for an IT support worker to join the PC support team in a company specifies that the applicant must be "willing to work flexible hours, be able to communicate well orally, have good written skills and get on well with a wide variety of people".
    Explain, giving examples, why **each** of these characteristics is important for someone working in such a role. (8)
    *AQA ICT1 Qu 8 May 2001*

4.  You have been asked to write a job description for a vacancy on a software company's help desk team.
    State, giving a reason for each one, **two** personal qualities that are relevant to the job, which you would ask for in the description. (4)
    *AQA ICT1 Qu 4 January 2003*

# Chapter 2 – ICT in Business and Commerce

No matter what career you take up, you will almost inevitably need to be able to understand and use information technology. ICT has changed and continues to change the way that business is done. This chapter looks at just a few of the businesses that have been revolutionized by the use of technology.

## ICT in banking

The banking industry makes extensive use of ICT in all its operations.

- Using telephone banking, a customer can ring in to check a balance or pay a bill, 24 hours a day, 365 days a year. One major bank has 750 phone banking staff taking up to 50,000 calls a day from 600,000 customers. As soon as the call is answered, the operator asks what service the customer requires, and selects one of 40 items on screen. The customer is then asked for their name and postcode, which enables their details to be retrieved in less than 2 seconds from the mainframe computer in Andover, Hants. As well as handling account queries and transactions, operators can access the bank's central credit-scoring system, empowering them to agree loans and overdrafts on the spot in many cases. If further discussion is needed, the system can arrange for the customer to visit their branch, by automatically booking a slot in the branch's electronic diary.

- Using ATMs, cash can be withdrawn at thousands of cashpoint machines all over the country.

- Using a debit card, purchases can be made at petrol stations, supermarkets, department stores, etc and the customer's account balance checked. If sufficient funds are available, the amount of the purchase is automatically debited to the account.

- Credit cards can be used to make purchases over the phone or via the Internet.

- Millions of cheques are processed each day using MICR (Magnetic Ink Character Recognition).

- Salaries and bills can be paid automatically by Direct Debit.

- Electronic smartcards such as Mondex store money on a microchip which can be topped up just like cash. Goods can be paid for by inserting the card into a reader and typing in the amount to be deducted. Such a card could eventually replace cash.

Banks and other organizations issuing credit cards commonly store details of customer purchases. This enables them to build up a profile of the customer's normal buying habits which can be used in different ways. For example, it makes it easier for the bank to identify a stolen card, if the purchases made are suddenly quite different or more is spent in a short period, than is normal for the customer. It also enables the bank to target certain customers with financial products or services that they wish to sell, and it helps them to make decisions on how much credit to allow a particular customer.

> ➤ **Discussion: What are the advantages to the bank, the employer and the employee of paying salaries by direct debit rather than using cash or cheques?**

## Shopping on the Internet

It is possible to buy almost anything from the latest CD to a skiing holiday or a set of saucepans over the Internet. Customers seeking the best deals can simply type, for example, 'saucepans' into a search engine such as Google and browse through sites to find what they are looking for at the lowest possible price.

*Figure 2.1: Searching for a product on the Internet*

Amazon is an example of a company doing all its business over the Internet, selling books, music, videos and more. Log on by typing in the address www.amazon.co.uk and you will see a screen similar to the following:

*Figure 2.2: A personalised screen on Amazon's site*

Notice that once you have bought anything from Amazon, they will use this information to suggest other purchases that you might like, or, as on the screen shown, offer you the chance to sell the products back once you have finished with them!

You can browse through new releases or search for a particular product. Once you have made your selection, added it to the shopping basket and proceeded to the secure checkout, your order details will be displayed on the screen. You'll receive an e-mail confirming your order the next day, and another when your goods have been dispatched.

## Advantages to business

For a business such as Amazon, this way of doing business has numerous advantages.

- There is a huge saving on overheads: no costly warehouse space, rent, heating or employee facilities;
- The 'virtual shop' can stock every one of the 16,000 or so CDs produced in the last year whereas a conventional store would stock only between 5-10,000;
- The shop has arrangements for 'Just In Time' delivery from its suppliers, so does not get left with books and CDs which it cannot sell;
- It is a valuable market research tool – a list of customers' names and addresses, purchases, likes, dislikes and suggestions can be built up at absolutely no cost and used to improve the service provided.

## Advantages to the customers

There are advantages to the customers, too. They can:

- Visit the shop without having to leave home, at any hour of the day;
- Hear snatches of a song before deciding to buy;
- Shop without being jostled by crowds, having to listen to music that is not to their taste.

Amazon estimate that the proportion of visitors to their site who make a purchase is much higher than for those who respond to a direct mail shot. Many of their customers return to make further purchases.

## Doing the weekly shopping online

It is no longer necessary to fight the crowds in Tesco on a Saturday morning. Customers can register and then do their grocery shopping from the comfort of their own home, to have it delivered for a modest £5.00 charge. To make the weekly order, the customer logs on, types in their user number and password, and has the latest up-to-date list of products and prices downloaded. The customer's shopping list is saved and can be recalled to help compile next week's list, a 'recipe for the week' can be downloaded and ingredients automatically put in the shopping trolley, quantities can be edited and notes added to any product ordered, such as 'Green bananas please'.

*Figure 2.3: Registering and ordering from Tesco Direct*

> ➢ **What kind of people do you think are most likely to use the Internet for their grocery shopping?**
> **What do you think are the advantages and disadvantages?**

## The drawbacks of online commerce

Inevitably, there are drawbacks to buying goods online. For one thing, there are worries about the security of giving a credit card number over the Internet. It is possible that hackers could retrieve thousands of credit card numbers and use them to order goods. Secondly, when companies post up information about new products and services, it is not only their customers who will visit the site – competitors will also be regular visitors, indulging in a little industrial espionage to make sure they don't get left behind.

Thirdly, because Internet sites can be accessed from all over the world, companies have to be aware of the laws regarding data protection in every country. Different countries have different laws regarding the holding and passing on of personal information about individuals.

Several companies have experienced problems with people who have set up web sites using their own company's trademark. They then demand large sums of money for the Web address, or collect credit card numbers from unsuspecting visitors to the site.

## Case study: Fake eBay site

A fake eBay site was launched in December 2002. The site was a replica of the real eBay.com site, but was registered to two men in Lithuania. When people logged on to the site, they were asked for details such as credit card number, bank account, driver's licence and social security numbers.

*Figure 2.4: eBay Home Page – genuine or an impostor?*

## Business-to-Business

One of the major growth areas on the Internet is trading between businesses – for example distribution and delivery of manufactured goods. International carriers can make huge savings by taking orders over the Internet, and customers can not only make savings but also get online information about exactly where their goods are, and when they are delivered.

## Finding new suppliers

The Internet is increasingly being used by businesses to find new suppliers of goods and services. Japan Airlines, for example, has used the Internet to post orders for in-flight materials such as plastic cups. On its Web site it advertises drawings and specifications (such as JAL's logo, which the cups must carry) in order to solicit business from any firm that comes across its site, rather than the usual Japanese suppliers.

## Setting up a Web site

It doesn't take much to set up a Web site – a PC and a modem, and a subscription to a Service Provider of about £10 per month will typically include space of between 5-10Mb to use for your own personal site. Huge, complex sites on the other hand can cost up to £500 per month – but savings can be impressive. BA estimates that if they can sell just 1% of tickets over the Internet, it will save them around £6m a year.

> ➤ **Discussion: Imagine you have been asked to set up a Web site for a small publisher specialising in 'A' Level textbooks. What features would you include on the Web site? Who would benefit from the Web site, and what would the benefits be?**

## Exercises

1. A large clothing retailer has decided to set up an on-line store.

   a) Explain **two** advantages to the retailer of using this method of selling as opposed to selling from a high street shop. (4)

   b) Explain **one** advantage to the customer of using the on-line store rather than a high street shop. (2)

   c) State **one** disadvantage to to the customer of using the on-line store rather than a high street shop. (1)

   d) Describe **two** ways in which the retailer could make use of the Internet to publicise its new service. (4)

   *AQA ICT1 Qu 9 January 2002*

2. Discuss in an essay the concept of a cashless society and the assertion that we will become one. You should refer to steps taken by banks and other financial institutions to move us towards a cashless society and explain why some people feel that it may never be possible to achieve such a goal. (15)

   *London Computing Paper 1 Qu 11 1996*

3. The use of Automated Teller Machines (ATMs), provided by banks and building societies, has become a common way for people to obtain cash.

   a) State

      i. **One** advantage to the bank or building society of installing ATMs. (1)

      ii. **Two** advantages to the customer of using ATMs. (2)

   b) The use of ICT has allowed banks and building societies to keep detailed records of purchases that people make using credit or debit cards. Explain **one** reason why this is a benefit. (2)

   *AQA ICT1 Qu 9 June 2002*

# Chapter 3 – ICT in Manufacturing

## Introduction

In the face of ever-increasing competition from international markets, many labour-intensive manufacturing companies face a stark choice: *automate*, or *evaporate*. Here are some of the many ways in which computers are used in the manufacturing world.

- Order entry and processing systems accept and process customer orders. A fully integrated system will also calculate the quantity and cost of materials needed to make the items ordered, produce reports on any shortages of materials in stock that need to be ordered and raise the purchase order. It will then track the progress of the order through the manufacturing process so that customer queries can be answered.

- Project management software provides management with the information necessary to keep projects within budget and on time. Reports can be produced showing actual costs versus projected costs, and the number of days ahead or behind schedule.

- Expert systems can be used in a multitude of ways from calculating the cost of a new multi-storey office block to detecting when a batch of beer is ready for the next stage of the brewing process.

- Computer-aided design systems are used in thousands of different applications from designing a new jumbo jet to the design of the most aerodynamic material for a ski racer's suit.

- Computer-aided manufacture enables components to be manufactured with the utmost precision.

- Robots are used in every kind of industry from car manufacture to sorting items on an assembly line.

## Case study: The sweet smell of success

Bass the brewers has built a machine that can perform the daunting task of smelling beer and deciding if it's up to snuff. The technology that makes this possible is neural computing, the revolutionary process that mimics the way the human brain works. The artificial nose makes a complex series of judgements based on the electrochemical stimuli received by its gas sensors, and could save the brewers a fortune.

"By detecting an over-active yeast or a weak crop of hops at an early stage in the fermentation process, the nose could save us having to throw away a whole batch – 345,600 pints of beer", explained Ian Morris of Bass.

It is not just brewers who are interested in the artificial nose. Manufacturers of instant coffee, perfume and other aromatic products are spending huge sums, in co-operation with researchers at several universities, to build a better-than-human olfactory sensor.

*Source: Garth Alexander, The Sunday Times 19 September 1993*

## Computer-aided design (CAD)

CAD systems allow designers and engineers to create designs on screen for thousands of products ranging from the tiniest computer chip to bridges, buildings and aeroplanes. The software allows users to create 3-dimensional 'solid' models with physical characteristics like volume, weight and centre of gravity. The models can be rotated and viewed from any angle, edited and stored. The computer can perform calculations to evaluate its performance under different stresses, or crash-test a new design of car before it is even manufactured.

Animation software can be used to enable a viewer to 'walk through' a 3-D model of say, a building, that exists only in the computer's memory.

CAD systems ('vector-based' graphics packages) store data in a different way from Paint ('bitmapped') packages. Paint packages store a picture as a two dimensional array, with each element of the array representing one pixel (dot) on the screen. A CAD package stores drawings as a collection of objects such as lines and circles, each represented by specifying coordinates, thickness and so on. This has many advantages, including the following:

- Drawings can be scaled or resized without distortion;

- Drawings are device independent; a drawing created using one type of VDU can be transferred to a screen of a different resolution without distortion;

- The files created tend to be smaller than for equivalent bitmapped images;

- Drawings can be made with a very high degree of accuracy by specifying coordinates.

*Figure 3.1: A simple drawing being made in AutoCAD*

## Computer-aided Manufacturing (CAM)

Computer-aided design is often linked to *computer-aided manufacturing* (CAM). CAD/CAM systems are used in the design and manufacture of thousands of applications from aeroplane and car parts to office furnishings and sports equipment. When the design of the product is completed, the specifications are input directly into a program that controls the manufacturing of parts.

A great advantage of these systems is their flexibility: individual items can be manufactured to a customer's exact specifications.

## Case study: Subcontracting sector uses ICT

Precimax was founded in 1988 and has grown to a 30-employee company with an anticipated turnover in 1997 of £1.4 million. It offers a full manufacturing service from initial design through to supply of fully-finished components and assemblies. Production is predominantly on CNC (computer numeric control) turning and machining centres, and programs can be created from customer drawings or directly from CAD via modem or disk. Batches range from one-off up to 5000, but are more typically in the 50 to 500 bracket. In size, turned components measure up to 250mm diameter.

Precimax is a major supplier of components for train braking and door systems and is currently producing parts for use in the platform edge doors for London Underground's new Jubilee Line extension. It also has a contract with a postal equipment manufacturer for monthly deliveries of rollers and other parts for letter-sorting machines.

Precimax uses Datatrack for Windows for keeping track of its annual 3000 orders. The system includes estimating and quoting, sales order processing, purchasing, job costing and delivery. The commercial director commented "A system to handle this level of business is absolutely essential. Without it, we would be lost. It enables us to control cost and better understand our trading and manufacture. It gives us accurate information, so we can communicate with our customers on costs and deliveries quickly and with confidence."

*Source: Machinery 5/19 December 1997*

➢ **Discussion: In what major ways are computers being used at Precimax?**

# Robots

The word 'robot' comes from the Czech word 'robotnik', meaning slave. Robots come in many different forms and shapes, but they all have the same basic components:

- Sensors, which capture information from the environment;
- A microprocessor to process the information;
- Actuators to produce movement or alter the environment in some way, for example by turning an electronic switch on or off.

Robots may be used for spray painting, spot welding and car assembly. They are also used as security devices inside homes and office buildings, as vehicles in space exploration, as intelligent wheelchairs for disabled people, and as underwater maintenance workers for oil rigs. Hundreds of applications use robots in one form or another.

# Why use robots?

- Robots can tirelessly perform repetitive and monotonous tasks, lift heavy loads and reach long distances. They are used, for example, by the US Navy to scrape and repaint ships.
- Labour costs can be substantially reduced. Robots are widely used in car manufacturing as well as in many other industries including printing and publishing. Robots can carry tons of paper coming off presses, bind and trim books and apply book covers. It has been estimated that each industrial robot will replace an average of six workers.
- Quality of work is consistent. A robot is never tired or bored or having an off day.
- Robots can work 24 hours a day, do not need breaks and do not go on strike.
- They can work in total darkness, at low temperatures, thus saving on electricity bills.
- They can be used in hazardous areas, such as fume-filled rooms or radioactive environments. Tests are currently being carried out to set robots to work on clearing mine fields.

➢ **Discussion: Robots are immensely expensive to buy and install, and need to be used for a high proportion of each day in order to recoup the cost. What happens when demand for a product slumps? Would a manufacturer be better advised to stick with manual workers, who can be laid off and rehired when times improve?**

## Exercises

1.  Computers and information technology are widely used in manufacturing industries. Give **three** different examples of their use in manufacturing, and in each case discuss
    (a)  The benefits to the company, the customers and the employees
    (b)  The possible drawbacks to the company, the customers and the employees. (12)
    *New question*

2.  Research an application of computers and ICT in manufacturing. Describe briefly the end product, the reasons for using ICT and the software and hardware used. (8)
    What group of people benefits most from the use of ICT in the application you have described? Is any other group of people disadvantaged? Briefly explain your answers. (4)
    *New question*

3.  Describe briefly **one** application for robots in industry. (2)
    Explain **two** advantages of using robots in the application you describe. (2)
    *New question*

4.  Some manufacturers are deciding to re-employ people on the shop floor and retire their robots. Give **one** argument to support this action and **one** argument against it. (2)
    *AEB Computing Paper 1 Qu 3 1996*

5.  The use of computer-controlled machinery in manufacturing and product assembly has become widespread. Give **two** benefits for the manufacturer, other than financial, and **two** implications for the employees of such automation. (4)
    *NEAB AS Computing Qu 3 1995*

# Chapter 4 – ICT in a Caring Society

## Introduction

In this chapter we'll take a look at some of the ways in which information technology is used in medicine, and the benefits that it has brought to people with disabilities.

## Computers in medicine

Computers have had a very significant impact on the quality of medical services. For example:

- Medical records stored in hospital information systems improve the quality of patient care. They are more accurate, they can keep track of prescriptions and tests administered, hospital admissions, dietary requirements and so on. Records are less likely to go astray than manual records and they can be made available to authorised people at any location.

- Databases of organ donors and patients needing transplants mean that when an organ becomes available, a match can quickly be found.

- Computerised devices such as pacemakers, artificial organs and prostheses (artificial limbs) have enabled tens of thousands of people to live longer and have a fuller life.

- Computerised monitoring devices can keep a 24-hour watch on critically ill patients and sound the alarm if vital signs change for the worse.

- Expert medical systems can help to diagnose diseases often at remote locations far from the care of a specialist. Vast amounts of data on symptoms and illnesses are stored in a 'knowledge base' which can help a doctor to arrive at a preliminary diagnosis.

- Surgeons can perform operations at remote locations using a remotely controlled robot arm. (See case study below.)

- Computers can model new drugs and test their effects, significantly reducing the time taken for new drugs to come onto the market.

---

### Case study: Robot surgeon operates

Surgeons in the US have successfully used computers and robots to take part in operations in a different continent.

Researchers from the influential Johns Hopkins University in Baltimore have revealed that they now have the technology to carry out "telesurgery" on patients anywhere in the world.

Already 17 patients undergoing surgery at Rome's Policlinico Casilino University have benefited from the technological advances.

US doctors used a combination of computers, telecommunications, videoconferencing and advanced surgical robots to guide surgery that was actually being carried out thousands of miles away.

None of the patients suffered any adverse effects.

Surgical robots augment a surgeon's ability by scaling down range of motion, providing three-dimensional vision and eliminating hand tremor.

The robotic systems consist of a surgeon's viewing and control console and a cart with robotic arms that sits next to the patient.

*Source: BBC news www.news.bbc.co.uk 5 June 2001*

---

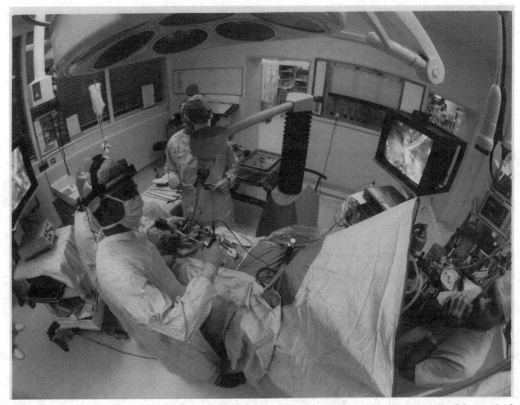

*Figure 4.1: The robot surgeon operates (Photograph by permission of Armstrong Healthcare Ltd)*

---

## Case study: Computer simulation cuts clinical trial cost of new drugs

The APACHE Simulator—a group of integrated clinical trial simulation services from APACHE's Health Outcomes Research division—is designed to help pharmaceutical and medical device manufacturers "cut clinical trial costs and boost effectiveness," notes Knaus. "Our goal is to help the industry bring consumers safe, effective new therapies more quickly and affordably.

Unlike the 'Space Cowboys' simulator, the APACHE Simulator isn't a machine per sé. It's APACHE experts using unique and proprietary databases such as the APACHE HIV Insight® database—and proprietary computer models such as the APACHE III methodology—to create powerful computer models that help APACHE clients identify what a particular drug or device can, should, and will do, in the real world.

By modeling and simulating all aspects of new and existing drug and device testing, evaluation and marketing—before the actual clinical trial begins—the APACHE Simulator enables manufacturers to eliminate unnecessary clinical trial costs.

*Source: www.apache-msi.com 31 August 2000*

---

## Expert systems used in medical diagnosis

Expert systems are computer programs that attempt to replicate the performance of a human expert on some specialised reasoning task. Also called **knowledge-based systems**, they are able to store and manipulate knowledge so that they can help a user to solve a problem or make a decision.

An expert system of this type is being developed in Australia to assist doctors in the diagnosis of melanoma, one of the most common types of cancer which manifests itself as dark patches similar to moles on the skin. In order to build the expert system, 45 different cancerous melanomas and 176 similar but benign non-melanomas were photographed and the images processed to remove hair, oil bubbles, etc. to extract the essential features. From these pictures and the known correct diagnoses, a set of 'rules' can be programmed into the expert system so that when presented with a photograph of a new skin lesion, the computer can make a diagnosis with a high degree of accuracy. The next step is to develop a real-time device.

1.  An image of the lesion is captured by the Polarprobe® camera system and downloaded onto the Polarprobe® computer system.

2.  Calibration is performed. Image preprocessing follows to mask out hairs and oil bubbles and to identify the boundaries of the lesion.

3.  The image is analysed by the Skin Polarprobe® software algorithms to extract diagnostic features of the lesion that facilitate the identification of melanoma using multiple discriminants such as colour segmentation, lesion patterns and geometry.

4.  The computer algorithms, developed in collaboration with CSIRO, compare the values with stored values inside the computer database. The stored values are based on a large amount of empirical data which has been collected in a data library by Polartechnics and the Sydney Melanoma Unit, Royal Prince Alfred Hospital.

5.  The Skin Polarprobe® computes the data using the detection algorithms and a decision is made as to whether the lesion is a melanoma or not.

6.  The physician is informed of the computer's diagnosis immediately.

*(Reproduced with permission from Polartechnics Ltd, Sydney, Australia)*

> ➤ **Discussion: What are the benefits and drawbacks of using such a system for the diagnosis of melanomas?**

## Computers and the disabled

About ten percent of people in Britain have some kind of disability. For many of them, new computer technology can dramatically improve their quality of life, their ability to communicate and their opportunities for independence and employment.

## Case study: Eyes in the sky

A satellite navigation system for the blind is expected to transform the way visually handicapped people get around towns and cities, and will make travelling to unfamiliar places overseas less of an ordeal and more of a pleasure. It is to be tested by several visually handicapped people in Birmingham.

The system hinges on the Global Positioning System (GPS) of satellites encircling the earth. Receivers picking up the signals from the satellites can calculate precisely where they are on earth. People from yachtsmen to motorists using in-car navigation devices now use the system.

The blind person's version is essentially a portable computer plus a satellite receiver. The computer, fitted with a speech synthesiser so that it can 'talk' to the user, contains electronic Ordnance Survey maps of an area or city. A blind person trained on a keyboard taps into the system his or her location and where they want to go, and it automatically plots the route.

Once this has been done, the user is ready to go and steps out of the house. The computer will then say things like "Walk 100 yards, turn left and then right". It will also inform you of landmarks on the way, such as a fire station, and mention the numbers of houses or buildings on a street.

*Source: Nick Nuttall, The Sunday Times, 27 March 1996.*

Today there are systems based on personal computers that can talk, listen, teach, communicate and translate. People with control over just an eyelid or a toe, for example, can communicate by means of the proper equipment attached to a PC

For example:

- Scanners can convert printed text to verbal output for the visually impaired;
- Voice recognition equipment converts speech to printed or displayed output for the hearing impaired;
- People with physical disabilities can use special pointing devices, pens or touch screens instead of keying devices for interacting with a computer;
- Vision systems have sensors built into special glasses;
- Implanted computerised devices can help physically impaired people to become more mobile.

## Exercises

1.  Computers and microprocessors are being used to help the physically disabled in many different ways. For each of **two** different types of handicap, briefly describe a way in which patients can be helped by this new technology. (4)

    *AEB Computing Paper 1 Qu 1 1995*

2.  Briefly describe **two** examples of how computers could aid surgeons performing operations. You must show clearly the role of the computer in your answer. (4)

    *AEB Computing Paper 1 Qu 6 1997*

3.  Research an application of information technology in one of the following areas: medicine, the home, education, helping people to overcome disabilities, environmental work. Prepare and deliver a short presentation. Your sources could include magazines and newspapers, TV programs such as Tomorrow's World, the Internet and library textbooks. (10)

    *New question*

# Chapter 5 – ICT in Education

## Computers in schools

In the 1980s money was found to put at least one microcomputer in every school in Britain. Only a few years ago in the late 1990s, computers seemed like the answer to all education's problems. All schools in the UK were connected to the Internet and huge sums of public money were spent on increasing the numbers of computers in schools.

Computers and ICT can bring benefits such as:

- The use of productivity tools like word processors, desktop publishing and spreadsheet software for use in projects and other school activities;

- The use of interactive teaching packages available on CD for many different subjects;

- Access to the Internet and thousands of online databases;

- Distance learning facilities for those who are unable to attend school or college, or for minority subjects (such as Russian or Japanese) which do not justify a full-time teacher in a single school;

- Links with other schools or colleges, or with industrial or business organisations;

- Special facilities available for students with disabilities – for example partially-sighted students may be able to change text size and background colour, blind people can use text-to-speech conversion packages, people with arthritis or cerebral palsy may control the computer by speaking to it instead of using the keyboard or mouse.

## Will computers replace teachers?

The fear is sometimes expressed that technology will make teachers redundant, and that pupils will lose the skills of social interaction as they become more and more isolated in their own little 'cyber-world'. Computer-aided learning packages have many advantages:

- Students can work at their own pace, repeating sections they don't understand;

- Computers are endlessly patient;

- The material is presented in a consistent way – you are not dependent on the skills of a particular teacher;

- Once the package is paid for, it can be cost-effective as fewer teachers are required.

At the same time, there are disadvantages in this method of learning. It can be very boring sitting in front of a computer screen, and a computer may not motivate students in the same way as a good teacher.

## Case study: An educational experiment

Professor Angrist, an economics professor at the Massachusetts Institute of Technology, conducted an experiment with schools in Israel to compare classes taught with and without information technology. He found that in fourth grade maths, where computers were used for instruction with one group of pupils but not with a similar control group, the children who had no computers actually scored better in test scores.

In a BBC interview on 26 December 2002 Sherry Turkle commented "You can get the machine to give you the questions at exactly your level, know exactly your level, drill you at exactly your level, and gradually introduce new material to bring you to a new level, and that's a great thing. But it's not such a great thing if you don't feel that there's also a person who is on your side and who is mentoring you and who cares about you."

> ➤ **Discussion: Do you think that computers could replace teachers for at least part of the timetable? Would this be desirable from the point of view of the school administration, the teachers, and the pupils?**

## Multimedia in schools

*Multimedia* is the combination of several elements such as text, graphics, animation, video and sound using a computer. To create or run multimedia software, a fairly powerful computer with a large memory, hard disk and a CD ROM drive is desirable. There are hundreds of CD ROMs available for every level of the National Curriculum, on virtually any topic from 'talking stories' for 6-year-olds, to The Complete Physics from BTC, which shows quality animations of solar eclipses and 'Algorithms and Data Structures' from Payne-Gallway Publishers for 'A' Level Computing students. (Figure 5.1.)

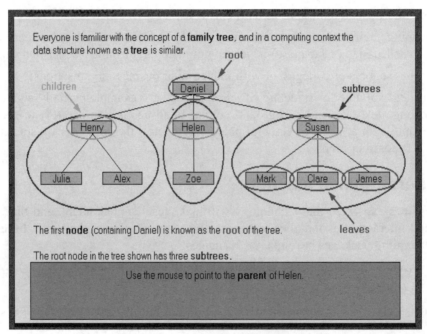

*Figure 5.1: Interactive multimedia tutorial*

## The Internet in schools

The Internet is without doubt a wonderful source of information on every imaginable topic. Using a search engine or web addresses which you have been given, it is possible to look up useful material for essays or projects for almost any subject. But giving pupils unlimited access to the Internet can bring its own problems. It is all too easy to spend hours aimlessly surfing the Internet without finding any really relevant information, which is simply a waste of time. Pupils may illegally download huge music files which fill up available disk space, or they may download material which contains viruses. Some students may cut and paste information from a web site into their homework without even reading it. Skills of reading information and critically judging whether it is relevant to what you want, up-to-date, accurate and impartial, are still essential but are sometimes ignored.

A further worry for teachers and parents is that children may be unloading unsuitable material, or even putting themselves in danger by contacting strangers in Internet chat rooms. The FBI in the US has statistics showing that the number of children lured away from home by people they have met online rose from 113 in 1996 to 1498 in 1999 and is still rising.

## Restricting access

One solution to the problem of students downloading unsuitable material or logging on to undesirable sites is to use filtering software, which can block access to inappropriate sites and content. Some filters only allow children to send and receive e-mail from specified addresses. However, not all filters work very well in blocking out all unsuitable material and they may block access to legitimate sites.

## Exercises

1.  A school wishes to allow its students unrestricted access to the Internet for research work during their lunchtimes. The headteacher is concerned that this might cause problems.

    State two problems that the headteacher might be concerned about, and for each one explain a measure that could be taken to prevent the problem. (6)

    *AQA IT01 Qu 7 January 2001*

2.  Describe briefly **five** ways in which information technology can aid pupils studying subjects **other** than computing or information technology. (5)

    *New question*

3.  Give **three** advantages and **three** disadvantages of computer-aided learning packages compared with conventional classroom teaching. (6)

    *New question*

4.  A local college has started running its courses on-line.

    Describe:

    (a) **Two** advantages to a learner of following an on-line course (4)

    (b) **One** disadvantage to a learner of following an on-line course (2)

    (c) **Two** advantages to the course organisers, at the college, of providing a course on-line. (4)

    *AQA ICT1 Qu 10 January 2003*

# *Chapter 6 – Role of Communication Systems*

## Introduction

The late 20<sup>th</sup> century became known as the 'information age'. It would be impossible to conduct modern day businesses without the use of communication technologies such as the telephone, fax machine and computer communications networks. Communications and computer technology have become inextricably linked, resulting in *telecommunications*, the transmission of data of all kinds (text, graphics, sound and video) over a variety of different communication channels such as public telephone lines, private cables, microwave and satellite. In this chapter we'll look at some of the important developments in communications.

## The Internet

The Internet is the largest wide area network in the world. In fact it is not a single network, but a collection of thousands of computer networks throughout the world. These linked networks are of two types:

- LAN (Local Area Network), covering an office block or University campus, for example;
- WAN (Wide Area Network) connecting computers over a wide geographical area, even over several countries.

All LANs and some WANs are owned by individual organisations. Some WANs act as **service providers**, and members of the public or businesses can join these networks for a monthly charge.

There is no central authority or governing body running the Internet; it started with an initial 4 computers in 1969 and grew over the next ten years to connect 200 computers in military and research establishments in the US. Today there are several million host computers, any of which could be holding the information you are looking for, and as many as 50 million people connected, any of whom could be future customers, friends or problem-solvers.

## The World Wide Web

The Web is a collection of pages stored on computers throughout the world, and joined by *hypertext* links. A hypertext link enables you to click on a word or graphic, and be taken automatically to the related Web page. It is the fastest-growing part of the Internet, owing much of its popularity to Web-browsing software such as Netscape, which enables you to quickly find references to any particular topic.

## Electronic bulletin boards

Electronic bulletin boards are Internet sites for groups of people with similar interests to exchange information and discuss issues. Bulletin boards are used by thousands of different user groups from University 'Open Learning' providers and software manufacturers' user groups to less savoury groups interested in terrorist activities or paedophilia.

## Intranets

An Intranet is a company-wide network run along the lines of the World Wide Web, making it possible to share documents, databases and applications. Intranets have the potential to revolutionise the way that organisations share information internally, just as the Internet will revolutionise the way that businesses communicate with external suppliers, customers and consultants.

The software to implement Intranets is already available. The latest Microsoft Office suite will let you surf Word and Excel documents, reading them in a local Web site just as if they had been produced by a Web page designer.

## Electronic mail (E-mail)

E-mail systems allow you to send memos, letters and files containing data of all types from your computer to any other computer with an e-mail address and a modem, simply by typing the recipient's name and pressing the 'Send' button.

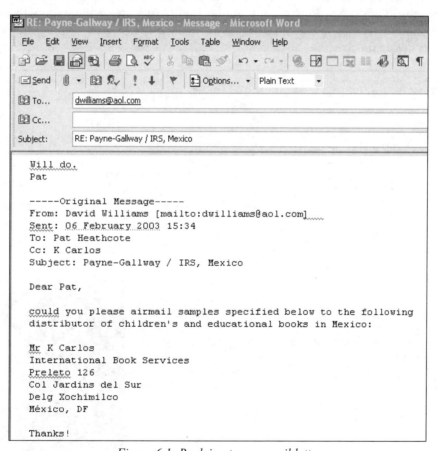

*Figure 6.1: Replying to an e-mail letter*

## E-mail facilities

Typical e-mail software such as Microsoft Outlook allows you to

- Type the address of a recipient in the **To...** box, write and send a message
- Read an e-mail that has been sent to you and then reply to it by clicking the **Reply** button, without having to type the recipient's address again. The original message appears under the reply, as in Figure 6.1
- Send a copy of the e-mail to any number of other recipients by putting their addresses in the **Cc...** box
- Forward an e-mail to someone else, with a message – for example Pat in the e-mail above may wish to ask someone else to deal with the request for samples
- Prioritise the message. Clicking on the **Importance:High** icon (an exclamation mark in Figure 6.1) will put this symbol beside the message in the list of new messages in the Inbox so that the recipient knows it is important.
- Attach a file such as a spreadsheet, a digital photograph, or another document. Clicking on the paperclip icon next to the **Send** button in Figure 6.1 will bring up a window in which you can select which file to attach. The recipient can then either save the file to their own hard drive or open it to view without saving it.

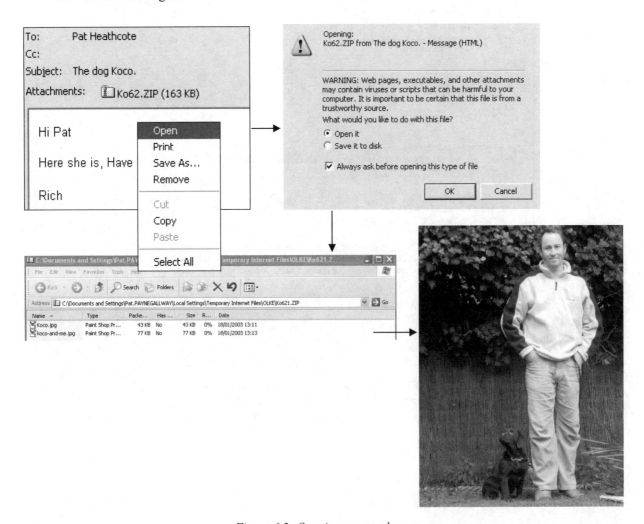

*Figure 6.2: Opening an attachment*

## Advantages and disadvantages of e-mail

E-mail has many advantages over both ordinary mail and the telephone. For example:

- A message can be sent anywhere in the world at the price of a local call, without having to leave your desk;
- The same message can be sent simultaneously to a group of people;
- The message will arrive in a few minutes, and can be picked up the next time the recipient looks at their e-mail;
- It is very easy to send a reply to an e-mail as soon as it is received, using a 'Reply' button;
- Large files such as spreadsheets and graphics can be sent as attachments.

Of course there is always a flip side – e-mails bring disadvantages such as:

- Information overload – some business people receive so many e-mails they find it hard to reply to them all and also get on with their other work;
- Viruses can be attached to e-mails, either accidentally or deliberately, and infect your computer;
- Sometimes important e-mails may be overlooked and not be read by the recipient if they are among several dozen received in a day, and the sender may be unaware of this;
- Employees may spend time sending personal e-mails to their friends when they should be working;

> **Discussion: Think of some other disadvantages of e-mail.**

## Case study: Monitoring employee e-mail

Monitoring employees e-mail is considered by many to be unethical and an invasion of privacy, but is considered legitimate by many companies who claim they need to know that their facilities are being used to further  business goals. Some also argue that they need to be able to search electronic mail messages for evidence of illegal activities, racial discrimination or sexual harassment. Others argue that the company needs access to business information stored in e-mails, just as if it were stored in filing cabinets.

> **Discussion: Many companies have stated policies regarding e-mail. Do you think employees should be granted privacy, or should companies have the right to monitor e-mail?**

## Hardware required to access the Internet

The basic hardware needed to set up online communications is a computer, a modem and a telephone line. The overall speed of online communication is governed by the speed of the modem and the speed of the communications link. An ordinary telephone line is the cheapest but not the fastest link. An ISDN line has a greater bandwidth and will send data much faster.

A **modem** (**Mo**dulator/**DEM**odulator) converts the data from your computer from digital form (0s and 1s) into analogue or wave form so that it can be sent over the telephone line, which was originally designed for speech. Modems typically transmit data at rates of between 28,800bps (bits per second) and 56,600bps. A second modem at the receiving end translates the analogue signal back into digital form.

*Figure 6.3: Modem*

Many computers come equipped with an internal **modem card** in one of the free expansion slots inside the computer.

## Software and services required to access the Internet

To connect to the Internet you need to sign up with an **Internet Service Provider (ISP)** who will supply you with a user account on a host computer and a complete software package that includes:

- A browser which enables you to download and view pages from the World Wide Web (see Chapter 22);
- Communications software which allows your computer to transmit and receive data using the Internet TCP/IP communications protocol (see Chapter 22);
- An e-mail package to enable you to send and receive e-mails;
- A newsreader which you use to read and post messages to the Usenet groups;
- An FTP client which you can use to download and upload files and software.

A good ISP should provide you with all of these at no charge. There are hundreds of ISPs in the UK including Virgin and BT who charge a monthly rate for unlimited access, and Freeserve from the High Street retailer Dixons, which is free. (Further details on http://www.freeserve.net ).

- Some users may want to install filtering software which blocks access to certain sites and let you set times during which the net can or cannot be used.

## Telephones

It seems incredible that only a decade or so ago, mobile phones were almost unknown. In little more than a decade, the mobile phone has changed from a yuppie toy to a vital piece of kit for 40% of Britons.

---

## Case Study: The Internet revolution

"We're at the beginning of the Internet revolution", says Brian Greasley, general manager of BT Cellnet's internet service provider, Genie Internet. He means that mobile phones, rather than the computers we've been using so far, are going to deliver that revolution.

"If you look at the Internet today, it's based on a PC platform of 350 million PCs worldwide. If you roll that figure forward to 2003, there will be around 400-500 million PCs. But there will be one billion mobile phones, and every one of them will have an Internet browser built in."

Greasley is referring, at least in part, to new "internet phones". They send information using a new standard called Wireless Application Protocol (WAP).

The new mobile phones will be used not just for talking – we'll use them to send messages, find out the latest news and football scores, access information and use services on the Internet.

And, here's the crunch, the amount of "bandwidth" these phones have – the amount of information they can receive or send in a second – will eclipse today's conventional phones. This summer, you could have the equivalent of an expensive ISDN line to your mobile phone. In the near future, you will quite easily have the kind of power that will make receiving high quality sound and video on the move quite straightforward and rewarding, reshaping the way we get information and entertainment.

*Source: Neil McIntosh, The Guardian 27 January 2000*

---

## Facsimile transmission (Fax)

The popularity of fax machines has exploded over the past decade. They are now regarded as indispensable by even the smallest business and have played a large part in speeding up business transactions. A fax machine scans and digitises images (text or graphics) on a page and transmits them in analogue form over a telephone line to another fax machine, which then reproduces a copy of the image on a piece of paper.

*Figure 6.4: Fax machine*

## Voice mail

Voice mail is a more sophisticated version of the telephone answering machine. A voice mail system can act as an automated switchboard so that when you dial a company number, you may hear a message along the lines of 'Hello – this is the Customer Service Department of XYZ. If you would like information on new services, press 1. If you have a query about your bill, press 2. For other information, press 3.'

A voice mail system also allows you to leave a recorded message for someone who is absent from the office. The recipient can then save it, delete it or forward it to someone else on another extension.

## Teleconferencing

Teleconferencing allows people in different physical locations to exchange ideas and information interactively using either the telephone or e-mail. A more advanced form of teleconferencing is videoconferencing, which allows participants to see and hear one another. A videoconferencing system includes video cameras, special microphones, large television monitors and a computer with a special device called a *codec* that can convert analogue video images and sound waves into digital signals and compress them for transfer over digital telephone lines. (An ISDN – Integrated Services Digital Network – line with a high bandwidth is required to transmit video.) At the other end, another computer reconverts the digital signals to analogue for displaying on the receiving monitor. Such systems are familiar from television programmes in which people on the other side of the Atlantic are interviewed from a studio in London, for example.

Microcomputer-based desktop videoconferencing systems are also available, where users can see each other and simultaneously work on the same document.

## Exercises

1. Many organisations have adopted e-mail as a method of communication only to find that it can have disadvantages.

   Describe **three** disadvantages of the use of e-mail, other than contracting viruses, for business communication. (6)

   *AQA IT01 Qu 6 June 2002*

2. What do the following features, available with most e-mail software, allow the user to do?

   (a) Forward

   (b) Reply

   (c) Send/Receive

   (d) Attach

   (e) Prioritise (4)

   *AQA IT01 Qu 6 January 2002*

3. A company specialises in organising international conferences for doctors. The company has decided to make use of the Internet for advertising and organising the conferences.

   (a) State, with reasons, the hardware that the company would need, in addition to their PC and printer, in order to connect to the Internet. (4)

   (b) State the purpose of the following software when used for the Internet:

   　　(i)　　Browser

   　　(ii)　　Editor

   　　(iii)　　E-mail software (3)

   (c) Explain **three** potential advantages for this company of using the Internet as opposed to conventional mail/telephone systems. (6)

   *NEAB IT01 Qu 7 1999*

4. Facsimile and computer based electronic mailing systems are different forms of message systems.

   (a) For each of these systems, describe **two** of the facilities offered. (4)

   (b) Discuss the relative strengths and weaknesses of each of these systems. (10)

   *NEAB IT01 Qu 7 1998*

# *Chapter 7 – ICT at Home*

## Introduction

Having an Internet connection at home may soon be as common as having a television. Indeed computers and digital broadcasting are gradually converging, with technology now available which allows consumers to buy a single box which enables them to watch hundreds of TV channels, play along with televised game shows, order goods and access the Internet. Via a set-top box containing a 40Gb hard disk, a processor and a digital receiver, users can store about 20 hours of digitally-received programmes onto the hard disk. The device requires a **modem** to connect the telephone cable to the Internet, and a **browser** for viewing Web pages operating over a broadband **Digital Subscriber Line (DSL)**.

*Figure 7.1: A set-top box*

Set-top boxes include the following features:

- they include an MP3 player for listening to and storing MP3 music
- they allow pausing and digital recording of live television programmes
- they include a keyboard for writing and receiving e-mails and faxes
- the screen can be split between TV and the Internet
- viewers will be able to watch digital TV and record to an integral hard disk at the same time
- 3D games can be played over the Internet
- they give access to interactive services such as online shopping or banking, or online voting with instant results. Future game shows with *Ask the Audience* features may attract greater participation with potentially 15 million online viewers who do not have to get up from the sofa in order to make that phone call
- the screen can have hot-spots with more specific information you can view and access, e.g. more localised weather forecasts or more information about news reports
- movies can be downloaded to enjoy when you have free time

---

### Statistics on Internet usage

Over the period July to September 2002 an estimated 11.4 million households in the UK could access the Internet from home, according to a recent survey. Among those who had accessed the Internet for personal use just over three quarters of adults (76%) had used it for e-mail, 71% used it to find information about goods and services and 36% used it to find education-related information. Of those purchasing goods and services, the most popular purchases were flights and holiday accommodation (31%, tickets for events (24%) and books and magazines (20%).

*Source: www.statistics.gov.uk*

---

## Using a search engine

It's easy to spend hours browsing the Web, jumping from page to page. To look up a particular topic you can use a search engine. There are several search engines such as google.com, yahoo.com, askjeeves.com and altavista.com.

Suppose you wanted to find out information about set-top boxes.

- Load Internet Explorer by double-clicking the icon.

- Click in the Address box to select the current address.

- Type **www.google.com** and press **Go**.

- In the Search box, type **set-top box** and click **Google Search**.

You will be presented with the first ten results, out of several hundred thousand.

---

### Case study: About Google

Google was founded in 1998 by two friends from Stanford University. By the start of 2002, 150 million queries were being entered into the Google search box every day. Many people think it is the best search engine on the Web.

A search engine creates an index as it "crawls" over the Web. Some Web crawlers index the pages by counting the number of times particular words appear in the code. For example, if a user enters the words "Friends Reunited" in the search box, a page containing the word "Friends Reunited" 10 times would appear above one containing the word 5 times. However, this makes it easy for unscrupulous Web page editors to fool the search engine into giving them high rankings. They repeat the same word many times, either on the page or hidden in the code.

Google works differently. It also looks at the contents of a page but it tries to see it from a user's point of view. For example, if a word appears in bold type on the page, it ranks that word as being particularly important for that page. If a word does not display on the page, it ignores it. Google also counts the number of links from other sites to that page, and how popular those other sites are.

These techniques help it to find the sites that are most likely to be useful to the user.

---

## Uses of the Internet

What else do people use the Internet for, besides e-mail, finding education-related information and ordering goods? Unfortunately one of the major uses of the Internet is to download unsavoury, pornographic or illegal material, or to commit fraud in one form or another. However there are hundreds of legitimate reasons why people log on. One phenomenally successful site has been **Friends Reunited**, which has turned Steve and Julie Pankhurst, the couple who founded, it into multimillionaires. In early 2003 the couple decide to put the site up for sale and are considering offers of £30 million from big Internet companies keen to acquire their database of 6.7 million e-mail addresses.

---

### Case study: Friends Reunited

Friends Reunited has a database of more than 45,000 schools. It invites members of the public to sign up with their old school and post an update on their lives – so far, more than 6 million have signed up.

Anyone who wants to make contact with an old acquaintance can then pay £5 for their e-mail address. Although only a tiny fraction of subscribers pay to obtain an e-mail address, the venture is hugely profitable.

Despite its popularity, the site has been blamed by marriage guidance counselors for wrecking relationships, as people contact childhood sweethearts.

Trade Unions also complained that message boards were full of defamatory remarks about teachers. One retired teacher from Doncaster sued and won £1,250.

*Source: Andrew Clark, The Guardian January 2003*

*Figure 7.3: The Friends Reunited site*

## Teleworking

Teleworking involves carrying out work away from the office and communicating with the employer through the use of computer and telecommunications equipment. Often teleworkers are based at home, but they can also work from telecentres, satellite offices or even on the move. A recent study by Sultzer Infra CBX found that there are over 1 million employees teleworking today in the UK. 52% of the working population expect to be homeworking by the year 2010.

(www.si-cbx.com/teleworking/twbody.html)

## Benefits of teleworking

- It may be easier to concentrate on work in a quiet environment at home than in a noisy office;
- Workers save on commuting time and costs, with the associated environmental benefits of keeping cars off the roads;
- Workers enjoy greater flexibility, and can arrange their working hours around other commitments such as picking children up from school;
- Employers save on the costs of office space and overheads such as heat and light;
- People in different locations can work in a team;
- People can be recruited from a much wider geographical area;
- People who are not able to take employment in standard office hours can be recruited.

## The problems of teleworking

- Management may fear difficulties in controlling a workforce that is not in the office;
- There is a problem in ensuring that remote staff understand corporate goals and retain a sense of loyalty to the organisation;
- Employees may feel isolated and miss the social environment of an office full of colleagues;
- Employees may find it difficult to work in teams, or to get help when they need it;

- Some teleworkers may find it difficult to separate home from work, and find work encroaching on their leisure or family time. Conversely, it may be difficult to concentrate on work with children making demands on a parent's time.

---

## Case study: Teleworkers use Modems not Motors

Average commuters add nearly five weeks to their working lives each year just travelling to their jobs.

And for those employees who travel to work each day by car, and buy a vehicle principally for commuting which they pay to park, that may also mean about £3,500 of their salary going to finance travelling costs.

Some workers in the South East of England, however, are adding as much as an extra third to their working lives by a lengthy commute and could also be spending up to a third of their incomes funding it.

New research contained in an RAC Foundation report, "Motoring Towards 2050 – An Independent Inquiry" also suggests that nearly 50 per cent of drivers are sympathetic to the idea of working from home and think that over half of the working population will do so by 2050.

A leaflet illustrates the costs to an average commuter who works 40 hours a week and spends another four hours travelling. If they run a car which has been bought for the purposes of getting to work and pay to park it, that can amount to over £3,500 each year. (Average household expenditure per car per week is £49.90 and a city centre season parking ticket around £1,000). The worst case scenario, "Didcot manager" uses the example of a married manager living in Didcot, Oxfordshire, who drives to the station, spends two hours every day travelling to Central London and back by rail and an hour on the tube (i.e.15 hours commute per week in addition to his standard working week of 43 hours) earning a gross salary of 26K. A calculation of his "true" hourly pay rate, which takes into account the time and money spent on travelling makes startling reading.

Didcot manager is left with £20,500 after tax, spends £4,000 per year on rail costs, £2,500 a year on the second family car which was bought specially for his journey to the station and £500 on car parking. He is then left with around £14,000 p.a. take home pay – or just under £5.00 an hour.

"Someone in this position might be better off, work fewer hours, be healthier and have a better quality of life by taking a lower paid job closer to home," commented Alan Denbigh, executive director of the Telework Association.

"But even the average commuter would be advised to persuade his employer to look at a scheme which allows him to work at least part of his week from home – increasing his productivity and efficiency, saving him money and improving his morale by allowing him to spend more time with his family".

*Source: Alan Denbigh 30/04/2002* www.tca.org.uk/news

---

## Exercises

1. 'Networked computer systems (e.g. Internet) will revolutionise the way we shop.' With the aid of specific examples, discuss this statement. Include in your discussion:

- The types of organisation likely to advertise on such systems.
- The capabilities and limitations of such systems for this activity.
- The potential security risks for the customers in using such systems.
- The organisational impact of such systems.
- The social impact of such systems.

(20)

*NEAB IT01 Qu 9 1997*

2. (a) Browsers and search engines are two items that are associated with the use of the Internet. Explain what is meant by:

    (i) a browser    (2)

    (ii) a search engine    (2)

  (b) In order to use the Internet, the owner of a PC at home normally needs to register with an Internet Service Provider (ISP). State two services, in addition to e-mail, that an ISP could provide.    (2)

  (c) Changes in technology now mean that it is no longer necessary to have a PC to be able to use some Internet services. Give two devices that can be used instead.    (2)

  (d) Explain why it is possible to send e-mail successfully to someone who has not got his or her PC switched on.    (2)

*AQA IT01 Qu 6 May 2001*

3. A major bookshop uses the Internet for an online bookshop. Give **three** advantages to customers of using the Internet to shop for books, and **three** advantages to the bookshop.    (6)

*New question*

4. A company sales manager is working away from home and the office for a week. Describe **two** ways in which he can use ICT to send data to the office.    (4)

*AQA ICT1 Qu 9 January 2003*

# Chapter 8 – Data, Information and Knowledge

## Input-process-output

Computers read incoming data called **input**, process or operate on it and produce **output**.

Examples of **input data** include:

- The mark achieved by candidate 1342 in A-level Information Technology Paper 1;
- The time at which Jane Rowe clocked in for work at McDonald's on Monday morning;
- The sale of a can of baked beans in a supermarket.

Examples of **output** that might be obtained from processing many items of similar data include:

- The percentage of candidates gaining 'A' grades in Information Technology in a particular year;
- The total number of hours worked last week by Jane Rowe;
- The total weekly cost of paying all employees;
- The total weekly value of goods sold in a supermarket;
- A list of items that need to be reordered.

## Data and Information

**Data** may consist of recorded facts, events or transactions. The data is entered into the computer by some means, for example using a keyboard or a bar code reader, as simply a string of characters which, without any context, are meaningless.

For example, hundreds of records in this format may be entered:

1903112281057

0435455729012

0130427136004

Without context, these are just meaningless strings of numbers. However, if you are told that the first ten characters represent the ISBN (unique International Standard Book Number) of a book, and the next 3 characters represent the quantity sold on a particular day, this might be useful information.

# Data + Context = Information

> ➤ **Discussion: The numbers 180173050484 might represent the birthdates of two different people. What else could they represent in three different contexts?**

Once the data has been input to the computer it can be processed in some way. It may be sorted, totalled or combined with other data to provide useful information. For example, the data on book sales described above may be combined with a file of book titles and a report produced showing the total monthly sales of each title in a bookshop.

**Information** is data that has been processed into a form that is useful, or data that has been given a meaning by putting it into context. Information is needed in organisations for the day-to-day running of a business ("How many cans of baked beans do we need to order today?") and to support decision-making and control. Information systems may also help managers to analyse problems, create new products, and find the best solutions to questions such as whether or in which direction to expand.

## Garbage in, garbage out

You may have heard the phrase *Garbage in, garbage out,* or GIGO for short. What does this mean? It implies that if you input wrong or inaccurate data to a computer, you will get wrong output, however accurately it is processed by the computer. If for example you entered

`0130427136400` instead of

`0130427136004`

in the example given above, the computer might report that the bookshop had sold 400 of that title, instead of only 4.

Companies can take measures which reduce the risks of entering inaccurate data, or recording data wrongly. For example, when you ring up to order something from a mail order house, instead of asking for your full address they will often just ask for your postcode and house number. This is looked up on a database of postcode addresses and the address is read out to you for confirmation. If it is correct, then the full address can be input automatically from the database and no errors will occur.

Other ways of ensuring that data is entered as accurately as possible include **validation** and **verification**. These techniques are covered in Module 2 (Chapter 16).

## The encoding of data

Data input to an ICT system may also take the form of pictures or sounds. For example, a picture taken on a digital camera may be stored in a computer's memory. A piece of music may be recorded digitally and saved as a file that can be downloaded from a website.

Whatever form the data takes – text, numbers, pictures or sounds – if it is to be stored and processed by a computer it must first be converted into a form that can be stored and processed by a computer. All data in a computer is stored in the form of electrical signals, which can be in one of two states, either on or off. These two states can be represented by the numbers 1 and 0, in the **binary** system. In Chapter 14 you will learn a little more about how characters can be encoded as combinations of 0s and 1s for storing in a computer. In Chapter 25 you will learn more about the binary system and how binary numbers can be used to represent pictures and sounds.

## Knowledge

Data and information are generally concerned with facts and figures. We all carry round a huge number of facts that enable us to function in our daily lives, but we also have a different kind of knowledge in the form of **rules**, or the likely effects of certain courses of action. For example:

- Students are likely to get a good grade in this course IF they attend regularly and IF they do all the homework set;

- A new restaurant is likely to succeed IF the food is good, the location is good and the price is reasonable;

- Double-clicking an icon in Windows will open an application.

'Knowledge workers' are generally people in professions such as engineering, medicine, management or teaching. Their specialised knowledge makes them experts in their field, able to create new products, provide services and make decisions, based on formal and informal facts and rules that they have learned through training or experience.

Many of these rules are based on probabilities, not certainties. Computers can be programmed with a 'knowledge' on particular subjects, consisting of facts, rules and probabilities, and then deliver advice to someone. These so-called 'expert systems' or 'knowledge-based systems', which store the knowledge of a human expert, are used in many areas such as medical diagnosis, oil exploration, the stock market and fault diagnosis of all kinds.

> ➢ **Discussion: A doctor could order various tests for a patient such as blood tests, X-rays and so on. From the results of the tests she would have *information* about the condition of the patient. What *knowledge* would she need to be able to make a diagnosis?**

## Access to knowledge

An example of a 'knowledge base' is the McAfee HelpDesk Suite. This software uses an expert system with a knowledge base containing instant answers to over 25,000 questions commonly asked by users having trouble with their hardware or software. The user simply loads the software and uses the 'Knowledge Wizard' to type in the problem. The software may then ask a series of questions before coming up with a diagnosis of the problem. (Figure 8.1.)

*Figure 8.1: McAfee HelpDesk Suite 'Knowledge Wizard'*

## Case study: Collecting information

Will Havercroft spends his days touring Britain looking for attractive towns for new Waterstones bookshops.

In an age of sprawling out-of-town shopping centres and vast indoor malls, finding new retail space is not a problem but Waterstones does not want anonymous sites in Arndale Centres. Mr Haverstock scours the country looking for unusual locations, such as an old church in Reading and a former cinema in Swansea.

In the last six months he has visited 70 towns from Dunfermline to Torquay. "I have been to many lovely towns I had not been to before, like Kings Lynn, Rugby and Bury St Edmunds. I think about whether it is an attractive place to shop which people who live nearby will travel to. I look at what sort of food is on sale and whether there are nice markets and restaurants. I look out for nice jewellery shops, as they are often a good indicator of the type of town it is, and I size up the competition.

I'm looking, wherever possible, for architecturally interesting buildings, but they must be adaptable for retail use."

*Source: The Guardian 2 January 1998*

➢ **Discussion: Mr Haverstock is visiting towns and gathering data to help aid management decisions. What other ways could he get data? What *knowledge* does he have which makes his visits a worthwhile exercise? Could this knowledge be coded and entered into a computer? If no decision is made for a year, is the information he collected still useful?**

## Sources of data

Data can be collected from many sources, either directly or indirectly. Data which is collected for a specific purpose is said to be collected **directly**. For example, the times at which an employee clocks in and out may be collected by punching a time card, and this data is used in the calculation of the weekly pay packet. Similarly, when a library book is borrowed, data about the book and the borrower is collected by scanning the bar codes of the book and the borrower's library card. This data is used directly to produce information on where a particular book is.

On the other hand, information can be derived from data which was originally collected for a completely different purpose – in other words, collected **indirectly**. For example a credit card company collects data about each transaction or purchase made so that the customer can be billed at the end of the month. This is the **direct** collection of data. At a later date, the data may be used to build a profile of the customer – perhaps they often use their credit cards for holiday travel, for example. The company could sell a list of all such customers to a travel company who would use it in a direct mail advertising campaign. This is the **indirect** collection of data – use of the data for a purpose other than the one for which it was originally collected.

➢ **Discussion: Think of several examples of data which is originally collected for one purpose, and then used for additional purposes.**

## Encoding information as data

Another way of looking at the difference between data and information is to regard data as an encoded form of information. *Information* about hours worked or grades achieved may be input as a string of numbers, i.e. *data* which is meaningful only when put into the correct context.

Precision may be lost when attempts are made to encode information as data. Although it seems desirable in some ways to hold as much information about people or things as possible there are problems in doing so, not only because it is difficult to maintain accuracy but for other reasons, as the following case study illustrates.

## Case study: 'Nightmare' scheme to track every pupil

Government proposals are afoot for a national computer record of the educational attainment of every child. Ministers plan to provide every child with a 13-digit identity number which would be used to track progress from the start of primary school through to University.

The Department for Education and Employment would control a central database with information on every pupil's social, economic and ethnic background as well as academic results and special educational needs.

A child's records would start with the score achieved in the proposed 'baseline' test at age 5, measuring elementary verbal and social skills. It would take in results of national assessment tests at 7, 11 and 14, GCSEs, A levels and vocational qualifications.

The file would also include more personal information such as a behaviour record, eligibility for free school meals and whether English was the child's native language.

But the Office of the Data Protection Registrar said the creation of a central databank about individual pupils raised 'nightmare' possibilities of abuse if it was not accompanied by adequate controls on access.

"There would have to be clear rules on access because this would set up a source of information that would be very attractive to somebody who might wish to find a particular child – for example a parent denied access because of violence."

The database on the other hand could reduce form-filling in schools by stopping repeated collection of the same data, and would provide the basis for much useful analysis.

*Source: The Guardian 1 January 1998*

➢ **Discussion: How could data about a pupil's behaviour be recorded? Who would decide what to encode? Would it be on a scale of 1 to 10?**

➢ **Are there any difficulties in recording a pupil's eligibility for free school meals?**

➢ **What are the benefits and dangers of this proposal to (a) the individual (b) society as a whole?**

## Quality of data

To be useful, data must be:

- Accurate;
- Up-to-date;
- Complete.

This is often hard to achieve. Encoding the information from a doctor's notes, for example, could lead to the coarsening of the precision and context of the data, just as the encoding of a pupil's behaviour in the case study above is not likely to give a complete or accurate picture in all cases.

There may be huge costs involved in keeping data up-to-date. Here are a couple of examples:

- An insurance agent may compile a list of which particular insurance company is most competitive for each of hundreds of different types of policy. But insurance companies change their rates all the time; in a few weeks, the research may have to be repeated.

- A company which markets the names and addresses of particular types of organisation, such as educational establishments or firms making agricultural equipment, may spend months gathering the information. But how can they be sure it is up-to-date? Colleges change their names, firms move or go bust and new ones start up. It is useful to **'date stamp'** each item of information, by recording the date that the information was last updated. Then at least someone can check each entry over a certain age.

## Exercises

1.  Describe, with the aid of examples, what is meant by *good quality* data. (6)
    *New question*

2.  Data input to an ICT system can take many forms such as pictures, sounds, numbers and letters. In all cases the data has to be encoded.

    Using an example, explain why data needs to be encoded. (2)
    *AQA ICT1 Qu 2 June 2002*

3.  Explain, using examples, the following terms as they are applied within ICT:

    (a)  Data (2)

    (b)  Information (2)

    (c)  Knowledge (2)
    *AQA ICT1 Qu 1 January 2002*

4.  The expression "Garbage in, garbage out" or "GIGO" is often used in connection with information processing systems.

    Explain, using an example, what is meant by this expression. (4)
    *AQA ICT1 Qu 2 May 2001*

# Chapter 9 – Information as a Commodity

## The importance of information

Almost overnight, it seems, success in almost any field has become impossible without information technology. In manufacturing, health care, education, policing, retailing, banking, farming and thousands of other fields, information is as valuable a resource as capital or people. Information is gathered about market trends, buying preferences, customer profiles; computers analyse, summarise and present this data to managers who use it as the basis for decision-making.

Accessible, accurate and up-to-date information can help to ensure that decisions of all kinds are likely to be correct, from how many thousands of a particular toy to manufacture in time for Christmas, to whether or not to open a new factory.

## Case study

A million Teletubby toys were manufactured for Christmas in 1997. The manufacturers got it wrong; a million would have been enough if only children wanted them, but adults (including large numbers of students, and people buying them as collectors' items) bought them as well, and three million toys were needed to satisfy demand.

In 1996 shortages of Buzz Lightyear cost Disney and Mattell £300 million in lost sales.

➢ **Describe some items of information that would help a manufacturer to accurately predict sales of a particular toy at Christmas time.**

## Collecting and analysing data

Data can be collected for a specific purpose, or it may be collected for one purpose and then used for some other purpose. If it is personal data, then care would have to be taken not to contravene the Data Protection Act ('Data must not be used for any reason incompatible with its original purpose').

Tesco's, for example, collects huge amounts of data on customer buying patterns through its Loyalty card. This massive amount of data can be analysed in thousands of different ways to help predict likely sales, or to suggest new marketing ploys. For example, a probably apocryphal tale is told of how a computer analysis of sales data showed that large numbers of disposable nappies were bought by men in their 20s and 30s on Friday evenings. This led the astute manager to position cans of beer in the same area of the store as nappies, on the basis that most men would pop a few cans in their shopping trolley as they were passing. Sales of beer rocketed!

➢ **Discussion: In the example discussed above, sales data is collected directly for the purposes of printing an itemised bill and keeping track of sales and stock levels. The data is used indirectly to target particular customers.**

**Think of other examples where data is collected for one purpose initially and then used for a different purpose.**

# Information as a commodity

Have you ever wondered why YOU in particular, or your family, are targetted for particular mail advertisements? Every time you make a credit card purchase, enter a competition or order goods by phone or mail, information about who you are and the products you bought goes onto a database. This information can then be used to direct advertising to the people who are most likely to be interested in particular products.

# Usefulness of data

Data is of poor 'quality' if it is out-of-date, inaccurate or incomplete. Companies who sell their products through direct mail, for example, need up-to-date lists of names and addresses of people who are likely to be interested in their product, and such lists are enormously valuable to them. But unless the list is kept up-to-date, it soon ceases to be of much value. People move away, grow old, die, or change their interests or purchasing habits.

Charities, for example, may sell their mailing lists to other charities, thus raising extra funds for themselves. Without knowing who on the list are regular donors and who is simply a 'one-off' donor of several years ago, the list is probably not very useful. The information can be 'date-stamped' by including for each person not only their address but the date of their last donation.

# Coding value judgements

What is a value judgement? The answer is, any description such as 'tall', 'dark', 'handsome', 'green-eyed', 'old'. If you have ever filled in a questionnaire on which you were asked to tick a box rating something from 'Poor' to 'Excellent' you will know how difficult this is.

---

> ➤ **Fill in the following questionnaire:**

*(1) The library facilities at school/college are:*

Excellent ☐  Good ☐  Fair ☐  Poor ☐

*(2) The computing facilities are:*

Excellent ☐  Good ☐  Fair ☐  Poor ☐

*(3) The amount of homework set on this course is:*

Far too much ☐  A bit too much ☐  About right ☐  Too little ☐

*(4) The course is:*

Very interesting ☐  Quite interesting ☐  Quite dull ☐  Very dull ☐

---

> ➤ **Discussion: Summarise the responses gathered from the class. Analyse the data and present a summary report.**
>
> **Notice how difficult it is to code such value judgements. To get a more accurate and complete picture, comments, exceptions or reasons need to be included, but these are very difficult to encode and analyse.**

## The benefits of ICT

Information technology systems have become indispensable in many businesses today. The benefits include:

- **Speed of processing.** Modern banking systems, for example, could not function without information technology. An MICR reader can sort and process over 2,400 cheques per minute.

- **Vast storage capacity.** Hundreds of thousands of transactions can be stored on disk for processing and analysing in organisations such as banks, building societies, government departments, hospitals and retail stores.

- **Ability to search and combine data in many different ways.** Retail stores can analyse purchases to identify trends and preferences. The police computers can analyse thousands of different pieces of information to help catch criminals.

- **Instant response.** Real-time systems such as airline reservation systems can give an instant response to a query about seat availability, and update their information as soon as a booking is made. When a customer pays for their groceries or other goods using a credit or debit card, the information on the card can be captured and the status of the account checked almost instantly. If sufficient funds are available, the transaction will be accepted.

- **Accurate results.** A computer can calculate the company payroll or the electricity bills for thousands of people with 100% accuracy every time.

- **Communication.** Electronic mail can be used to keep people in different branches of an organisation in touch. Data and information can be sent from one branch to another.

- **Improved company image.** A company can use word processors, desktop publishing and presentation graphics to enhance its image.

---

## Case study: Ford and Microsoft invest in joint venture

By March 2000 Ford's customers will be able to order new vehicles from web sites including Microsoft's www.carpoint.com and Ford's www.ford.com. The jointly-developed *Carpoint* software system will provide access to real-time information such as vehicle availability and delivery schedules, and will be integrated with manufacturer and dealer systems.

The new system will enable customers to customize a car to their own requirements, and manufacturers and dealers hope that the system will give them greater insight into customer buying patterns and preferences. The software will include an online management system to enable dealers to respond to Internet-based queries, and vehicles will continue to be delivered through dealers.

➢ **Discussion: What benefits will the new system bring to dealers, manufacturers and customers? Can you foresee any problems arising from the new system?**

---

## Limitations in the use of information technology systems

New systems nearly always have some drawbacks. These could include:

- Job losses among employees;

- Faults in the software may mean the new system does not work as planned, which may lead to chaos, loss of customers and low employee morale;

- Inadequate hardware may lead to bottlenecks in the flow of data around an organisation;

- Managers may be simply overloaded with information. It is not uncommon for an individual in an organisation to receive several hundred e-mails in the space of a week. If he or she goes away for a week's holiday, it can be almost impossible to catch up with the backlog.

- It may be difficult to extract data from a system in the form required by a user. If the requirements of a new system have not been correctly specified it may not be possible to produce the information that management subsequently finds they need.

- The information can only be as good as the data that is input – garbage in, garbage out, as the saying goes. If employees are not aware of how important it is to enter data accurately, or there are insufficient checks built in to the system to ensure accurate data entry, the information produced may be useless. The difficulty of coding value judgements and the problems of aging data are described above. Poorly designed data entry forms can also contribute to problems of inaccurate data entry.

## Exercises

1. With the aid of an example, describe **one** problem which may arise when coding a value judgement.

(2)

*NEAB IT01 Qu 2 1996*

2. A college maintains an extensive database of its full-time students. The database contains personal data, the courses students attend, and higher education or employment applications.

   (a) Describe how the college might keep the personal data of the students up to date. (3)

   (b) The college wishes to sell the personal data to a local sports retailer. An agreement is to be written between the college and the retailer. Describe **three** issues, relating to the data, that should be included in the agreement. (3)

   *NEAB IT01 Qu 4 1997*

3. A travel firm arranging package holidays in Spain for the 2001 season uses data obtained from a survey of their customers' favourite holiday resorts in 1997. Explain

   (a) why the data from 1997 might not be suitable for use to predict the requirements for 2001,

   (b) what the effect on the company might be if it used the 1997 data. (4)

   *AQA IT01 Qu 3 May 2001*

4. State three factors that affect the value and importance of information. Give an example that shows clearly how each factor affects the information's value.

   *AQA IT01 Qu 4 January 2001*

# *Chapter 10 – Computer Crime and the Law*

## Computer crime and malpractice

New technologies generally create new opportunities for crime; as soon as one avenue is blocked to the criminal, another one is discovered. As information technology has spread, so too have computer crime and abuse. The Internet, for example, is used not only by innocent members of the public but also by fraudulent traders, paedophiles, software pirates, hackers and terrorists. Their activities include planting computer viruses, software bootlegging, storing pornographic images and perpetrating all sorts of criminal activities from credit card fraud to the most complex multinational money laundering schemes.

**Computer crime** involves an illegal activity.

**Computer malpractice** in law involves professional negligence when providing computer-related services. If you provide services to someone, you have a legal responsibility (a duty) to exercise reasonable care in providing the services. For example:

- if you provide consulting services, your duty is to take reasonable care to provide good advice;

- if you provide data backup and archiving services, your duty is to take reasonable measures to ensure that you copy the right data and that you keep it safe.

- Software developers who do not properly test their software and distribute it full of bugs may be guilty of malpractice.

However, lawsuits in malpractice cases are not common and often fail.

The term 'computer malpractice' is also used to describe negligent behaviour by employees relating to their use of computers – for example, failing to keep a password secure or failing to adhere to company procedures by, for example, sending offensive material in e-mails, reading other people's confidential e-mails or leaving computers logged on and unattended.

## Hacking

Hacking is defined as unauthorised access to data held on a computer system. The extent of hacking is extremely difficult to establish as it is usually only discovered by accident, with only about two percent of security breaches discovered as a result of positive action on the part of security staff. (*Digital Crime* by Neil Barrett, page 40.)

Hacking is often perpetrated by employees of a company who have acquired inside knowledge of particular user Ids and passwords. The ability of such hackers to carry out illegal actions without being detected is often hampered by the audit and monitor software that all computer operating systems supply.

The motive behind hacking can often be mischievous rather than anything more sinister: computing students who are learning about operating systems may take delight in penetrating a University's security system to prove that it can be done, or to gain access to exam questions and answers.

*Figure 10.1: Results of a survey carried out by Mathew Bevan*

In November 1997 Mathew Bevan, a 23 year-old computer technician obsessed with the X-Files and the search for alien spacecraft, and Pryce, a teenager working independently, walked free after a 3-year-long case against them collapsed. They had quite separately penetrated US Air Force computers, Mathew partly motivated by a belief that a captured alien spacecraft was being held secretly at a remote Nevada airbase, and Pryce by an interest in Artificial Intelligence. They were traced not by infowar techniques but by traditional police methods, when Pryce boasted to an undercover informant of his activities on an Internet chat line and gave him his London phone number. They were charged with three offences under the Computer Misuse Act 1990, but eventually it was decided that they in fact presented no threat to national security and they were acquitted after the prosecution offered 'No Evidence'.

Mathew Bevan is now forging a career in Information Security and has a web site www.kujimedia.com full of interesting information which you might like to look at. You can find a myriad of stories and views about hacking, as well as interesting statistics. Look at the FAQ page for more details on the case.

## Theft of data

Data can be stolen by illegally accessing it, or by stealing the computer on which the data is stored. In December 1990 Wing Commander Farquhar's notebook computer was stolen from his car when he left it unattended for a few minutes. It contained the preliminary Allied invasion plan for the impending Gulf war, and could have had potentially disastrous consequences.

## Fraud on the Internet

The most common form of fraud on the Internet takes place between traders that appear to be legitimate and innocent purchasers of goods that are offered for sale. A trader could for example represent himself as a particular organisation (say, Comet) but in fact be entirely unconnected. They could then take orders and payment for goods and not deliver them.

*Figure 10.2: Legitimate online merchandising*

Another type of trade involves the purchase of software, which the buyer provides payment for and then expects to be able to download. The fraudulent trader can take the money and then develop a persistent 'fault' which means that the software arrives scrambled or is not transmitted at all.

---

## Case study: Cyber theft to net millions

Online retailers are set to lose almost £100 million in business over Christmas and New Year in 2002 as gangs of fraudsters cash in on the Internet sales boom. As more than 10 million have shopped by computer, there has been a corresponding increase in computer crime. In some scams, the criminals set up a bogus but professional-looking web site offering desirable goods at well below High Street prices. Buyers input their details – including billing address and security numbers- but when they try to purchase something, the site will tell them their card cannot be processed. The criminals running the site keep the information for six to eight weeks, then use it fraudulently. Retailers can be alerted to fraudsters by looking for people who order high-value goods and ask for them to be delivered to an address different from the billing address, but this system breaks down at Christmas when many people shop in this way.

The actual fraud accounts for only part of the cost to retailers. The security set up by retailers costs millions more in lost potential sales as retailers often find it cheaper to turn down orders which could be thought suspicious, rather than double-checking the honesty of the purchaser.

*Source: Tony Thompson, Observer 22 December 2002*

---

## Viruses

Viruses are generally developed with a definite intention to cause damage to computer files or, at the very least, cause inconvenience and annoyance to computer users. The first virus appeared at the University of Delaware in 1987, and since then the number of viruses has escalated to over 9000 different variations in 1997. The virus usually occupies the first few instructions of a particular program on an 'infected' disk and relies on a user choosing to execute that program. When an infected program is executed, the virus is the first series of instructions to be performed. In most cases the virus's first action is to copy itself from the diskette onto the PC and 'hide' within obscure files, the operating system code or within unused disk blocks which are then marked as being 'bad' and unavailable for reuse. The virus can then proceed to perform any of a number tasks ranging from the irritating to the catastrophic such as reformatting the hard disk.

Some viruses lie dormant, waiting to be triggered by a particular event or date – the 'Friday 13th' virus being a well-known one. The virus then infects other diskettes, perhaps by modifying operating system programs responsible for copying programs. From there, the next PC to use the diskette will be infected.

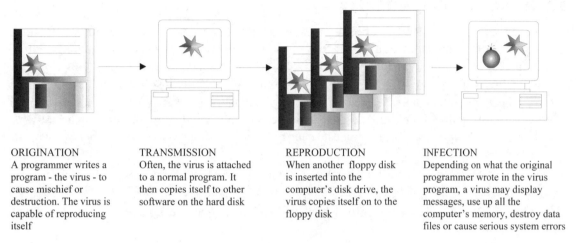

ORIGINATION
A programmer writes a program - the virus - to cause mischief or destruction. The virus is capable of reproducing itself

TRANSMISSION
Often, the virus is attached to a normal program. It then copies itself to other software on the hard disk

REPRODUCTION
When another floppy disk is inserted into the computer's disk drive, the virus copies itself on to the floppy disk

INFECTION
Depending on what the original programmer wrote in the virus program, a virus may display messages, use up all the computer's memory, destroy data files or cause serious system errors

*Figure 10.3: How a virus works*

## 'Logic bombs'

A 'logic bomb' is similar to a virus and is sometimes delivered by means of a virus. The 'bomb' can be written to destroy or, worse, subtly change the contents of an organisation's computer systems. However, it does not begin this activity until signalled to do so by the hacker or extortionist, or it may be activated if a cancelling signal fails to arrive. In many cases the bomb itself is not actually planted; a warning message alerting the organisation to the placing of a bomb is usually sufficient to persuade vulnerable institutions to hand over huge sums of money. Estimates suggest that at much as £500 million has been handed to extortionists threatening attacks on computer installations between January 1993 and June 1996.

## Digital crime and the law

The rapid progress of computer technology has led to the need for new laws to be introduced so that all perpetrators of computer crime can be prosecuted. Laws in the US impact on computer users in this country, since the majority of systems and Internet content is American. A general approach to a common standard for Internet-related laws throughout the European Union formed part of a proposed European Commission directive discussed by member states in October 1996.

## The Computer Misuse Act of 1990

In the early 1980s in the UK, hacking was not illegal. Some universities stipulated that hacking, especially where damage was done to data files, was a disciplinary offence, but there was no legislative framework within which a criminal prosecution could be brought. This situation was rectified by the Computer Misuse Act of 1990 which defined three specific criminal offences to deal with the problems of hacking, viruses and other nuisances. The offences are:

- unauthorised access to computer programs or data;
- unauthorised access with a further criminal intent;
- unauthorised modification of computer material (i.e. programs or data).

To date there have been relatively few prosecutions under this law – probably because most organisations are reluctant to admit that their system security procedures have been breached, which might lead to a loss of confidence on the part of their clients.

---

## Case study: Online blackmailers

A Sunday Times investigation in 1996 established that British and American agencies were investigating more than 40 'attacks' on financial institutions in New York, London and other European banking centres since 1993. Victims have paid up to £13m a time after the blackmailers demonstrated their ability to bring trading to a halt using advanced 'information warfare' techniques learnt from the military.

Criminals have penetrated computer systems using 'logic bombs', electromagnetic pulses and 'high emission radio frequency guns' which blow a devastating electronic 'wind' through a computer system. They have also left encrypted threats at the highest security levels, reading: "Now do you believe we can destroy your computers?"

In most cases victim banks have given in to blackmail rather than risk a collapse of confidence in their security systems.

➢ **Under which clause of which act could a hacker leaving a threatening message as described above, be prosecuted?**

---

## Software and music copyright laws

Computer software is now covered by the Copyright Designs and Patents Act of 1988, which covers a wide range of intellectual property such as music, literature and software. Provisions of the Act make it illegal to:

- copy software;
- run pirated software;
- transmit software over a telecommunications line, thereby creating a copy.

Software can easily be copied and bootlegged (sold illegally). In addition, the programming *ideas* and *methods* can be stolen by a competitor. Microsoft was sued (unsuccessfully) many years ago by Apple Computers for copying the 'look and feel' of their graphical user interface. It is possible for an expert programmer to 'reverse engineer' machine code to establish the specific algorithms used, so that they can be copied. Some software manufacturers put 'fingerprints' into the code – little oddities which do not affect the way the program runs – so that if the same code is found in a competitor's program, they can prove that it was illegally copied.

Recently there has been a lot of publicity about the illegal downloading of music from the Internet.

---

## Case study: Spears warns against piracy

Britney Spears is among the pop stars fronting a new advertising campaign aimed at warning people against online piracy.
Rapper Nelly and hip-hop star Missy Elliott will also be featured in the campaign, which will be screened on TV in the United States over the next few months.
It has been funded by the world's biggest record labels to educate people about illegally downloading music off the internet, which is being blamed for a dip in sales.

➢ **Who are the stakeholders (the people affected) in this story? Who are the victims?**

---

## Exercises

1. The Computer Misuse Act defines three types of offence. With the aid of examples, describe each of these **three** types of offence. (9)

   *NEAB IT01 Qu 7 1997*

2. The illegal use of computer systems is sometimes known as computer-related crime.
   (a) Give **three** distinct examples of computer-related crime. (3)
   (b) Give **three** steps that can be taken to help prevent computer-related crime. (3)

   *NEAB Sample Paper IT01 Qu 4*

3. Explain using examples, the difference between malpractice and crime as applied to Information Systems. (4)

   *AQA ICT1 Qu 8 June 2002*

4. Explain, using examples, four different ways in which the Internet is being used to support illegal activities. (8)

   *AQA ICT1 Qu 4 January 2002*

# Chapter 11 – Protecting ICT Systems

## Internal and external threats to ICT systems

Data and programs within an information technology system are vulnerable to deliberate and accidental destruction or loss, both from within an organisation and from outside it. At one end of the scale it may be a floppy disk which after months of loading your project without complaint, comes up with a message 'Disk unreadable'. At the other end of the scale criminal syndicates hacking into major organisation's computer systems can steal millions of pounds, for example by transferring money to phoney accounts or making fraudulent credit card purchases. What can be done to protect systems against loss?

**Internal** threats to ICT systems include:

- Hardware failure. A disk head crash, for example, can make the contents of a hard disk unreadable.

- Faulty procedures. A poorly trained employee who does not fully understand how to make entries into an Accounts system can wreak havoc over quite a short period of time.

- Natural disasters. Fire, flood, hurricanes and earthquakes can destroy a building, taking every last customer record with it.

- Employees using laptop computers outside the office may neglect to take backups and lose data through loss of or damage to hardware;

- Dishonest employees. Computer systems are vulnerable to fraud and theft of data both from inside and outside the organisation.

**External** threats to ICT systems include:

- Hackers gaining entry to company databases and stealing or corrupting data or using the information gained to carry out fraudulent transactions;

- Viruses being downloaded from the Internet;

Unless systems are perceived to be secure, companies may suffer from a lack of confidence in a particular company. Banks, for example, are generally reluctant to disclose how much money they have lost through insecure systems. Many people are unwilling to give credit card numbers when making purchases over the Internet.

---

### Case study: Safety and Privacy of NHS records

Computer records, coded with each patient's unique NHS number and accessible via a UK-wide network, NHSNet, will be linked to patients' names by a new tracking system, the NHS Strategic Tracing Service. Ross Anderson, a computer security expert at Cambridge University says that plans to protect privacy will not work. The proposed use of Smart cards to access the system and firewalls between NHSNet and the Internet will be inadequate because of the large number of health staff involved. The stakes are high, because it is vital for public health that individuals are confident their privacy will be respected.

The NHS executive says security for the tracking system will follow two basic principles: access will occur only where there is a clear need, and all transactions will be strictly monitored.

Why would anyone want to steal NHS data? Here are some possible reasons:

1. Insurance companies may want to know how big a risk you are.
2. Extremist anti-abortionists may want to know who has terminated a pregnancy.

---

3. Blackmailers could access health records of public figures.

4. Information could be used to make obscene phone calls, or even identify subjects for stalking or attacks.

5. Lawyers may want to contact certain kinds of patients to suggest litigation.

6. Companies selling drugs and medical appliances could try to market directly to relevant people.

7. Funeral parlours may try to find out who is seriously ill.

*(Adapted for an article in The Guardian, January 29 1999)*

## Measures to protect ICT systems from illegal access

Measures that can be taken include:

- Physical restrictions to the building and/or computer departments. Most medium- and large-size organisations require all employees to wear an ID badge and all visitors to sign in and wear a temporary ID while on the premises. The Computer department is commonly protected from access by a locked door which can only be opened by authorised personnel.

- When using a computer terminal, employees are normally required to sign on with a user-id and password. Company policy commonly states that passwords must not be written down, must not be composed of common names, words or dates and must be changed frequently.

- Access to various data files on the computer can be restricted to those people who need it, identified by their user ID. Any piece of data in a database can have restrictions placed on who can look at it and who can change it, by setting appropriate access rights. Restrictions can also be placed on the location and time at which terminals can be used to access certain data, so that for example a user in the Sales Department will not be able to access any data after 6pm, and will not at any time be able to access Personnel records.

- Special software can be installed on a computer system which will maintain an 'audit trail' of who has logged on, from which terminal and for how long. This will enable any unusual activity to be spotted and investigations made.

- Data can be encrypted before being transmitted. Data is 'scrambled' using an encryption technique so that even if it is intercepted it cannot be read without decoding it first. It is then decrypted at the receiving end. Cryptography researchers are constantly coming up with better techniques for encrypting data. Strong encryption means that the code is virtually impossible to crack, whereas weak encryption means that it would be difficult for most individuals or companies to decrypt , but it could be done by an organisation with sufficient resources and motivation.

## Case study: Numbers up as encryption code cracked

The code used by the majority of major financial institutions and e-commerce Web sites has been broken.

Researchers led by the Dutch National Research Institute for Mathematics and Computer Science have determined the two prime numbers used to generate a single 512-bit RSA key.

The breakthrough was announced by RSA, the authors of the system used by many companies, websites and banks to encrypt financial data. It's the code that secures your credit cards when you buy online.

It wasn't easy. It took scientists at eleven sites in six countries seven months and 292 different computers, working for 35 years of computing time, to find the two 155 digit-long prime numbers needed.

RSA continually challenges its researchers to break its codes, which depend on the multiplication of two prime numbers. By proving it is possible to factor the RSA key, the researchers have reinforced the view that current codes are not strong enough. Criminals with access to enough computing power could, it appears, interfere with banking and e-commerce transactions.

*Source: Ben Hammersley, The Times 'Interface' 1 September 1999*

> ➤ **Discussion: In some countries *strong encryption* is illegal because governments want to be able to decode messages from terrorists, drug traffickers or other criminals. However, *weak encryption* is not sufficient to prevent determined criminals from stealing confidential data such as credit card numbers used over the Internet.**
> **Do you think strong encryption should be legal in this country?**

## Types of backup

### Online backup

Backup of all data on a company database is crucial. Many companies cannot afford to lose even a few minutes worth of online transactions, let alone a day's worth. One method of ensuring that data is not lost if for example a disk head crashes, or a bomb is exploded in the vicinity, is to write each transaction to three separate disks more or less simultaneously. Two of the disks will be at the main computer centre, so that in the event of one disk drive failing, the data is safe on the other drive until the problem is fixed. The third disk drive will be situated at a remote, secure location so that if the whole computer centre is destroyed the data is still safe.

### Periodic backups

For many companies it is sufficient to make daily backups of all data files. Data is transferred, maybe overnight, to a backup tape or disk and the backup copy is then stored in a fireproof safe. It is necessary to have the previous day's backup copy stored securely, preferably offsite to guard against data loss in the case of fire.

A relatively recent development is the technique of backing up files onto the Internet, so that your files are safely tucked away overnight in San Diego or somewhere truly remote. America's biggest backup provider, @Backup (www.backup.com) enables a user to download a compact little application and then backup important files in off-peak hours. One reason that this method has been slow to catch on, apart from the cost of the phone calls, is the worry about security. @Backup claims that its encryption is so tight that even its own staff cannot tell what is in the files backed up on its hardware.

### Backing up laptop data

Having a laptop computer stolen while travelling on business can be disastrous. The NetStore Group provides a backup service called PCRefresh, which for a monthly fee backs up any changed files on a laptop automatically every day. Using this service a laptop user anywhere in the world can be supplied with a new machine with the original data already installed.

## Other security measures

Other measures to guard against accidental or deliberate destruction of data include:

- Installing virus checkers on all networks. Viruses are small programs written by sad people who wish to cause others disaster or at least inconvenience and annoyance. New viruses are constantly being written and software companies such as Network Associates issue regular updates of their anti-virus software which can be downloaded from the Internet. Many companies forbid employees to download games and other free software from the Internet as it is prone to virus attack.

- Careful vetting of staff before hiring can help to ensure that potential hackers or fraudsters are not employed. When an employee is fired for any reason it is common in some organisations for them to be escorted immediately from their desk out of the building so that they are not given the chance to destroy data in a 'revenge attack'. Their user-id is removed from the system at the same time.

- Staff training to ensure that all employees who use the computer know the correct procedures and understand the importance of following them can prevent data from being corrupted by faulty data entry, for example.

- Careful siting of the mainframe computer in a large organisation to minimise danger of flooding, with smoke alarms and automatic fire-quenching systems installed. Frequently mainframes are sited in anonymous, unmarked buildings to minimise the threat of extremist attacks.

## Issues surrounding access to the Internet

With so much material on the Internet, there are other considerations beyond merely making the transfer of data secure.

- Parents and schools do not want children accessing, for example, pornographic material. They also want to protect children who post material on the Internet for a school project being contacted by undesirable strangers.

- Companies want some control over e-mails and jokes being sent over the Internet from their offices.

Many organisations including businesses, schools and colleges set up their own company-wide **intranet**. This is effectively the same as providing all the facilities commonly used on the Internet, such as browsing software and e-mail facilities for internal use. A proxy server to control access to the Internet and to control access from outside, together with other hardware and special software can be used to maintain security. This is known as a **firewall**. Using an Intranet, a school for example can control what is accessible to pupils which will prevent unsuitable material being downloaded.

## Case study: Caught on the Net

In December 1999 twenty-three office staff at the New York Times were fired after company managers discovered they had been e-mailing smutty jokes, jokes about bosses and pornographic pictures while tapping away on-screen.

The New York Times has a policy specifying that "communications must be consistent with conventional standards of ethical and proper conduct, behaviour and manners". Staff are banned from using their computers to "create, forward or display any offensive or disruptive messages".

In 1997 Norwich Union paid £450,000 in an out-of-court settlement and had to make a public apology when an e-mail on the intranet disparaging a competitor got out. Workers in the city have been sacked for downloading and distributing pornography. Working with a sexually explicit screensaver could constitute harassment if it offended other staff.

Employers are advised to spell out what is and is not acceptable. Abuse of e-mail, for example, may be treated as a disciplinary offence if employees breach them.

*Source: Helen Hague, The Guardian 3 December 1999*

## Exercises

1. (a) State the **three** levels of offence under the Computer Misuse Act of 1990. Illustrate each answer with a relevant example. (6)

    (b) Describe **four** separate measures that can be taken to prevent accidental or deliberate misuse of data on a stand-alone computer system. (8)

    *NEAB IT01 Qu 5 1999*

2. A company offering security services for ICT systems includes the following quotation in its advertisements. "You're protected against hackers, viruses and worms. But what about the staff in the sales department?"

    Describe **three** ways in which a company's own staff can be a weak point in its ICT systems.

    (6)

    *AQA ICT1 Qu 6 January 2003*

# *Chapter 12 – Data Protection Legislation*

## Personal privacy

The **right to privacy** is a fundamental human right and one that we take for granted. Most of us, for instance, would not want our medical records freely circulated, and many people are sensitive about revealing their age, religious beliefs, family circumstances or academic qualifications. In the UK even the use of name and address files for mail shots is often felt to be an invasion of privacy.

With the advent of large computerised databases it became quite feasible for sensitive personal information to be stored without the individual's knowledge and accessed by, say, a prospective employer, credit card company or insurance company to assess somebody's suitability for employment, credit or insurance.

## Case study: James Wiggins – a true story

In the US, James Russell Wiggins applied for and got a $70,000 post with a company in Washington. A routine pre-employment background check, however, revealed that he had been convicted of possessing cocaine, and he was fired the next day, not only because he had a criminal record but because he had concealed this fact when applying for the job. Wiggins was shocked – he had never had a criminal record, and it turned out that the credit bureau hired to make the investigation had retrieved the record for a James Ray Wiggins by mistake, even though they had different birthdates, addresses, middle names and social security numbers. Even after this was discovered, however, Wiggins didn't get his job back.

If the pre-employment check had been made *before* Wiggins was offered the job, he would not have been offered it and no reason would have been given. The information would have remained on his file, virtually ensuring that he would never get a decent job – without ever knowing the reason why.

## The Data Protection Act

The Data Protection Act 1984 grew out of public concern about personal privacy in the face of rapidly developing computer technology. It provides rights for individuals and demands good information handling practice.

The Act covers 'personal data' which are 'automatically processed'. It works in two ways, giving individuals certain rights whilst requiring those who record and use personal information on computer to be open about that use and to follow proper practices.

The Data Protection Act 1998 was passed in order to implement a European Data Protection Directive. This Directive sets a standard for data protection throughout all the countries in the European Union, and the new Act was brought into force in March 2000. Some manual records fall within the scope of the Act and there will also be extended rights for data subjects.

# The Data Protection Principles

The Data Protection Act became law on 12th July 1984 and was updated in 1998.

Once registered, data users must comply with the eight Data Protection principles of good information handling practice contained in the Act. Broadly these state that personal data must be:

1. fairly and lawfully processed;
2. processed for limited purposes;
3. adequate, relevant and not excessive;
4. accurate;
5. not kept longer than necessary;
6. processed in accordance with the data subject's rights;
7. secure;
8. not transferred to countries without adequate protection.

# Useful definitions from the 1984 Act

| | |
|---|---|
| **'PERSONAL DATA'** | information about living, identifiable individuals. Personal data do not have to be particularly sensitive information, and can be as little as a name and address. |
| **'AUTOMATICALLY PROCESSED'** | processed by computer or other technology such as document image processing systems. The Act doesn't currently cover information which is held on manual records, e.g. in ordinary paper files. |
| **'DATA USERS'** | those who control the contents and use of a collection of personal data. They can be any type of company or organisation, large or small, within the public or private sector. A data user can also be a sole trader, partnership, or an individual. A data user need not necessarily own a computer. |
| **'DATA SUBJECTS'** | the individuals to whom the personal data relate. |

(More information can be found on the web site http://www.dataprotection.gov.uk which contains a lot of information on this topic.)

# Data Subjects

We are all 'data subjects'. All types of companies and organisations ('data users') have details about us on their computers. This growth of computerised information has many benefits but also potential dangers. If the information is entered wrongly, is out of date or is confused with someone else's, it can cause problems. You could be unfairly refused jobs, housing, benefits, credit or a place at college. You could be overcharged for goods or services. You could even find yourself arrested in error, just because there is a mistake in the computerised information.

## The Data Protection Registrar

The Act established the office of **Registrar**, whose duties include:

- Maintaining a register of data users and computer bureaux and making it publicly available.
- Disseminating information on the Act and how it works.
- Promoting compliance with the Data Protection Principles.
- Encouraging the development of Codes of Practice to help data users to comply with the Principles.
- Considering complaints about breaches of the Principles or the Act.
- Prosecuting offenders, or serving notices on those who are contravening the Principles.

*Figure 12.1: The Data Protection Registrar's Home Page*

## A data user's Register entry

With few exceptions, all data users have to register, giving their name and address together with broad descriptions of:

- Those about whom personal data are held;
- The items of data held;
- The purposes for which the data are used;
- The sources from which the information may be obtained;
- The types of organisations to whom the information may be disclosed i.e. shown or passed on to;
- Any overseas countries or territories to which the data may be transferred.

# Exemptions from the Act

- The Act does not apply to payroll, pensions and accounts data, nor to names and addresses held for distribution purposes;
- Registration may not be necessary when the data are for personal, family, household or recreational use;
- Subjects do not have a right to access data if the sole aim of collecting it is for statistical or research purposes, or where it is simply for backup;
- Data can be disclosed to the data subject's agent (e.g. lawyer or accountant), to persons working for the data user, and in response to urgent need to prevent injury or damage to health.

Additionally, there are exemptions for special categories, including data held:

- in connection with national security;
- for prevention of crime;
- for the collection of tax or duty.

# The rights of data subjects

The Data Protection Act allows individuals to have access to information held about themselves on computer and where appropriate to have it corrected or deleted.

As an individual you are entitled, on making a written request to a data user, to be supplied with a copy of any personal data held about yourself. The data user may charge a fee of up to £10 for each register entry for supplying this information but in some cases it is supplied free.

Usually the request must be responded to within 40 days. If not, you are entitled to complain to the Registrar or apply to the courts for correction or deletion of the data.

Apart from the right to complain to the Registrar, data subjects also have a range of rights which they may exercise in the civil courts. These are:

- Right to compensation for unauthorised disclosure of data;
- Right to compensation for inaccurate data;
- Right of access to data and to apply for rectification or erasure where data are inaccurate;
- Right to compensation for unauthorised access, loss or destruction of data.

---

## Case Study: A universal entitlement card

Richard Thomas, the new Information Commissioner, is stimulating debate on proposals for an entitlement card which were issued by the government in July 2002. The proposals, if implemented, would affect all individuals in the U.K.

Richard Thomas is inviting views from a cross-section of relevant parties at a conference entitled 'Entitlement card - the issues' at the Institute of Civil Engineers in London on January 15th 2003. The conference has been arranged to encourage a comprehensive debate to assist his formal response to the Home Office consultation exercise which ends on January 31st 2003.

The conference will seek to examine whether the stated benefits of a 'universal' entitlement card (which include reducing fraud and providing simpler access to public and private sector services) are sufficient to outweigh the identified data protection and wider privacy concerns.

One issue of concern is the development of a proposed 'central register' of all card holders. Key questions need to be answered in relation to what safeguards can be built in to place strict controls over the amount of personal information it will hold and the purposes it could be used for. Other worries include the need to ensure the accuracy of personal information held on the proposed central register and increasing the possible risks of identity theft.

*Source: www.dataprotection.gov.uk  January 2003*

**Discussion: What are the benefits and drawbacks of a 'universal' entitlement card to (a) the individual and (b) the state?**

**Look up 'universal entitlement card' in a search engine such as Google and read some opinions on this topic.**

## Exercises

1.  A company is storing details of its customers on a database. Describe **three** obligations the company has under the Data Protection Act. (6)

    *NEAB  Computing Paper 1 Qu 7 1997*

2.  Data protection legislation was introduced into the UK in 1984; it has since been superseded by the 1998 Act.

    (a)  State why the legislation was originally introduced. (1)

    (b)  State what type of data is the subject of the Data Protection Act 1998. (2)

    (c)  A company wishes to collect data from order forms submitted by its customers to sell to other companies.
    State **two** actions the company must take so that it can legally collect and sell that data. (2)

    (d)  The Data Protection Act gives individuals the right to see what data is being held about them.

        (i)  State how an individual must ask to do this. (1)

        (ii)  Could an individual have to pay to receive a copy of his or her data? (1)

    *AQA ICT1 Qu 7 January  2002*

# Chapter 13 – Health and Safety

## Computers and health

Computers can be held responsible for a whole raft of health problems, from eyestrain to wrist injuries, back problems to foetal abnormalities, stomach ulcers to mental collapse. Articles appear regularly in the newspapers relating stories of employees who are suing their employers for computer-related illnesses.

Not so long ago it was thought that the widespread use of these fantastic machines, that could perform calculations and process data with lightning speed and complete accuracy, would free up humans to work maybe only two or three hours a day, while the computer did the lion's share. In fact, people seem to be working harder than ever, trying to keep up with the output of their computers. Human beings are the weak link in the chain, needing food, rest, a social life; prone to headaches, stress, tired limbs and mistakes.

*Figure 13.1: Stress at work*

## Stress

Stress is often a major factor in work-related illness. Simply thinking about computers is enough to cause stress in some people. It is stressful to be asked to perform tasks which are new to you and which you are not sure you can cope with. It is stressful to know that you have more work to do than you can finish in the time available. It is stressful, even, to have too little to do and to be bored all day.

The introduction of computers into the workplace can have detrimental effects on the well-being of information workers at many different levels in an organisation. For example:

- Some companies may use computers to monitor their workers' productivity, which often increases their stress levels. Symptoms include headaches, stomach ulcers and sleeplessness.

- Many people are afraid of computers and fear that they will not be able to learn the new skills required, or that their position of seniority will be undermined by younger 'whizz kids' with a high level of competence in ICT

- It can be almost impossible for some people to get away from work. Pagers, mobile phones, laptop computers and modems mean that even after leaving the office, there is no need to stop work – indeed, should you even *think* of stopping work? As a busy executive, can you afford to waste 45 minutes on the train to Ipswich reading the newspaper or just gazing out of the window, when you could be tap-tap-tapping on your laptop, or infuriating your fellow passengers by holding long and boring conversations on your mobile phone?

• 'Information overload' means that managers are often bombarded with far more information than they can assimilate, producing 'information anxiety'. Try typing the words 'Information Overload' into one of the World Wide Web's search engines and within seconds, it will have searched millions of information sources all over the world and come up with thousands of references all presorted so that those most likely to be of interest are at the top.

• A survey of 500 heads of ICT departments revealed that over three quarters of respondents had suffered from failing personal relationships, loss of appetite, addiction to work and potential alcohol abuse. The continuing developments within ICT ensure that it is always in the minds of business executives and also that it is blamed for most corporate problems. The very speed of development, for which ICT is now famous, and the need to keep pace with this is also a major contributing factor to ICT stress-related illness.

---

## Case study: Information overload

*Val Kerridge is an ICT manager in an Engineering company:*

"I have to monitor everything to do with computers that might affect the firm, from fax-modems to new operating systems or network capabilities. I'm always being asked what I think of new hardware or software products, so I feel obliged to read everything – computer magazines, e-mails, user group communications on the Internet, mailshots from suppliers – there was so much it made me ill. I couldn't sleep properly, I had constant headaches and neck pains from staring at a screen, and I never had time to eat properly in a 12 to 14 hour day at the office."

*Peter Harris is a management consultant:*

"I was away for four days and when I came back, there was a huge pile of mail and faxes and dozens of e-mail messages. I couldn't tell from the titles whether they were important or not, and I spent 10 hours or more in front of a screen dealing with it all. I didn't know what information overload was until I came across the research and then I thought, 'Yes, that's me.'

When I go into organisations I find it very common in all departments. There's too much information and not enough communicating.

I now have a survival strategy. I am very strict with the amount of information I use. I scan it and throw it away or file it. I've learned to say 'No, I don't need that information'".

➢ **Discussion: Do you suffer from computer-related stress? How can it be alleviated?**

---

## Repetitive strain injury (RSI)

RSI is the collective name for a variety of disorders affecting the neck, shoulders and upper limbs. It can result in numbness or tingling in the arms and hands, aching and stiffness in the arms, neck and shoulders, and an inability to lift or grip objects. Some sufferers cannot pour a cup of tea or type a single sentence without excruciating pain.

The Health and Safety Executive say that more than 100,000 workers suffer from RSI. It is not a new disease; Bernard Ramazzini, an Italian physician, noted of scribes and notaries in 1717:

> "The diseases of persons incident to this craft arise from three causes … constant sitting … the perpetual motion of the hand in the same manner, and the attention and application of the mind … constant writing also considerably fatigues the hand and the whole arm on account of the continual tension of the muscles and tendons."

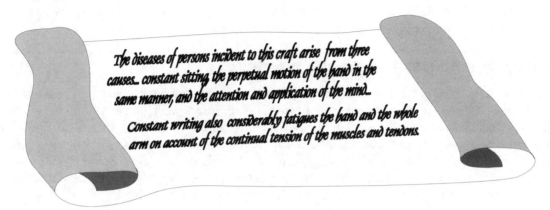

*Figure 13.2: Recognition of RSI is not new!*

Now, as then, the constant pain "can be removed by no medicines".

## Case study: Bank staff 'driven to injury'

Keyboard operators at the Midland Bank's factory-style processing centre at Frimley, Surrey developed severe cases of repetitive strain injury after their work rate was sharply increased, a court was told yesterday.

Five former part-time workers who put cheque details into computers are claiming compensation for upper limb disorders including aches, stiffness and shooting pains in their arms, fingers, wrists, shoulders and necks.

The five former Midland workers, all women, were required to key in transaction records at an intensive stroke rate, on inadequately designed equipment, with a poor working posture and negligible training.

There was a lack of breaks or variation of tasks and there was strong pressure on staff to maintain and increase speed. The fastest operators – who keyed four strokes a second with their right hand, while holding cheques in their left – were awarded gold badges and their names were publicised by the bank.

In 1989, the Midland Bank had to pay £45,000 compensation to an RSI sufferer.

*Source: Seumas Milne, The Guardian November 25 1997*

➢ **What factors were cited as contributing to the onset of RSI among the employees?**

## Eyestrain

Computer users are prone to eyestrain from spending long hours in front of a screen. Many computer users prefer a dim light to achieve better screen contrast, but this makes it difficult to read documents on the desk. A small spotlight focussed on the desktop can be helpful. There is no evidence that computer use causes permanent damage to the eyes, but glare, improper lighting, improperly corrected vision (through not wearing the correct prescription glasses), poor work practices and poorly designed workstations all contribute to temporary eyestrain.

## Extremely low frequency (ELF) radiation

In normal daily life we are constantly exposed to ELF radiation not only from electricity mains and computer monitors but also naturally occurring sources such as sunshine, fire and the earth's own magnetic field. Research into the effects of ELF radiation is increasing and seems to indicate that it may be connected to some health problems. Several studies have tried to establish whether there is a link between monitor use and problems in pregnancy such as early miscarriages. The results are not clear-cut, because although some studies seem to show a correlation between an increased rate of miscarriages and long hours spent at a VDU in the first trimester of pregnancy, other factors such as stress and poor ergonomic conditions could have played a part.

---

## Case study: Health risks of mobile phones

Research is continuing into the question of whether mobile phones are a health hazard. There are two direct ways by which health could be affected as a result of exposure to radiation from handsets. These are by thermal effects caused mainly by holding handsets close to the body and as a result of possible non-thermal effects from both handsets and base stations. There are also possible indirect effects. There is evidence that using a mobile phone while driving increases the risk of accidents. Some people's well-being may be adversely affected by the environmental impact of mobile phone base stations situated near their homes, schools or other buildings, as well as their fear of perceived direct effects.

*Source:* Report by Independent Expert Group on Mobile Phones, April 2000)

http://www.iegmp.org.uk/report/text.htm

**Discussion: Look up the report and use a search engine to find other sites giving more information about the risks of mobile phone use. Are children at greater risk than adults? Is the use of a hands-free kit safer than a handset while driving?**

---

## Computers, health and the law

Occupational health and safety legislation in Britain is researched, guided and structured by the Health and Safety Executive (HSE), a government body. An EEC Directive on work with display screen equipment was completed in the early 1990s, with member states required to adapt it to become part of their own legislation. As a consequence, the Health and Safety at Work Act of 1974 incorporated legislation pertaining to the use of VDUs, and the relevant section is now referred to as The Health and Safety (Display Screen Equipment) Regulations 1992.

This legislation is intended to protect the health of employees within the working environment, and employers, employees and manufacturers all have some responsibility in conforming to the law.

**Employers** are required to

- Perform an analysis of workstations in order to evaluate the safety and health conditions to which they give rise;
- Provide training to employees in the use of workstation components;
- Ensure employees take regular breaks or changes in activity;
- Provide regular eye tests for workstation users and pay for glasses.

**Employees** have a responsibility to

- Use workstations and equipment correctly, in accordance with training provided by employers;
- Bring problems to the attention of their employer immediately and co-operate in the correction of these problems.

**Manufacturers** are required to ensure that their products comply with the Directive. For example, screens must tilt and swivel, keyboards must be separate and moveable. Notebook PCs are not suitable for entering large amounts of data.

Screen must **tilt**..

.. and **swivel**

*Figure 13.3: Workstations must be ergonomically designed*

---

### Classrooom menace: ignore it and you may end up in court

Schools should not only teach children good posture and ensure they take regular screen breaks, but also scrutinise the equipment they provide. Chairs and screens should be adjustable for each child and foot- and back-rests may be needed.

"Some schools may be buying laptops because they are relatively cheap and easy to store but they are terrible for kids and long-term use. The screens are too low and the little workstations sold for them put kids into horrid positions," says Ms Martin, a specialist remedial therapist with extensive experience teaching RSI victims.

Tom Jones, of Thompsons solicitors, the UK's largest personal injury law firm, says schools ignoring RSI may find themselves in court.

"Schools have a duty of care over computer use in the same way they have at a school rugby match."

*Source: Caroline Palmer, The Guardian 2 December 1997*

---

## The ergonomic environment

Ergonomics refers to the design and functionality of the environment, and encompasses the entire range of environmental factors. Employers must give consideration to

- **Lighting**. The office should be well lit. Computers should neither face windows nor back onto a window so that the users have to sit with the sun in their eyes. Adjustable blinds should be provided.

- **Furniture**. Chairs should be of adjustable height, with a backrest which tilts to support the user at work and at rest, and should swivel on a five-point base. It should be at the correct height relative to a keyboard on the desk.

- **Work space**. The combination of chair, desk, computer, accessories (such as document holders, mouse and mouse mats, paper trays and so on), lighting, heating and ventilation all contribute to the worker's overall well-being.

- **Noise**. Noisy printers, for example, should be given covers to reduce the noise or positioned in a different room.

- **Hardware**. The screen must tilt and swivel and be flicker-free, the keyboard must be separately attached.

- **Software**. Software is often overlooked in the quest for ergonomic perfection.  The EEC Directive made a clear statement about the characteristics of acceptable software, requiring employers to analyse the tasks which their employers performed and to provide software which makes the tasks easier. It is also expected to be easy to use and adaptable to the user's experience.

## Software can be hazardous to your health

Bad software can be extremely stressful to use. Software that slows you down by crashing frequently, giving incomprehensible error messages, using non-standard function keys and displaying badly structured menus, for example, can leave a user longing to throw the computer from the nearest window. Repeated failure with a new software package very quickly becomes frustrating, boring and depressing. Feelings of inadequacy and alienation mean that people may begin to dread their daily encounters with the computer and productivity suffers.

Human-computer interaction is a growing field of study within computing and seeks to understand, among other things, what makes software difficult or unpleasant to use, and how it can be improved. The principles of good, usable software design are based on extensive research.

Interface design also covers aspects such as the use of colours which minimise eyestrain, the use of shortcut keys for experienced users, and the ease with which data can be entered. A screen in which default values are already entered (such as today's date on an invoice entry form), which has fields appearing in the correct order (e.g. the same order as the printed form from which data is being entered) and which has list boxes or combo boxes from which the user can select, will make the software much easier to use.

## Exercises

1.  A company provides all new employees with an induction booklet including guidelines for working with ICT.

    State, giving a reason for each one:

    (a)  **three** health and safety guidelines (6)

    (b)  **two** guidelines to protect the company's data (4)

    *AQA ICT1 Qu 8 January 2003*

2.  The introduction of computer terminals and personal computers has been associated with a number of physical health hazards.

    (a)  State **three** health hazards which have been associated with prolonged use of computers. (3)

    (b)  Describe **five** preventative actions which may be taken to avoid computer-related health hazards, explaining clearly how each action will assist in preventing one or more of the hazards you have described in part (a). (10)

    *NEAB IT01 Qu 6 1998*

# ICT1 – Sample Questions and Answers

1.  (a)  Information processing is concerned with:

    Input

    Processing

    Output

    Feedback

    Briefly describe these four elements of information processing, using a diagram to illustrate your answer. (6)

    (b)  Explain the difference between 'knowledge' and 'information'.

    *NEAB IT01 Qu 1 1998*

*Notes:*

In Chapter 8 you will find a block diagram which shows the stages of Input, Processing and Output. *Feedback* is an easy concept to understand and as it has not been explicitly covered in the text, you will have to use common sense to add it to the diagram. Feedback always goes back from the output to the input phase and the purpose of it is to have some effect on the input. Think of occasions on which you have been asked for feedback, perhaps on the quality of a product or the 'A' Level course you are studying. In your written explanation, try and give enough detail to score the marks – it is all too easy to write a superficial answer which will not satisfy the mark scheme. For example if you write 'Feedback is the response from the user to the output he/she receives' this will probably get you one mark, but not the two marks allocated.

In part (b), remember that knowledge consists of the facts and rules that you know about a particular topic.

*Suggested answer:*

(a)  **Input** is the capturing of the raw data or facts representing events occurring in organisations. (1)

**Processing** is the conversion of these raw facts into a form that is useful for some purpose, for example by summarizing, finding subsets of data satisfying some given criteria (e.g. all items which need reordering). (1)

**Output** is the production of reports (on-screen or hard copy) from the processed information which goes to the end-user. (1)

Feedback is the response to the output that a user receives, which is returned to appropriate members of the organisation to help them refine or correct the input phase. (2)

(1)

(b)  Information is data which has been processed into a meaningful and useful form whilst knowledge is a set of concepts, rules and procedures used by people to create, collect, store and share information. (2)

2. A multi-national organisation maintains an information technology system which holds a large amount of vital and sensitive data.

    (a) Describe **three** steps which should be taken to protect the data against deliberate theft or corruption. (6)

    (b) Describe **three** steps which should be taken to protect the data against accidental loss. (6)

    *NEAB IT01 Qu 4 1996*

*Notes:*

It always helps when answering questions to try and relate them to your own personal experience and use any knowledge gleaned from the course combined with a large dose of common sense – don't leave home without it. Have you ever visited a large organisation? What happens as you enter the front door? Would it be possible to get into their Computer Department? If you had a few week's work experience with such an organisation, what would prevent you from looking at or corrupting sensitive data?

For Part (b), be aware that you will not get full marks with one-word answers or short phrases without some explanation or expansion of your answer. Often one mark goes for the phrase such as 'Take regular backups' or 'Staff training' and the second mark for further explanation. Think what else you can say about backups. For example how often will they be done, what will they be stored on, where will they be kept? Get used to allowing your mind to float around a subject, exploring it from different angles.

*Suggested answer:*

(a) Physical restrictions can be placed on the building so that anyone entering has to sign in or show an ID badge. This will prevent unauthorised people from gaining access to computer terminals inside the building. Physical access to sensitive areas can be restricted to badge-holders or more sophisticated techniques such as iris recognition technology.

Each employee can be given a user-id and password which has to be frequently changed and not written down anywhere. Access rights to data can be made dependent on the user-id of the person signing on.

Staff should be carefully vetted before they are hired to ensure as far as possible that they are honest and reliable and not likely to indulge in hacking or theft of data. They can be asked to sign a document laying down the company's regulations and code of practice. If staff are fired for any reason they should be escorted from the building immediately and their user-id removed from the system so that they have no chance for 'revenge attacks'.

(You could also gain points for describing data encryption, call-back system for logging on, keeping an audit trail etc if you are familiar with these techniques.)

(b) Periodic backups of the data could be made. For example a backup of all files that have changed could be made every evening onto a backup tape which is stored in a secure, fireproof safe. Once a week an extra backup copy could be stored off-site.

Accidental loss may be caused by not following correct procedures for example when updating files. Therefore training the staff to follow correct procedures will help to protect against accidental loss.

Staff should be forbidden to bring in disks from outside the organisation to reduce the risk of introducing viruses. Virus detection software may be installed on the company network to guard against the risk of destructive viruses being accidentally downloaded from the Internet or introduced from a floppy disk.

3.  Give two advantages and one disadvantage of a firm using electronic mail as a method of keeping in touch with its large number of travelling salespersons. (3)

*NEAB Specimen Paper IT01 Qu 2*

*Notes:*

Before you put pen to paper consider what you are comparing electronic mail with. Contact by letter? By mobile phone? By a note in the internal mail to be picked up on return to the office? By fax? Be careful to avoid answers such as 'quicker', 'cheaper', 'more reliable' which will not score any marks. Can you think of any facilities that e-mail has which are not available with other means of communication? What scenario are you imagining for these salesmen? Do they return to the office every day, or are they away for several days at a time? Try to put yourself in the position of the salesperson (or the boss) before you start to answer the question.

*Suggested answer:*

Advantages: Using e-mail the same message can be sent to a group of salespersons in a single operation, thus saving the time that would be spent writing or telephoning each individual.

The salesperson can look at his/her e-mail messages at a convenient time, and so would not be interrupted by a telephone call in the middle of a meeting with a client.

(Could also say: Compared with sending a letter, the advantages are that e-mail will arrive far quicker, and the sender will know that the message has been received at the salesperson's computer – if it is not, a message such as 'e-mail returned' is sent back to the sender.)

Disadvantage: The salesperson may not look at his/her e-mail regularly – it is reliant on following good practice and checking e-mail, maybe on a laptop, at least once a day.

---

4.  Recent changes in communications technology have resulted in a blurring of the distinction between telecommunications and computing. Information services are starting to be provided on what is becoming known as the Information Super Highway (ISH).

    (a) State the minimum facilities needed to gain access to these services. (3)

    (b) Identify and briefly describe three types of information service you would expect to find when linked to the ISH. (6)

*NEAB IT01 1998*

*Notes:*

'Facilities' refers to the hardware and software needed to access the Internet. (*Information Super Highway* is not a phrase that has stood the test of time.) This should be straightforward to answer – you need to mention 3 different things to get 3 marks. Part (b) will be easier if you have spent time using the Internet. You will get one mark for naming an information service and two marks for a brief description making two good points.

*Suggested answer:*

(a) Hardware needed: A PC with a modem, and a telephone line or ISDN connection.

   Software: Browser such as Internet Explorer.

(b) Home shopping: Can browse through a catalogue, select goods and transfer them to a 'shopping basket', then proceed to 'checkout' and give credit card details and delivery address. Goods will be delivered to address.

   Entertainment: Videos, music and games software can be downloaded and saved.

   News service: the BBC and national newspapers have online news so that you can check weather, football or cricket scores, current affairs as the news breaks.

   (Could also describe online banking, stock market dealing, software help, university places, job vacancies etc.)

5. Briefly describe **two** social impacts and **two** organisational impacts commonly identified as a result of introducing computerised information systems into business organisations. (8)

*NEAB IT01 Qu 2 1998*

*Notes:*

The Mark Scheme specifies that "There must be a clear statement of the issues. Whilst lengthy discussion is not required, short phrases of 4 or 5 words are unacceptable at A Level." You will get no marks for writing, for example, "The business will become more efficient and it will be easier and quicker to find out information."

The key to getting good marks on questions like this, which look superficially easy, is to first consider very carefully what the question means. Is it asking for the social impact on the employees or the general public? When you have decided, imagine a particular business, and consider how computerisation affects that business. What are you envisioning when you consider the social impact of introducing a computerised information system? A person in the stock room at a garage, who has to know whether a particular part is in stock? A car salesman who has a customer wanting a silver Puma with blue interior and who wants to know the delivery time? These examples may help with the organisational impact. They may not have much of a social impact so now think of another situation. What about a Travel company who has information available over the Internet on holidays available at short notice? What about telephone banking? What about e-mail? Use your own personal experience wherever possible.

*Suggested answer:*

**Social impacts:** Computerised information systems may have the effect of shifting the locations of work. For example many high street banks may close, and employees lose their jobs unless they are willing to relocate to say the Scottish highlands where the new telephone banking centre is set up. Some employees in other organisations may be able to work from home using a PC and modem, linked to the company network, so they will not need to travel to work. This may be convenient but may result in a feeling of isolation.

(Could also discuss issues of stress from speed of change or information overload when a manager is required to deal with 50-100 e-mails every day.)

**Organisational impacts:** The type of work done by employees often changes, and this may mean that training programmes have to be introduced. The organisation may become 'flatter' as all levels of worker in the company use the computerised information system and there is less need for middle managers.

The skill level of the workforce may rise and it may be harder to recruit people with the right skills than for the unskilled workforce previously required.

---

6. List **six** factors which could give rise to health or safety problems associated with the use of information technology equipment. (6)

*NEAB IT01 Qu 3 1996*

*Notes:*

The question says 'list' so you don't need a long explanation of each point you make. Generally it is not considered very hazardous to health to sit down at a computer for the duration of an ICT lesson or for long enough to type up your homework, so you probably need to be thinking of people whose job it is to enter data at a computer all day long.

*Suggested answer:*

Incorrect positioning of computer facing window can lead to eyestrain from screen glare.

Incorrect seating position can lead to backache.

Constant typing with inadequate breaks can lead to RSI (repetitive strain injury).

Printer noise can contribute to stress.

Badly designed software can cause stress and a desire to throw the computer out of the nearest 6<sup>th</sup> floor window.

Trailing electric cables can be a safety hazard.

---

7.  A software house is advertising for an analyst programmer to join one of their development teams. State four personal qualities that the company should be looking for in the applicants. (4)

*NEAB IT01 Qu 2 1999*

*Notes:*

The word 'team' should give you at least one clue. Also, what does an analyst programmer do? Analyses systems, of course … and how is this carried out? Think of the people in your class you would most like to have in your team for a joint assignment and you've probably got the answer.

*Suggested answer:*

Ability to work as part of a team, *(but this on its own won't score you the mark!)* i.e. exchange views, share information, listen to the other team members' ideas.

Good oral communication skills, able to interact easily and confidently with users, ask the right questions and understand the user's requirements.

Good written communication skills for documenting results of interviews, writing technical documentation for programmers.

Good problem-solving abilities since systems analysis is a high-level skill requiring insight as well as technical knowledge.

*(Could also mention: ability to work under pressure and meet deadlines; organisational management skills, i.e. ability to take orders and give them, be responsible for own work and delegate where necessary.)*

---

8.  Many market research firms use questionnaires as a means of gathering raw data for companies about the popularity of their products.

    (a)  Explain why Information Technology is widely used in Market Research. (4)

    (b)  Once the data has been collected, it can be used to give the client information about their products. Explain the difference between information and data in this context. (4)

*NEAB IT01 Qu 4 1999*

*Notes:*

In part (a), try to think how Market Research would be done without using computers. The data would be collected on forms, then presumably answers would be totted up manually (how long would that take??), calculations laboriously worked out … with quite a few mistakes probably creeping in and a few made-up results along the way. Now think of reasons why computers are used for this task.

In part (b) be careful to avoid answers such as "data is raw data, and information is data which has been processed" for which you will get no marks. Many great minds have struggled to explain the difference between data and information and not all of them agree but you will have to try and add something of note to the debate!

*Suggested answer:*

    (a)  Data can be input directly from the documents on which it is collected, thus avoiding transcription errors and allowing more accuracy.

The data will be processed very much more quickly which is important to companies which require feedback quickly so that they can respond to consumer demands.

*(could also mention that the data can be manipulated more easily using statistical packages, graphs can be produced, etc. to present the information in a variety of ways for different audiences e.g. management, the general public. Or, that a far greater volume of results can be handled than would be possible manually so more accurate results will be achieved.)*

(b) The data is the raw facts or figures which are fed into the computer, and which have no meaning until a context is given to them. Information is data which has been processed to give it meaning. For example the numbers representing answers to the questions on the questionnaire (data) are input and processed, and information is produced such as '83% of the population do not think that the shape of a toothbrush is an important factor in deciding whether to purchase.'

---

9. The personnel department of a large company keeps records on all the employees of the company. These records contain personal data and details of the employees' position, training and medical history. The company is registered on the Data Protection Register and has to abide by the principles of the 1998 Data Protection Act. Three of these principles are:

- "Personal data shall be adequate, relevant and not excessive in relation to the purposes for which they are processed";

- "Personal data shall be accurate and, where necessary, kept up to date";

- "Appropriate technical and organisational measures shall be taken against unauthorised or unlawful processing of personal data and against the accidental loss of or destruction of, or damage to, personal data".

For each of the principles stated above, describe what the company must do to comply with them. (6)

*AQA ICT1 Qu 10 June 2002*

*Notes:*

Your answers to this question must relate to what actions the company must take in this particular situation, as it applies to each of the given principles. For the first principle, for example, you could say that the company must not hold irrelevant data such as the fact that the employee's husband is in jail, since this fact has no bearing on the employee herself. Thinking of an example always helps to clarify the issue in your own mind – if you can't think of an example, then you don't really understand the principle.

*Suggested answer:*

The company must not keep irrelevant data such as the fact that the employee threw soup over the Mayor at a demonstration against congestion charges.

The company must make sure the data is accurate – for example by validating and verifying the data that is entered so that their date of birth or date of joining the company is accurate.

The company must make sure the data is secured against unauthorized access, for example that it is protected by passwords against another employee illegally accessing their private records.

# Section 2

## Information: Management and Manipulation

# Chapter 14 – Introduction to Computer Systems

## The components of a computer

All computers, whatever their size or function, have certain basic components. They have input devices for reading data into main memory, a central processing unit (CPU) for processing the data, output devices for printing, displaying or outputting information, and storage devices for permanent storage of programs and data.

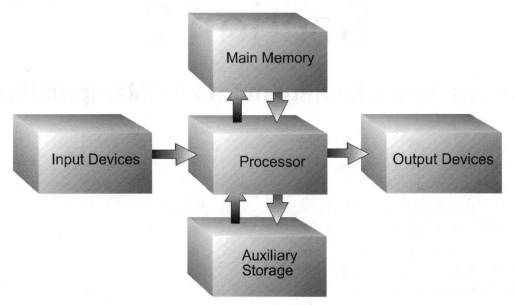

*Figure 14.1: Block diagram of a computer system*

## Input and output devices

Input devices include the keyboard, mouse, barcode readers or scanners and many other devices. We will be looking at some of these and their uses in more detail in the next chapter. Output devices include various types of printer and plotter as well as the VDU (screen).

> ➢ **Discussion: Can you think of some other input devices? In what circumstances or environment is the device you have named appropriate?**

## The processor

The processing power of a computer is measured in terms of its speed of operation, the amount of memory it has, and the number of input/output devices it can handle. All computer operations are under the control of the CPU, which has the following functions:

- It controls the transmission of data from input devices to memory;
- It processes the data held in main memory;

- It controls the transmission of information from main memory to output devices.

Most computers use integrated circuits, or chips, for their CPUs and main memory. A chip is about ½" square and can hold millions of electronic components such as transistors and resistors. The CPU of a microcomputer is called a **microprocessor**. The CPU and main memory of a PC are commonly held on a single board called a main circuit board.

## Main memory

Instructions and data are held in main memory, which is divided into millions of individually addressable storage units called **bytes**. One byte can hold one character, or it can be used to hold a code representing, for example, a tiny part of a picture, a sound, or part of a computer program instruction. The total number of bytes in main memory is referred to as the computer's memory size. Computer memory sizes are measured as follows:

| | | |
|---|---|---|
| 1 Kilobyte (Kb) | = | 1,000 bytes (or to be exact, 1024 bytes) |
| 1 Megabyte (Mb) | = | 1,000,000 (1 million) bytes |
| 1 Gigabyte (Gb) | = | 1,000,000,000 (1 billion) bytes |
| 1 Terabyte (Tb) | = | 1,000,000,000,000 (1 trillion) bytes |

As with processing power, the amount of memory that comes with a standard PC has increased exponentially over the past 20 years. In about 1980, BBC microcomputers with 32K of memory were bought in their thousands for home and school use. In 1981, Bill Gates of Microsoft made his famous remark "640K ought to be enough for anybody". In 2003, a PC with 256Mb of memory is standard, costing around £500- £1,000 including bundled software.

## RAM and ROM

There are basically two kinds of memory; Random Access Memory (RAM) which is the ordinary kind of memory referred to above, used for storing programs which are currently running and data which is being processed. This type of memory is **volatile** which means that it loses all its contents as soon as the machine is switched off.

Read Only Memory (ROM) is the other type of memory, and this is non-volatile, with its contents permanently etched into the memory chip at the manufacturing stage. It is used for example to hold the **bootstrap loader**, the program which runs as soon as the computer is switched on and instructs it to load the operating system from disk into memory. To assist software development, some types of ROM are programmable (PROM) and may also be erasable (EPROM).

## Auxiliary storage

All standalone PCs come equipped with an in-built hard disk, the capacity of which is also measured in bytes. A typical storage capacity for the hard disk supplied with a desktop PC is between 20 and 40 gigabytes. The hard disk is used for storing software including the operating system, other systems software, application programs and data.

A PC may have other storage **devices** such as a CD-ROM drive, a CD-RW/DVD combi drive (a device which can write to CDs and read DVDs), a floppy disk drive and a Zip drive.

- CDs have a capacity of approximately 650Mb.
- Many PCs and laptops have a combi CD-RW and DVD drive, which can read from and write to a writeable CD and play back DVDs.

- Many PCs also have a drive for Zip disks, which have a capacity of 100Mb or 250Mb.
- Floppy disks consist of a thin sheet of mylar plastic encased in a hard 3½" casing. The standard High Density disk has a capacity of 1.44Mb.

*Figure 14.2: Hard disk and floppy disk*

## Internal storage of data

One of the things that many people find most amazing about computers is their seeming ability to understand and interpret all kinds of information fed in via a keyboard, mouse, scanner, microphone or sensor of some kind.

All digital computers use the **binary** system for representing data of all types – numbers, characters, sound, pictures and so on. A binary system uses just 2 symbols to represent all information. The symbols could be anything like a dot and dash (as in Morse code), + and -, or 0 and 1. The great advantage of the binary system is that the digits 1 and 0 can be represented by electrical circuits that can exist in one of two states – current is either flowing or not flowing, and a circuit is either closed or open, on or off.

A closed circuit allowing current to flow represents 1

An open circuit represents 0

*Figure 14.3: Electrical circuits can represent 1 or 0*

## The ASCII code

A binary digit (1 or 0) is known as a '**bit**', short for **BI**nary digi**T**. In most computers today, bits are grouped together in 8-bit **bytes**. A byte can hold $2^8$ different combinations of 0s and 1s, which means that, for example, 256 different characters can be represented.

Over the years, different computer designers have used different sets of codes for representing characters, which has led to great difficulty in transferring information from one computer to another. Most personal computers (PCs) nowadays use the ASCII code (American Standard Code for Information Interchange), but many mainframe computers use a code called  EBCDIC (Extended Binary Coded Decimal Interchange Code — pronounced EB-SUH-DICK or EB-SEE-DICK according to taste).

ASCII originally used a 7-bit code, but a later version that is now more common uses 8 bits. The 128 different combinations that can be represented in 7 bits is plenty to allow for all the letters, numbers and special symbols, and the extra 128 combinations are used for symbols such as Ç, è, ü, ©, ®, Œ, etc.

> ➢ **Discussion: About how many different combinations of 0s and 1s are required to represent all the keys on a keyboard? (Remember to include uppercase and lowercase letters.)**

The ASCII codes are shown below.

| Character | ASCII | Char | ASCII | Char | ASCII | Char | ASCII |
|---|---|---|---|---|---|---|---|
| space | 0100000 | 8 | 0111000 | P | 1010000 | h | 1101000 |
| ! | 0100001 | 9 | 0111001 | Q | 1010001 | i | 1101001 |
| " | 0100010 | : | 0111010 | R | 1010010 | j | 1101010 |
| £ | 0100011 | ; | 0111011 | S | 1010011 | k | 1101011 |
| $ | 0100100 | < | 0111100 | T | 1010100 | l | 1101100 |
| % | 0100101 | = | 0111101 | U | 1010101 | m | 1101101 |
| & | 0100110 | > | 0111110 | V | 1010110 | n | 1101110 |
| ' | 0100111 | ? | 0111111 | W | 1010111 | o | 1101111 |
| ( | 0101000 | @ | 1000000 | X | 1011000 | p | 1110000 |
| ) | 0101001 | A | 1000001 | Y | 1011001 | q | 1110001 |
| * | 0101010 | B | 1000010 | Z | 1011010 | r | 1110010 |
| + | 0101011 | C | 1000011 | [ | 1011011 | s | 1110011 |
| , | 0101100 | D | 1000100 | \ | 1011100 | t | 1110100 |
| - | 0101101 | E | 1000101 | ] | 1011101 | u | 1110101 |
| . | 0101110 | F | 1000110 | ^ | 1011110 | v | 1110110 |
| / | 0101111 | G | 1000111 | _ | 1011111 | w | 1110111 |
| 0 | 0110000 | H | 1001000 | ' | 1100000 | x | 1111000 |
| 1 | 0110001 | I | 1001001 | a | 1100001 | y | 1111001 |
| 2 | 0110010 | J | 1001010 | b | 1100010 | z | 1111010 |
| 3 | 0110011 | K | 1001011 | c | 1100011 | { | 1111011 |
| 4 | 0110100 | L | 1001100 | d | 1100100 | | | 1111100 |
| 5 | 0110101 | M | 1001101 | e | 1100101 | } | 1111101 |
| 6 | 0110110 | N | 1001110 | f | 1100110 | ~ | 1111110 |
| 7 | 0110111 | O | 1001111 | g | 1100111 | del | 1111111 |

*Figure 14.4: ASCII codes*

> ➢ **Discussion: The name JACK can be held in 4 bytes of a computer's memory. What will be the binary code representing this name? (You can assume that the leftmost bit in each byte is 0.)**

Note that a particular binary pattern in 4 consecutive bytes could represent 4 characters, a number, a sound, a tiny portion of an image or an instruction to the computer. Its interpretation depends entirely on the context in which it is read.

## Exercises

1. Find some advertisements for PCs and write down the specifications and prices. Are prices still falling and computers still becoming more powerful? (6)

   *New question*

2. State **two** types of data, other than alphanumeric, that can be stored in a computer file. (2)

   *AQA ICT2 Qu 1 May 2001*

3. A company is replacing the personal computers used by its employees. The staff have been offered the choice of a desktop personal computer, or a laptop computer.

   Describe one advantage, and one disadvantage, to the staff of their choice. Your advantages and disadvantages must be different in each case:

   (a) a desktop personal computer (4)

   (b) a laptop computer (4)

   *AQA ICT2 Qu 6 January 2003*

# Chapter 15 – Data Capture

## Keyboard data entry

The keyboard is the most common input device, suitable for a wide range of applications from entering programs to typing all kinds of documents using a word processor, or entering personal details of customers or patients at a hospital, etc. Data entered at a keyboard is commonly copied from a source document, and as such has disadvantages:

- It is easy to make **transcription** errors – that is, copy the data wrongly from the document.

- It is time-consuming.

- Data entry operators who enter data all day every day are prone to **repetitive strain injury** (RSI), a condition which renders them unable to do any further data entry or even perform everyday tasks such as pouring a cup of tea.

## Key-to-disk systems

In organisations where large amounts of data are collected on forms which then have to be keyed in for later processing (a **batch processing** system) an entire computer system consisting of a processor, dozens of terminals and central disk storage may be dedicated entirely to data entry. One terminal is nominated as the supervisor's terminal, from whose screen the supervisor can see exactly what every data entry operator is working on and how many keystrokes per hour and how many errors everyone is making. Completed batches of data are stored on disk from where they are either downloaded to the main computer over a communications link, or transferred to magnetic tape which is physically removed and taken to the main computer room.

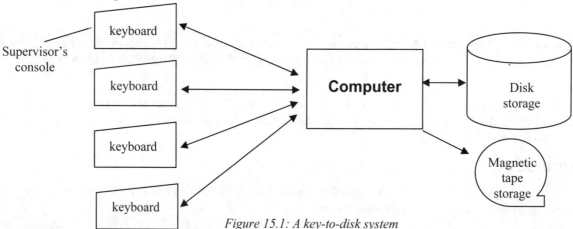

*Figure 15.1: A key-to-disk system*

Using a key-to-disk system, each data entry operator calls up the data entry program for her particular batch of data (e.g. payroll data entry, Council Tax payments, student grant applications) and keys in the data, which is automatically validated by the computer program.

When the batch of data has been entered and stored on disk, the source documents are passed to a second data entry operator who switches her machine to **verify** mode and keys in the data a second time. The keystrokes are compared with the data already stored on disk and any discrepancy causes the machine to beep so that the error can be corrected.

Banks, for example, no longer process routine transactions (such as paying in cheques) in branches. Instead, the work is sent to giant processing centres where the staff do nothing but key in data.

"It's like a factory", said one Barclay's worker. "There's just crates and crates of work everywhere. They call them customer service centres, but you never see a customer".

The trend is raising health and safety concerns among the banking unions. Four employees at one Midland Bank processing centre took their employer to court in 1998 claiming they developed repetitive strain injury (RSI) after being required to key in 2000 cheque details per hour.

In order to ensure the accuracy of the data entered, it is commonly **batched** and **verified** – that is, entered twice by different operators with the second version being automatically compared with the first version and any discrepancies brought to the operator's attention. (See **batch processing** in Chapter 24.)

## Voice data entry

The user speaks the text into a microphone and special software such as IBM's VoicePad or Dragon's Naturally Speaking interprets the text and displays it on a screen, where it may be edited using the keyboard and exported to a word processing package such as Word. The accuracy of the voice recognition system is improved by 'training' it to a particular user's voice – an embarrassing process of speaking a given set of a few hundred short sentences to your computer, repeating any that are not accurately interpreted.

*Figure 15.2: Voice recognition: not always 100% accurate!*

## Scanners and OCR

An optical scanner can be used to scan graphical images and photographs, and software can then be used to edit or touch up the images. Scanners can also be used to read typed or even hand-written documents and OCR (Optical Character Recognition) software can then be used to interpret the text and export it to a word processor or data file. Scanners are also used to input large volumes of data on preprinted forms such as credit card payments, where the customer's account number and amount paid are printed at the bottom of the payment slip.

## Case study: Automating college enrolment

Enrolling thousands of college students on hundreds of different courses is a year-long administrative headache for colleges. Unravelling the mysteries of what students and staff have written on the enrolment forms and then entering all this information onto computer, checking it and resolving it can take weeks. One college has slashed this time and eliminated many of the errors by investing in a scanning solution from Formic.

Formic has a proven track record in scanning survey questionnaires using graphical imaging and intelligent character recognition technologies which produce clean, validated data with minimal human intervention. Its new ACE product (Automated College Enrolment) links a scanner with a digital camera and identity card printer to offer immediate and complete enrolment in the presence of the student.

Students select their courses with the help of teaching staff, who then attach official peel-off stickers to the form. Stickers are preprinted with course names and barcodes for reliable scanning. This simple procedure has eliminated much administrative frustration of trying to identify which course a student really meant to enrol for, and made it impossible for students to enrol on courses that do not exist.

Students present themselves at the enrolment desk for their form to be scanned by computer. Handwriting is converted to letters and numbers, answers are checked and validated against a postcode database. This way, all omissions and inconsistencies are picked up and resolved while the student is still there. Finally, a plastic identity card is produced bearing the student's name, enrolment number and smiling face in full colour etched securely into its tough surface. The same digital picture is stored for use later. The whole process typically takes two to three minutes from start to finish.

*Source: Tim Macer, Formic magazine*

➤ **Discussion: What are the benefits of the scanning system? What output could be obtained from the information gathered at enrolment time? What other use could be made of the digital photographs?**

## Mouse, joystick, light pen, touch screen

The mouse and its variants such as a trackball is well known to all users of PCs. A light pen is a device which incorporates a light sensor so that when it is held close to the screen over a character or part of a graphic, the object is detected and can be moved to create or modify graphics.

A touch screen allows the user to touch an area of the screen rather than having to type the data on a keyboard. They are widely used in tourist centres, where tourists can look up various local facilities and entertainments, in fast food stores such as McDonald's for entering customer orders, in manufacturing and many other environments.

## Magnetic Ink Character Recognition (MICR)

All banks use MICR for processing cheques. Along the bottom of a cheque the bank's sort code, customer account number and cheque number are encoded in special characters in magnetic ink. The amount of the cheque is encoded in magnetic ink when it is handed in at a bank. The cheques can then be processed extremely fast by high-speed MICR devices that read, sort and store the data on disk. MICR has several advantages for processing cheques:

- It is hard to forge the characters;
- The characters can be read even if the cheque is crumpled, dirty or smudged;
- The characters are readable by humans, unlike bar codes.

## Magnetic stripe

Cards with magnetic stripes are used as credit cards, debit cards, railway tickets, phone cards and many other applications such as customer loyalty cards. The magnetic strip can be encoded with up to 220 characters of data, and there are over 2.4 billion plastic card transactions every year in Britain, with 83% of adults owning at least one card. The information provided when someone signs up for a loyalty card with Sainsbury, Tesco, Boots or W.H.Smith, for example, plus a few months of shopping records, can provide a detailed portrait of customers' habits.

The day is not far off when you will be able to wake up on Saturday morning (or whichever is your regular shopping day) to an e-mail from Sainsbury suggesting what you need to buy this week.

Nevertheless, three factors threaten to destroy the lucrative business that high street banks have made out of plastic: crime, the cost of cash and competition. In 1996 card fraud cost the banks £97.1 million, with £13.3 million of it from fake magnetic stripe cards. The 220 characters are simply too easy to copy, which is why the stripes will eventually disappear and be replaced by a chip, which is almost impossible to fake.

## Smart cards

Smart cards look similar to plastic cards with a magnetic stripe, but instead of (or as well as) the magnetic stripe, they contain a 1-millimetre square microprocessor embedded in the middle, behind a small gold electrical contact. Instead of swiping the card, you plug it into a reader.

Chip cards cost only about £1 to produce, and can hold typically 4K bytes of data. They are already used in banking, healthcare, telecoms, transport, Pay TV, and as store loyalty cards. By 2004 there will be nearly 2 billion smart cards in use worldwide, according to some estimates.

They have the advantage of being:

- Reliable
- Low cost
- Easy to use
- Fast
- Anonymous
- Secure

*Figure 15.3: A Smart card*

> ➤ **Discussion: It has been suggested that other information such as kidney donor record and driving licence could be held on the same chip card that allows you to withdraw cash and pay for goods.**
> ➤ **What would be the benefits of doing this?**
> ➤ **What other information would it be useful to hold on a card of this sort?**

## Optical Mark Recognition (OMR)

An optical mark reader can detect marks made in preset positions on a form. It is widely used for marking multiple-choice exams and market research questionnaires.

## Bar code reader or scanner

Bar codes appear on almost everything we buy. The pattern of thick and thin bars represents the 13-digit number underneath the bar code. There are four main pieces of information on a bar code;

The first two (or sometimes three) digits indicate in which country the product has been registered. The code for the UK and Ireland is 50.

The next five digits represent the manufacturer's code – Cadbury's for example is 00183.

The second group of five digits represents the product and package size, but not the price.

The last digit is a check digit, which is calculated from the other digits in the code and ensures that the barcode is keyed in or read correctly.

*Figure 15.4: A product bar code*

## Benefits of using bar codes

The major benefit of using bar codes at point of sale is that management is provided with very detailed up to date information on key aspects of the business, enabling decisions to be made quicker and with more confidence. For example:

• Fast-selling items can be identified quickly and automatically reordered to meet demand.

• Slow-selling items can be identified, preventing a build-up of unwanted stock.

• The effects of repositioning a given product within a store can be monitored, allowing fast-moving more profitable items to occupy the best space.

• Historical data can be used to predict seasonal fluctuations very accurately.

Bar code scanners are relatively low cost and extremely accurate: only about one in 100,000 entries will be wrong.

"Add on 5" can be used to provide additional information.
Add on 2 is used with periodicals to denote the week or month of issue.

*Photograph courtesy of Scanner Technologies*

*Figure 15.5: A bar code scanner*

> ➤ **Discussion: A supermarket has a file of all stock items, which is on-line to the point-of-sale terminals at each checkout. What data is held on the stock file? What processing takes place when an item is scanned by the barcode reader? What is the output from the process?**

## Other uses of bar codes

Bar codes can be used in a wide range of applications that require fast and accurate data entry. These include:

- Warehousing. Bar-coded containers of raw materials are stored in racks of bins which are also bar coded. When goods are put into the warehouse, the computer system instructs an automatic crane to retrieve the nearest available empty bin. The filled bin is then returned to an empty location. The crane relies entirely on bar codes to move goods in and out.

- Transport and distribution. All major road freight carriers now use bar codes. Individual packages are bar coded as are depot consignments. The exact location of any package is known at any one time together with details of the type of service used. Individual customers can be billed quickly and missing parcels traced more easily.

- Manufacturing. Very accurate data relating to work in progress can be obtained using bar codes as the data entry method. Management can obtain up to date data on the progress of unfinished goods, enabling bottlenecks and over-production to be reduced and production efficiency to improve.

- Marketing. Many polling companies now use bar-coded multiple choice questionnaires to enter data quickly and accurately. Survey times can be dramatically reduced.

- Medical. Bar codes are commonly used to identify blood and other samples. Hospital patients' and outpatients' records are increasingly bar coded for fast retrieval and better accuracy.

- Libraries. Bar codes are used to record loans and provide more information on stock.

- Banking, insurance and local government. Bar codes are used extensively for accurate document control and retrieval. Many cheque book covers, insurance claim files and council tax forms are bar coded.

## Hand-held input devices

Portable keying devices are commonly used in such applications as reading gas or electricity meters, where the meter reader displays the next customer name, address and location of meter on a small screen, then reads the meter and keys in the reading. At the end of the day all the readings can be downloaded via a communications link to the main computer for processing.

## Exercises

1. Speech recognition systems for Personal Computers are now becoming more affordable and useable.

    (a) State **two** advantages to a PC user of a speech recognition system. (2)

    (b) Give **two** different tasks for which a PC user could take advantage of speech recognition. (2)

    (c) Speech recognition systems sometimes fail to be 100% effective in practice. Give **three** reasons why this is so. (3)

    *NEAB IT02 Qu 6 1999*

2.  A village store has just installed a computerised point of sale system including a bar code reader.

    (a)  Describe **two** advantages that the store gains by using a bar code reader attached to a computerised point of sale system.  (4)

    (b)  Describe **one** disadvantage to the store of using a bar code system.  (2)

    *AQA ICT2 Qu 10 January 2001*


3.  A scanner is to be purchased for use with a personal computer.

    (a)  State one item of software that should be supplied with the scanner, and state why it is needed.  (2)

    (b)  A map has been scanned and its image saved in a file.

    State **three** ways that the image of the map could be manipulated before it is printed.  (3)

    *AQA ICT2 Qu 3 January 2003*


4.  Describe briefly an appropriate application for each of the following methods of input:

    (i)  MICR

    (ii)  Key-to-disk

    (iii)  Video camera

    (iv)  Touch screen

    (v)  Smart card  (10)

    *New question*

5.  (a)  Why is MICR used in preference to OCR in cheque processing systems?  (1)

    (b)  Why is OCR used in preference to MICR in invoicing systems?  (1)

    (c)  (i)  What is Optical Mark Reading (OMR)?

    (ii)  Give **one** situation where OMR might be used.  (2)

    *NEAB Computing Paper 2 Qu 3 1997*

# Chapter 16 – Verification and Validation

## Data capture

In the last chapter we looked at different input devices and situations in which they would be appropriate. The particular method used to capture data will be chosen because it offers advantages in terms of speed, accuracy, and/or cost.

Methods of 'direct data capture' which cut out the need to key in data from input documents are likely to have all these advantages, and so are becoming more and more common. However, we are a long way off from escaping the chore of filling in forms of one sort or another, a large number of which will then have to be keyed into a computer system.

> ➤ **Discussion: Name (a) some applications which use direct data entry, eliminating the need for keying in data and (b) applications which require data to be keyed in.**

## Types of error

Figure 16.1 shows an example of an order form filled in by customers of a mail order company.

| ORDERED BY | | | | | | |
|---|---|---|---|---|---|---|
| MR/MRS/MISS/MS | | | CUSTOMER NO | | | |
| SURNAME | | | POST TO: | | | |
| ADDRESS | | | MANSION HOUSE, MAIN STREET | | | |
| | | | BANSTEAD | | | |
| | | | LAKE DISTRICT | | | |
| POSTCODE | | | LA31 8TR | | | |
| DAYTIME TEL NO | | | | | | |

| PAGE NO | CODE | COLOUR | SIZE | QTY | DESCRIPTION | PRICE |
|---|---|---|---|---|---|---|
| | | | | | | |
| | | | | | | |
| | | | | | | |
| | | | | | | |
| | | | | | GOODS TOTAL | |
| | | | | | P & P | £2.50 |

CARD NO.    VALID FROM    EXPIRY DATE    TOTAL PAYABLE

*Figure 16.1: A Mail Order form*

The information from this form will be keyed in to the computer and then processed to produce a set of documents including a delivery note and invoice for the customer, as well as updating stock and sales records. There are several possible sources of error before the data are processed:

- The customer could make a mistake, entering the wrong product codes, adding up the total cost wrongly, forgetting to enter their address or card expiry date, etc.;

- The person keying in the data could make a **transcription** error, keying in the wrong product code or quantity, misreading the customer's name, adding an extra couple of 0's to the total price by keeping a finger down too long, and so on;

- A form could be blown into the bin by a sudden draught as a fan starts up or someone flounces out, slamming the door – or the operator might decide the writing was so bad it simply wasn't worth the effort of struggling with, and bin it;

- A bored keypunch operator, chatting to a colleague, could enter the same form twice without realising it;

- A faulty connection between hardware components such as the processor and the disk drive could mean that some characters are wrongly transmitted.

Now clearly a mail order company would not stay in business very long if this was how the operation worked! So what can be done to minimise the possibility of error?

## Batch processing

In a batch processing system, documents such as the sales orders described above are collected into batches of typically 50 documents. A **data control clerk** has the responsibility of:

- counting the documents;

- checking each one visually to see that the customer has entered essential details such as their name and address, card details if that is the payment method, and total payable;

- calculating a control total of some crucial field such as Total Payable, for the entire batch of 50 documents;

- calculating **hash totals** of other fields such as size or quantity (see below);

- filling in a batch header document which will show, for example:

  ❑ batch number

  ❑ number of documents in batch

  ❑ date received

  ❑ control total

  ❑ hash total

- logging the batch in a book kept for this purpose.

A hash total is a sum of values calculated purely for validation purposes. For example, if the sizes of all garments ordered on a batch of forms (12, 10, 12, 34, 36, etc.) are added together and the total entered on the batch header and keyed in, the computer will be able to perform the same calculation and if the figures don't match, then the batch must have an error in it somewhere.

Control totals and hash totals have a similar purpose: the data from the batch header is keyed in as well as the contents of all the documents in the batch, and the computer performs the same summing calculations that the data entry clerk made manually. If there is any discrepancy, an error is reported and the batch is rechecked. The difference between the two types of total is only that a hash total has no meaning, whereas a control total (e.g. number of documents in the batch) does.

The stages in batch processing are discussed in Chapter 24.

# Validation checks

As the data is being keyed in, a computer program controlling the input can perform various validation checks on the data. For example:

1. **Presence check.** Certain fields such as customer number, item code, quantity etc must be present. The data control clerk may have visually checked this but the program can perform a second check. Also, if this is a new customer, a number could be automatically assigned.

2. **Format check** (also called **picture check**). For example the code perhaps has a pattern of 2 letters followed by 4 numbers. The quantity and price must be numeric.

3. **Range check.** The expiry date of a card must have a month number between 1 and 12, and the date must be later than today's date.

4. **File look-up check.** If the customer has filled in their customer number, the computer can look this up on the customer file and display the name and address. The data entry operator can check that it tallies.

5. **Look-up list check**. A list of valid values may be displayed for, say, colour and the operator selects from the list.

6. **Check digit check.** (see below).

7. **Batch header checks.** The total number of records in the batch should be calculated by the computer and compared with the figure on the batch header. The control totals and hash totals are also calculated and compared.

# Check digits

Code numbers such as a customer number, employee number or product number are often lengthy and prone to error when being keyed in. One way of preventing these errors occurring is to add an extra digit to the end of a code number which has been calculated from the digits of the code number. In this way the code number with its extra check digit is self-checking.

The best-known method of calculating check digits is the modulus-11 system, which traps over 99% of all errors. The calculation of a check digit is shown below.

1. Each digit of the code number is assigned a 'weight'. The right hand (least significant) digit is given a weight of 2, the next digit to the left 3 and so on.

2. Each digit is multiplied by its weight and the products added together.

3. The sum of the products is divided by 11 and the remainder obtained.

4. The remainder is subtracted from 11 to give the check digit. The two exceptions are:

   - If the remainder is 0, the check digit is 0, not 11.
   - If the remainder is 1, the check digit is X, not 10.

Example:

To calculate the check digit for the number 1587:

| | | | | |
|---|---|---|---|---|
| Original code number | 1 | 5 | 8 | 7 |
| Weights | 5 | 4 | 3 | 2 |
| Multiply digit by its weight | 5 | 20 | 24 | 14 |
| Add products together | | $5 + 20 + 24 + 14 = 63$ | | |
| Divide by 11 | | 5 remainder 8 | | |
| Subtract remainder from 11 | | $11 - 8 = 3$ | | |

Check digit = 3. The complete code number is 15873.

To check that a code number is valid, it is not necessary to recalculate the check digit completely. If the check digit itself is assigned a weight of 1, and the products of the digits (including the check digit) and their respective weights are calculated, their sum will be divisible by 11 if the check digit is correct.

All books have an ISBN number which has a modulus-11 check digit. Try checking whether the ISBN number 1858051703 is valid.

## Verification

Verification is the process of entering data twice, with the second entry being compared with the first to ensure that it is accurate. It is common in batch processing for a second data entry operator to key in a batch of data to verify it. You have probably come across another example of verification when setting a password; you are asked to key the password in a second time to ensure that you didn't make a keying error the first time, as it is not echoed on the screen.

## Detecting transmission errors

In order to guard against the possibility of data being wrongly transmitted between the various hardware components of a computer, a **parity bit** is added to each character. In an even parity machine, the total number of 'On' bits in every byte (including the parity bit) must be an even number. When data is moved from one location to another, the parity bits are checked at both the sending and receiving end and if they are different or the wrong number of bits are 'On', an error message is displayed.

Thus a character code of 1101010 will have a parity bit of 0 appended to it, and a character code of 1101110 will have a parity bit of 1 appended.

Data is transmitted over a transmission line between computers in **blocks** of say 256 bytes. A **checksum** may be calculated by adding together the numeric value of all the bytes in a block, and this sum is transmitted with the data, to be checked again at the receiving end.

## Accuracy and validity

When primary data is collected for surveying prospective customers or following the launch of a new product, for example, the research organisation has to be careful that the sample of the population chosen to be asked questions accurately reflects the whole population. If for example the researcher collects data from random members of the public in a town between 10am and 12 noon each morning for a week, they are probably going to interview mainly pensioners or people not currently employed.

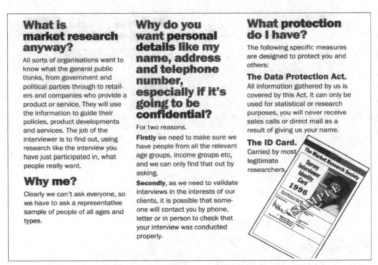

*Figure 16.2: A Market Research Society card*

> ➤ **Discussion: Look back at the order form shown in Figure 16.1. Is it possible that some of the data entered on the form could be *valid* but *inaccurate*?**

## Exercises

1.   *(see case study below)*

## Case study: Market research survey

The National Readership Survey is a survey about the newspapers and magazines people read (and the ones they don't), how much television they watch, and how much they listen to the radio. The research is used by publishers and editors to help them identify, for instance, what people of different ages are interested in, so they can produce newspapers and magazines to suit their readers.

The people to be interviewed (35,000 annually) are a cross-section of the population, and in order to make sure that a representative sample is chosen, interviewees are asked questions about their age, occupation, income and other descriptive details. They are also asked for their name and telephone number. Each interviewer is equipped with a battery-powered laptop computer with a single floppy disk drive and a modem. The program for each particular survey is posted to them in advance together with a list of addresses to visit and a list of questions to ask. The interviewer types the respondent's answers straight into the computer from where the data is saved onto the floppy disk. Each evening the data is transferred by telephone link to the company's mainframe computer. The data is analysed and distributed within two weeks of collection.

> ➤ **Questions:**
>
> a.   How can a householder be sure that the interviewer is genuinely employed by a Market Research Organisation? (1)
>
> b.   Name **two** advantages of entering data straight into the computer rather than onto hand-written forms. (2)
>
> c.   Describe briefly **two** advantages and **two** disadvantages of using laptop computers that have only a single floppy drive and no hard disk. In each case say whether the advantage or disadvantage is to the market research company or to the interviewer. (4)
>
> d.   The interviewees' names, addresses and telephone numbers are stored on the mainframe computer system, but held separately from the answers given in the interview and not linked to them in any way. Why are interviewees asked to supply this information? Explain why names and addresses are held separately from the rest of the data. (3)
>
> e.   The survey includes questions on which sections (home news, foreign news, sport, computers, finance etc) people read in newspapers and also questions on major purchases made by members of the household over the past year or two. How would this information be useful to the organisations which use the data? (2)

2.   A well designed information system should be able to check that input data is valid, but it can never ensure that information is accurate.

   (a)   Explain the distinction between accuracy of information and validity of data. Illustrate this distinction with a suitable example. (4)

   (b)   Describe **two** ways in which data capture errors may arise, together with techniques for preventing or reducing these errors. (4)

   *NEAB IT02 Qu 6 1997*

3. Most banks and building societies now offer cash withdrawal facilities through the use of Automatic Teller Machines (ATMs). The data that needs to be entered before a transaction can take place will include the customer's account number and Personal Identification Number (PIN).

   (a) (i) State **three** validation checks that should be made on the customer's account number. (3)

       (ii) State **one** validation check that should be made on the PIN. (1)

   (b) These transactions will normally involve transmission of data from and to an ATM via a communications link. State **one** security precaution that should always be taken, giving a reason why it is needed. (2)

   *NEAB IT02 Qu 8 1999*

4. A company that organises music festivals sells tickets via the Internet. An on-line booking form has to be completed to reserve the tickets.

   (a) State **three** fields other than Name, Address and Postcode that you would expect to find on the booking form. (3)

   (b) Name and describe a different validation check for each of the fields you have chosen. (6)

   *AQA ICT2 Qu 7 May 2001*

5. A school uses an information system to store details of students' examination entries and results. As part of this system a program is used to check the validity of data such as candidate number, candidate names and the subjects entered.

   (a) Suggest **three** possible validation tests which might be carried out on this data. (3)

   (b) Explain, with an example, why data which is found to be valid by this program may still need to be verified. (2)

   *NEAB IT02 Qu 5 1996*

6. With the aid of an example, distinguish clearly between a batch/control total and a hash total. (4)

   *NISEAC Computing Paper 2 Qu 3 1996*

7. Explain the difference between the terms verification and validation when applied to data. Illustrate your answer with an example of each. (4)

   *AQA ICT2 Qu 6 May 2002*

# Chapter 17 – Introduction to Databases

## What is a database?

A database is a collection of data. It may be something as simple as a list of names and addresses or details of the CDs in your personal collection, or it may contain details of all the customers, products, orders and payments in a large organisation. The word database often now refers to data held on a computer but non-computerised databases also exist. Some smaller schools, for example, may hold a card index file with details about all the pupils in the school. A school library may hold a card-index file with details about each book.

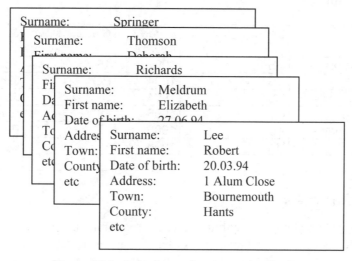

*Figure 17.1: A database of names and addresses*

## Retrieving information from a database

The main difference between computerized and non-computerised databases is the speed with which data can be accessed. Information that would previously have taken weeks or even years to gather and collate can now be gathered in a few seconds. A doctor's surgery, for example, may hold details on each patient. To find the names and addresses of all patients over 65 in a manual system would involve a painstaking search through every record. The answer could be retrieved from a computerized database in a second or two.

A computerized database also makes it possible to analyse data in ways that were previously unthinkable. Retail stores such as Tesco and Sainsbury's collect data on customer purchases every time a loyalty card is used. This data can be held in a database and used to build up a profile of what each customer is likely to purchase. Health Authorities can carry out complex analyses linking various illnesses to other factors such as diet or environment. Police databases are used to build up profiles of crimes and criminals and come up with possible suspects.

## Databases vs. Database Management Systems

The software that is used to access, update and manipulate the data in a computerised database is known as a Database Management System. There are many different ways in which data can be organised in a database, but by far the most common is the **relational database model**. Microsoft Access is an example of a Relational Database Management System (RDBMS).

## Flat files

A flat file is a database held in a single file. This allows only very simple structuring of the data, and the software that accesses and updates the data is commonly called a File Management System.

File management systems (such as the one which forms part of the integrated package MS Works) have been around for a number of years and differ from true Database Management Systems in that the data stored in one file cannot easily be linked to data stored in another file. These so-called 'flat-files' are useful for storing data such as a list of contact names and addresses, a list of student grades or details of a video collection. A spreadsheet can be used as a flat-file database, with a column representing a field and a row representing a record.

| Video number | Title | Country | Date released | Classification | Star |
|---|---|---|---|---|---|
| 1 | A Few Good Men | US | 1992 | 15 | Tom Cruise |
| 2 | The Mask | US | 1994 | PG | Jim Carrey |
| 3 | The Flintstones | US | 1994 | U | John Goodman |
| 4 | Trainspotting | UK | 1996 | 18 | Ewan McGregor |
| 5 | Crocodile Dundee | AUS | 1986 | 15 | Paul Hogan |
| 6 | Elizabeth | UK | 1998 | 15 | Cate Blanchett |
| etc | | | | | |

## Problems with flat files

There are several drawbacks to holding anything except very simple data in a single file. As an example, consider a file that contains details about customer orders for an electrical goods store. If all the data is to be held in a single file, the file needs to contain details of the customer (such as name and address), the items ordered, the employee who sold the item and probably the supplier of the item as well. We could end up with a file of data similar to that shown below:

ORDERTABLE

| OrderNo | OrderDate | ItemNo | Description | Price | Supplier | Customer | Employee Firstname | Employee Surname | Date Employed |
|---|---|---|---|---|---|---|---|---|---|
| 1 | 10/01/00 | 54112 | Oven | 475.00 | Atag | Harris | James | Noakes | 09/10/99 |
| 2 | 10/01/00 | 87123 | Dihswasher | 260.00 | Phillips | Jenner | Rebecca | Maynard | 01/02/98 |
| 3 | 11/01/00 | 44433 | CD Player | 500.00 | Toshiba | Bemrose | James | Nokes | 09/10/99 |
| 4 | 11/01/00 | 81723 | Dishwasher | 260.00 | Philipps | Akbar | Rebecca | Maynard | 01/02/98 |
| 5 | 11/01/00 | 54112 | Oven | 475.00 | Atag | Payne | James | Noaks | 01/01/99 |
| 6 | 11/01/00 | 18293 | Hairdryer | 24.50 | Phillips | Campbell | Paul | Smith | 05/06/97 |

We would also need to hold details of the customer such as their title and initials, address and phone number, and additional details both on the item sold and the employee. Even with the small number of fields shown it is obvious that the file has serious shortcomings. These are described in the following paragraphs.

## Redundant data

The table contains a vast amount of repeated data. Names, prices and dates are all stored several times, wasting disk space and slowing down any queries that we might make to retrieve information from the table. Data entry will be time-consuming since every time an order is entered, the employee's name, date of employment and other details will have to be typed in as well. The description and price of the item will also have to be typed in along with the supplier details. If we sell 500 dishwashers, the price, description and supplier details will have to be recorded 500 times.

## Errors on input

Typographical errors are bound to occur if all these details have to be entered every time a sale is made. In the table above, employee *Noakes* has had his name spelt wrongly twice. A query to find out the total value of sales made by Noakes will not find them all – he will not be pleased when his bonus for selling goods worth over £2000 per day is wrongly calculated as a result!

## Problems with updating data

Suppose Rebecca Maynard, one of the employees who has made thousands of sales since she was employed, gets married and changes her name. Instead of having to make this change only once, every record that contains her name would have to be updated. Similarly, if details such as address and telephone number of each employee were stored (which they certainly would be), these details would have to be changed in every record if the employee moved or changed their phone number.

## Problems with modifying data

With a single table, problems arise if records need to be added or deleted. When a new employee joins the sales force, there is no way of adding their details to the database until they make their first sale. Similarly, if a record is to be deleted, information will be lost. For example if record number 3 is deleted the information about the price and supplier of the CD Player will be lost.

## Summary

In summary, the problems that arise with flat file databases are:

- Redundant data, which makes the file large, wasting space on disk, and also makes it slow to retrieve information;
- Errors which arise from typing the same data many times in different records;
- Difficulties in updating and modifying data.

These problems can be solved in the most efficient way possible by using multiple tables to store the data.

## Using multiple tables

We can move the data about employees into a separate table. At the same time, we will give each employee a unique ID number since it is quite possible that the store could hire two people with identical names and with the current information stored there would be no way of distinguishing between them.

The two tables shown below hold the same data as before.

EMPLOYEETABLE

| EmployeeID | Employee Firstname | Employee Surname | Date Employed |
|---|---|---|---|
| 1 | James | Noakes | 09/10/99 |
| 2 | Rebecca | Maynard | 01/02/98 |
| 3 | Paul | Smith | 05/06/97 |

ORDERTABLE

| OrderNo | OrderDate | ItemNo | Description | Price | Supplier | Customer | EmployeeID |
|---|---|---|---|---|---|---|---|
| 1 | 10/01/00 | 54112 | Oven | 475.00 | Atag | Harris | 1 |
| 2 | 10/01/00 | 87123 | Dishwasher | 260.00 | Phillips | Jenner | 2 |
| 3 | 11/01/00 | 44433 | CD Player | 500.00 | Toshiba | Bemrose | 1 |
| 4 | 11/01/00 | 81723 | Dishwasher | 260.00 | Philipps | Akbar | 2 |
| 5 | 11/01/00 | 54112 | Oven | 475.00 | Atag | Payne | 1 |
| 6 | 11/01/00 | 18293 | Hairdryer | 24.50 | Phillips | Campbell | 3 |

What we have done is leave the employee ID in the ORDERTABLE to act as a pointer to which employee sold the item. All the information about a particular employee can then be looked up in the EMPLOYEETABLE.

Using the same principle, we could set up a separate table for Item to hold the description, price and supplier, and a fourth table to hold details of customers. We would need to assign each customer a unique ID number just as we did for employees, and leave the ItemNo and CustomerID as pointers in ORDERTABLE.

> ➤ **Discussion: What would each of the four tables EMPLOYEETABLE, CUSTOMERTABLE, ITEMTABLE and ORDERTABLE look like, holding the same information as the single table that we started with? Show the contents of each table.**
>
> **Notice that this structure does not allow for an order consisting of more than one item! You would need yet another table to cater for this, or there will still be redundant data on the tables. Try using another table called ORDER-LINE, or ignore this complication for now.**

It is quite likely that details on each supplier would be held as well. A further table could be set up to hold these details.

This principle of giving each *entity*, (or *object* or *thing*) its own table and linking the tables by means of a pointer like EmployeeID or CustomerID is the principle behind **relational databases**. Relational database management systems (RDMSs) such as MS Access make the process of referring to several different tables to look up data completely transparent to the user.

## Solving the problems of single table databases

One of the problems with holding the data in a single table was the amount of redundant data that needs to be stored. Using a separate table for each entity means that the information only needs to be entered once. This also avoids the problems of typographical errors arising from typing the same data in many different records.

The difficulties which arise in modifying and updating data in a single table also disappear when multiple tables are used. We can, for example, add a new employee as soon as they are hired, before they have made a sale.

In the next chapter we will look in more detail at how to design the best database structure for a particular application.

# Flat file information storage and retrieval systems

Before database management systems became popular, it was common practice for each department in a large company to keep their own data on separate files. Thus for example the Payroll department would keep data on employees and their salaries, tax information and so on. The Personnel Department might have a very similar file holding much of the same information, but with some non-overlapping fields. The Sales Department might have a file holding sales figures from which employee bonuses were calculated, which would have to be passed to the Payroll Department.

*Figure 17.2: Data files in a traditional flat file system*

This type of system (the 'traditional file approach') is also loosely known as a 'flat file information storage and retrieval system'. In addition to the problem of redundant data being stored in several different files, problems arose when it became necessary to add new fields to a file, because all the programs using the file had to be updated to reflect the change even if they did not use the new fields.

The advantages of a database system over such a system may be summarised as:

- data independence                        i.e. the structure of the database does not affect the programs which access the database;

- quality of management information        information is more useful as it is based on a single, comprehensive set of data;

- control over redundancy                   the data is not stored several times in separate files

- consistency of data                       because the data is stored only once, there is no possibility of holding different data on different files (e.g. different addresses for the same employee);

- more information available to users       because the data is held in a single, company-wide database, all users have access to it;

- greater security of data                  a database management system enables different levels of access to be specified so that users can only view or update the parts of the database that they are authorised to access or change;

- less time spent inputting data            because it is held only once, there is no duplication of effort inputting the same data into different files.

## Exercises

1. Explain by means of an example:
    (i) what is meant by *data redundancy* in a flat file information and retrieval system; (2)
    (ii) how data in such a system might become *inconsistent*. (2)

    *New question*

2. A publishing company keeps records of all the books they publish, and the authors of each book in a flat file system, for the purposes of calculating royalty payments to each author. Each author is paid a royalty based on an agreed percentage of gross sales over the previous 6 months. An advance on royalties is paid when a manuscript is delivered and this is deducted from the first royalty payment. (Only one column is shown for address to save space in the example but there will in practice be several columns).

    The file called BOOK contains fields as shown below. Some sample contents are also shown.

BOOK

| Book No | Title | Author | Address1 | Date Published | Royalty% | Advance |
|---------|-------|--------|----------|----------------|----------|---------|
| 156 | Basic Spreadsheets | Donaldson,G | 3 Elgar Close | 01/03/99 | 7.5% | £0 |
| 157 | Programming in Visual Basic | Noakes,K | White House | 01/04/99 | 10% | £500 |
| 160 | Intermediate Spreadsheets | Donaldson,G | 3 Elgar Close | 01/02/00 | 8% | £250 |
| 163 | Basic Windows 2000 | Woods,R | 6 Bullen Ave | 01/03/00 | 10% | £0 |

    (i) Explain, with reference to the above table, what is meant by *redundant data*. (2)

    (ii) Describe briefly **two** problems which arise from holding the data in a single table. (2)

    (iii) Show how the data could be rearranged in two tables to solve these problems. (4)

    *New question*

3. A company is experiencing difficulties with its computerised flat file information storage and retrieval system. Describe **three** benefits that the company would gain by converting to a relational database system. (6)

    *AQA ICT2 Qu 5 January 2001*

# Chapter 18 – Relational Databases

## Relational databases

Within a relational database, data is stored in **tables**. A very simple database such as one that contains a list of names and addresses may have all the data stored in a single table, whereas a more complex database such as the one discussed in the previous chapter holding details of customers, orders, employees, items for sale and suppliers will require several tables.

## Putting data into the correct tables

When you set out to design a database for a particular application, how do you know how many tables to use, and what data to put in which table? The answer lies in the fact that the database will be storing information about real-world objects or entities such as students, subjects and teachers, or doctors and patients at a GP's surgery. Relationships exist between these entities – for example a student can study many subjects, and a subject may be studied by several students. A doctor will be responsible for many patients but a patient will only see one doctor.

Databases have to store information about these different objects and the relationships that exist between them. Generally the commonsense rule to follow is: *create a table for each separate entity in the database.*

### Example 1: A library database

Let's see how this works in practice. Suppose you are going to build a database to keep track of books in a library, and who has books out on loan. We will assume that a borrower may have several books out on loan at any one time. The two obvious entities in this system are BORROWER and BOOK, so we will create a table for each of these entities. Next you have to decide what fields to put in each table. One rule is that each record in the table must have a unique identifier by which it can be distinguished from every other record in the table. It is usually a good idea to use a simple numeric identifier.

The BORROWER table could have the following fields:

> BorrowerID  (This is the unique identifier, also known as the *primary key*)
> Surname
> Firstname
> Title
> AddressLine1
> AddressLine2
> Town
> County
> Postcode
> DateofBirth


The BOOK table could have the following fields:

> BookID  (The unique identifier or *primary key* – it could be the accession number of the book)
> DeweyCode
> Title
> Author
> DatePublished
> Publisher

Using **standard database notation**, these tables can be described as follows:

BORROWER (<u>BorrowerID</u>,  Surname, Firstname, Title, AddressLine1, AddressLine2, Town,
     County, Postcode, DateofBirth)
BOOK (<u>BookID</u>, DeweyCode, Title, Author, DatePublished, Publisher)

(Note that the table name is shown in uppercase and the primary key is underlined.)

You may be able to think of several other fields that we could have on each table.

The next problem is that these tables do not tell us anything about who has which books on loan. To solve this, we can look at 3 different possibilities:

Option 1. On the BORROWER table, add fields showing which books the individual has out on loan and when they are due back;   *or*

Option 2. On the BOOK table, include fields to show whether the book is out on loan, who has borrowed it and when it is due back;   *or*

Option 3. Create a brand new table holding details about books on loan.

Option 1 is a bad one because we don't know how many fields to set aside for books that have been borrowed. The majority of borrowers may have no books on loan at any particular time, many borrowers may have just one or two, and a few borrowers may have the maximum, say 6 books, out on loan. It will be a waste of space to allow 6 fields for books borrowed, (not to mention 6 more for date due back) on every customer record. It will also be very difficult to query the database to find who has a particular book out, since we won't know which of 6 fields to look in.

Option 2 is better, and will involve adding 2 extra fields to the BOOK table – BorrowerID and DateDue. BorrowerID acts as a pointer or link to the BORROWER table and all the details about the borrower can be looked up as required. It will be easy to query the BOOK table to find out who has the book out on loan.

The only drawback to this solution is that most libraries have tens of thousands of books on the shelves and relatively few out on loan at any one time. Therefore, queries to find out who has overdue books, or when a particular book is due back, may take a very long time because so many records have to be searched. Let's look at Option 3.

Option 3 involves creating a new table which we will call LOAN. This needs only 3 fields:
BookID  (This is also a *foreign key* because it is a primary key of the BOOK table, not this one)
BorrowerID (This is known as a *foreign key* because it is a primary key of another table, not this one)
DateDue

This is the best solution to the problem. The LOAN table will be relatively small, queries will be performed very quickly, and there is very little redundant data. (this solution does use one more field in total and the tables will take up a little more space than the two tables for Option 2 but the benefits far outweigh the disadvantages.) The table will be structured as follows:

LOAN (<u>BookID</u>, BorrowerID, DateDue)

Note that BookID is a unique primary key only if the loan records are deleted as soon as the book is returned. If the loan record remains on the table, no one else will be able to borrow the book because the database will not allow two records which have the same primary key to be added to the table!

**Example 2: A vet keeps a database to hold information about the treatments that each animal has had. Owners are notified when, for example, a cat is due to be vaccinated against cat flu. What tables are required for this application, and what fields should be specified on each table?**

When designing a database it is important to have a clear idea of what information you hope to get out of it. There is no point collecting and keeping data unless it is required on a report or as part of an answer to a query.

Step 1.    Identify the entities. Obvious entities include PET, OWNER, VISIT and possibly TREATMENT. There may be other entities such as DRUG.

Step 2.    Decide what fields need to be held on each table. Identify a primary key for each table.

Step 3.    Make sure the relationships between the tables are correctly represented by means of foreign keys linking the tables together.

As a first try, the tables might have fields defined as follows:

**PET**

>      PetID          *(Primary key)*
>
>      Type of animal (Dog, Cat, etc)
>
>      Breed
>
>      Date of Birth

**OWNER**

>      OwnerID   *(Primary key)*
>
>      Surname
>
>      Initials
>
>      Title
>
>      Address (probably split into 4 or 5 fields)

**VISIT**

>      PetID          *(Part of Primary key)*
>
>      Date          *(Part of Primary key)*
>
>      Flu Vaccine (Y/N)
>
>      Other treatments (Notes)

Notice that in the VISIT table, the PetID on its own is not sufficient to uniquely identify the record, since a pet may have several visits. Assuming that an animal only ever has one visit on a particular date, the two fields PetID and Date together form a unique identifier and can be used as the primary key.

Looking at Step 3, we must make sure that the relationships are correctly represented.

---

➢   **Discussion: What additional field(s) need to be added to which table(s) to represent the relationship 'One owner may have several pets'?**

---

## Creating a database table in MS Access

We have seen that before you can begin to store data in a database table, you have to specify the format of a record in the table. Each record in the table will have the same format or structure, specified by defining the characteristics of each field in a record. You must specify:

1.  The **order** in which the fields are stored in the record.

2.  The **name** of each field.

3.  The **field type**. The database software will offer a number of field types including

    *   Text (also referred to as Character or Alphanumeric)

    *   Numeric (integer, or real with a specified number of decimal points)

    *   Date (in a number of different formats)

    *   Yes/No (or True/False)

    *   Memo (for writing notes about a client, for example).

4.  For some types of field such as a text field, the field length. This should be large enough to hold the maximum expected length of data – for example, 20 characters could be allowed for a surname.

Once the structure of the database table has been specified, the empty table can be given a name and saved.

## The significance of field types

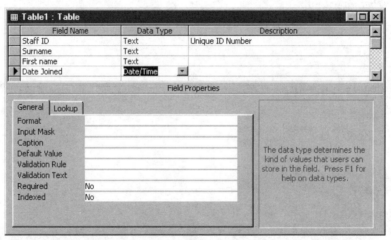

*Figure 18.1: Specifying the structure of a record in a database file*

Does it really matter whether you specify a date or numeric field as a text type, or a field such as a telephone number as numeric? The answer is YES – for several reasons.

*   Certain field types are automatically validated when the user enters data. Thus, if you specify a field named Date of Birth as a date field, the software will not allow a user to enter 31/2/76 because this is not a valid date. If you have specified the field as a text field, no automatic validation is possible.

*   Similarly, if a field is defined as currency or numeric, the user will not be able to enter a non-numeric character in the field by mistake.

*   On the other hand, it is unwise to define a telephone number as numeric because a user may want to leave a space or hyphen between the area code and the rest of the number, and a numeric field will allow only numbers and a decimal point to be entered.

- Numeric fields are held differently inside the computer from text fields, and if the field will be involved in any type of calculation, it MUST be defined as numeric (or date, or currency) or an error will be reported when the computer tries to perform the calculation.

- The length specified for a text field should also be chosen carefully and documented for future reference. If a student ID, for example, is defined as 6 characters in one file and 10 characters in another file, errors will occur when the two files are linked through this common ID number.

## Primary key

Each individual row or record in a database file needs to be given a unique identifier, and this is termed the **primary key**. It needs to be carefully chosen so that there is no possibility of two people or items being confused; Surname, for example, is no use as an identifier. The primary key sometimes consists of more than one field: for example several stores in a national chain may each have a store number, and each store may have Departments 1,2,3 etc. To identify a particular department in a particular store, the primary key would be composed of both Store number and Department number.

> ➤ **Discussion: What would be a suitable primary key for:**     **a book in a bookshop?**
>                                                                    **a book in a library?**
>                                                                    **a hospital patient?**
>                                                                    **a car owned by a car-hire firm?**

## Exercises

1. Express in standard database notation the tables for PET, OWNER and VISIT described in this chapter.      (3)

   *New question*

2. A video and games rental shop uses a database package to record membership details of customers who wish to borrow videos or games. The following details must be entered for each new member; full name, address, postcode and date of birth.

   (a) Name and describe a validation check that could be used when data is first entered into the following fields for a new member. Your validation check must be different in each case.

       (i)    Full_Name      (2)

       (ii)   Postcode      (2)

       (iii) Date_of_Birth      (2)

   (b) The database package automatically generates a membership number. Explain why this is required.      (2)

   *AQA ICT2 Qu 7 January 2001*

# Chapter 19 – Tables, Forms, Queries and Reports

## The basic components of a database

The four basic components of a database are:

- tables
- forms
- queries
- reports

In order to demonstrate how each of these components is used, we will build a simple database of library borrowers, books and loans as described in Chapter 18.

## The tables for the Library application

Three tables are needed for this application which we will call **tblBorrower**, **tblBook** and **tblLoan**. The structure of each table is shown below.

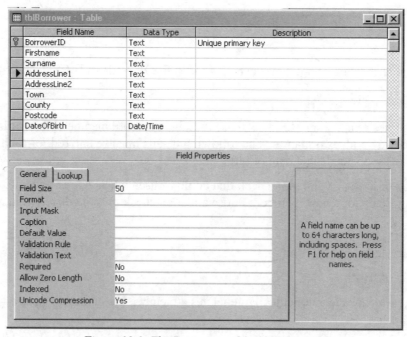

*Figure 19.1: The Borrower table (tblBorrower)*

Data can be entered into this table in one of two ways: straight into the table in what Access calls Datasheet view, or using a form specially designed for the purpose. In Figure 19.2 two records have been added in Datasheet view.

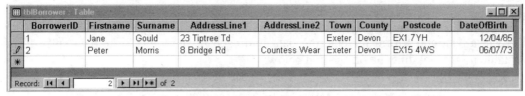

*Figure 19.2: Data entered into **tblBorrower** in Datasheet view*

Next we will create the structures for tblBook and tblLoan.

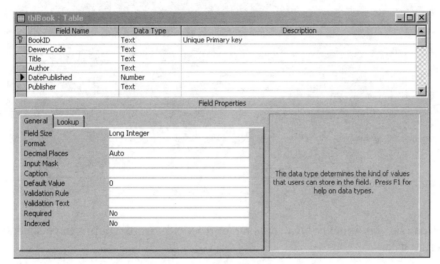

*Figure 19.3: The Book table (tblBook)*

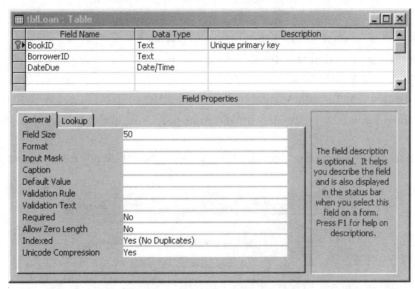

*Figure 19.4: The Loan table (tblLoan)*

Note that the primary key of the loan table is BookID. This is sufficient to uniquely identify the record provided that a Loan record is deleted from the table as soon as the book is returned by the borrower. Both BorrowerID and BookID are *foreign keys* because they are primary keys in tblBorrower and tblBook respectively.

# Forms

We can create a data entry form for entering data into each of the tables. The data entry form for the Borrower table might look like the one shown below:

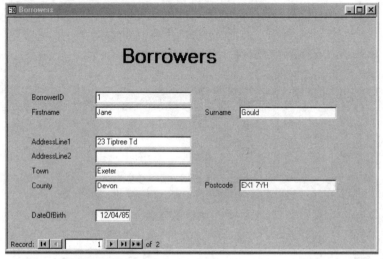

*Figure 19.5: Data entry form for Borrowers*

A form like this can be very quickly created using an Access 'wizard'. Forms have several advantages as a means of entering data:

- they present a much more attractive appearance to the user;

- the fields can be placed on the form in a convenient order for data entry;

- some fields can be given default values so that the user rarely has to enter a value – for example, the town could default to 'Exeter' if this was a library in Exeter;

- validation can be performed automatically on certain fields – for example the program could check that the date of birth is within a particular range;

- forms can be created which contain fields from several different tables – we will do this below;

- several data entry forms can be created for different purposes, each showing just the relevant fields from the table(s).

If we use a wizard to create a form for inputting Loan details, the following form is created:

*Figure 19.6: First attempt at form for entering Loans*

This is not a good form because it gives the user no opportunity to check the name of the borrower or the title of the book. These details are not held on the Loans table – they are on tblBorrower and tblBook. We need to combine the data from the three tables before creating the form, and to do this, we use a **query**.

## Queries

Queries are very powerful tools in a database. They are most commonly used to find subsets of the data, such as for example all loans for books which are overdue, or all borrowers over 16 years old. Reports or mail-merge letters can then be created from these subsets of the data.

In a multi-table database queries can pull together all the information needed from different tables, creating a new **answer** table from which forms and reports can be created. When data in the original tables (called the **base** tables) changes, the changes will automatically be reflected in the answer tables. Queries can also be used to summarise data, delete or update all records satisfying particular criteria, append data to one table from another, or make a brand new table.

We'll look at how a query can combine data from tblBorrower, tblBook and tblLoan. First of all the relationships between the three entities needs to be defined.:

> One borrower may have many books on loan;    (a one-to-many relationship)
>
> Each book may appear on one loan record.    (a one-to-one relationship)

The relationship between Borrower and Book can be specified in Access (using **Edit**, **Relationships**) and is depicted as shown below:

*Figure 19.7: Setting up relationships between entities*

The query is now created as shown below, using fields from all three tables. The query has been saved with the name **qryLoanForm** and this will also be used by Access as the name of the Answer table from which our new form will be created.

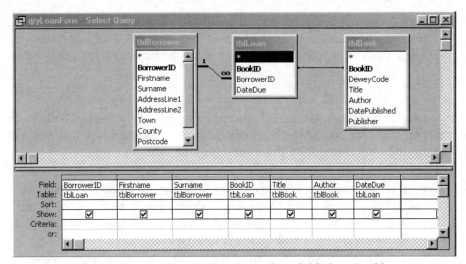

*Figure 19.8: Creating a query to combine fields from 3 tables*

*Note: When a book is returned, the Loan record for that book must immediately be removed from the Loan table, or it will not be possible to add a new Loan record for the book. if, say, the same Borrower wants to take it out again the next day.*

## Creating the Loan form from the new query

Now the new form can be created using the new query as the source. A possible layout is shown below. As soon as the user enters the BorrowerID, the borrower's name is automatically shown, and similarly, the book title and author are shown when the BookID is entered.

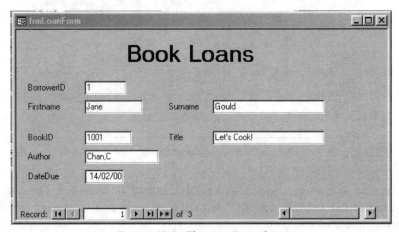

*Figure 19.9: The new Loan form*

## Reports

Queries are commonly used to pick out records satisfying particular criteria and to sort or summarise them ready to be printed on a report. For example, suppose we wanted a list, sorted by borrower name, of all books overdue by more than one week. These borrowers could then be mailed a postcard reminding them to return their books.

The first step is to perform a query to pick out the fields that are needed on the report and to set the criteria, expressed in the DateDue column as *<Date()-7* (Note that *Date()* gives today's date.) The report will be sorted in the order in which the fields appear on the query unless we specify otherwise. In the example below we have specified that the records are to be sorted in ascending order of Surname and Firstname.

*Figure 19.10: Query to find overdue books*

Now a report can be created based on the records in the Answer table.

| Overdue books | | | | 22 February 2000 | | | |
|---|---|---|---|---|---|---|---|
| ID | Surname | Firstname | Address | BookID | Title | Author | DateDue |
| 6 | Arnot | Mark | 7 Exe Vale Road | 1009 | Wild Swans | Chang | 10/02/00 |
| | | | Exeter | | | | |
| | | | Devon        EX8 7HG | | | | |
| 4 | Baker | Neil | 7 School Lane | 1011 | Business Information | Cleary,T | 09/02/00 |
| | | | Countess Wear | | | | |
| | | | Exeter | | | | |
| | | | Devon        EX11 9KP | | | | |
| 4 | Baker | Neil | 7 School Lane | 1010 | The Road Ahead | Gates,Bill | 09/02/00 |
| | | | Countess Wear | | | | |
| | | | Exeter | | | | |
| | | | Devon        EX11 9KP | | | | |

*Figure 19.11: A report on overdue books*

## Selecting a suitable output format

Reports can contain any data from any table or combination of tables, sorted and summarised as required. The report can be suitably **formatted** by selecting appropriate headings, fonts, spacing and sequence of fields across the page. In the example above the address fields have been arranged in just two columns so that the fields fit across the page.

*You can download all the instructions to build this database in Access 2000 or 2002 from the web site* <u>www.payne-gallway.co.uk</u>

## Exercises

1. Explain how data can be retrieved from a database in order to produce meaningful information. (4)

   *New question*

2. A **report generator** allows a user to generate a report by specifying the fields required on the report. Name **four** other parameters a user might specify in order to create a report in the desired format. (4)

   *New question*

3. Describe briefly two different uses for **queries** in a database management system, giving an example of each. (4)

   *New question*

4. Give **four** reasons why data is normally entered into a database by means of a specially created form rather than directly into the tables. (4)

   *New question*

# Chapter 20 – Systems Software

## What is an operating system?

Computers require two types of software: **applications software** such as word processing, spreadsheet or graphics packages, and **operating systems software** to control and monitor the running of application programs, and to allow users to communicate with the computer.

The operating system consists of a number of programs which are typically 'bundled' with the hardware; in other words, when you buy a new PC, for example, you will also be supplied with a CD containing the latest version of the Windows operating system. This then has to be installed by running a special installation program supplied on the CD, which will copy the operating system to your hard disk and customise it to your particular hardware configuration.

The part of the operating system that manages the computer's resources (the CPU, memory, storage devices and peripherals) is called the **kernel** (or **supervisor** or **control program**). Each time you switch on your PC, the kernel will be copied from the hard disk into memory, which takes a couple of minutes.

## Functions of an operating system

Obviously, the operating system (OS) for a standalone microcomputer system will be very much simpler than that of a supercomputer which is controlling hundreds of terminals and running many different kinds of job simultaneously. Nevertheless, all operating systems perform certain basic functions, including:

- **Memory management.** Most computers nowadays are capable of holding several programs in memory simultaneously, so that a user can switch from one application to another. The operating system has to allocate memory to each application – as well as to itself!

  If the OS detects that there is insufficient memory to load an application that the user has asked for, it may swap another application (or part of it) out to disk temporarily, and reload it when required, swapping something else out to disk. This takes time, which is why increasing memory may have the effect of speeding up the computer's performance.

  The technique of swapping part of the contents of memory out to disk is known as **virtual memory**, because it makes the computer appear to have more memory than it actually does.

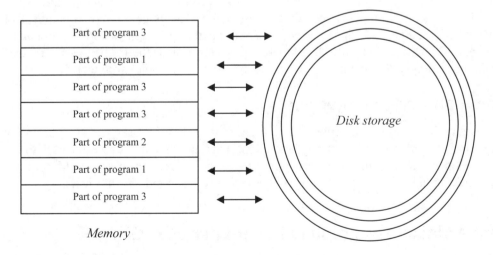

*Figure 20.1: Virtual memory*

- **Resource allocation and scheduling**. In larger computer systems which are capable of running several programs at once (**multiprogramming**), the OS is responsible for allocating processing time, memory and input-output resources to each one.

- **Backing store management**. The OS controls the transfer of data from secondary storage (e.g. disk) to memory and back again. It also has to maintain a directory of the disk so that files and free space can be quickly located.

- **Interrupt handling**. The OS detects many different kinds of interrupt such as for example a user pressing the Enter key on the keyboard, a printer sending a message that it is out of paper, the real-time clock interrupting to indicate that the processor should be allocated to the next user in a multi-user system, a hardware or software malfunction.

- **Allowing a user to communicate with the computer**. The user gives instructions to the computer to start a program, copy a file, send a message to another user, and so on by typing in commands recognised by the operating system or by using a mouse to point and click in a graphical user interface such as Windows 2000.

## Utility programs

As well as the basic operating system, the systems software available to users includes numerous **utility programs**, such as:

- **Virus checkers** which check disks and memory for viruses and delete them if detected;

- **Security and accounting** software which checks user IDs and passwords, counts and reports the number of attempts made to log on under each user ID, the amount of processor time used at each session, total login time and so on;

- **File management utilities** which attempt to repair corrupted files, reorganise files on disk so that free space is 'defragmented' (which can improve performance), 'zip' (compress) files so that they occupy less space if for example you want to make a backup copy of a large file onto a floppy disk.

## The DOS operating system

Two operating systems currently dominate the microcomputer world: Windows and the Apple Macintosh (MacOS) operating system.

In 1981, IBM purchased from a tiny company called Microsoft Corporation an operating system which it called PC-DOS (Personal Computer Disk Operating System) for its new microcomputer. Bill Gates, the head of Microsoft, retained the right to sell the same operating system to other computer companies, under the name MS-DOS (Microsoft Disk Operating System), with the result that it rapidly became the most popular operating system in the world, with over 150 million copies sold worldwide.

## The command-driven interface

DOS was essentially a command-driven interface, meaning that the user had to type in commands in exactly the correct syntax to perform any operation. This allows complex commands to be entered to customise the operating system for a particular user, and experienced users could perform operations faster using DOS than by using a mouse and menus or icons in a Windows interface.

## The Apple Macintosh graphical user interface (GUI)

While Microsoft were developing their DOS operating system, the Apple Computer Corporation were working on a completely different way of communicating with a microcomputer. In 1984, Apple brought out their most powerful PC, the Macintosh, complete with the WIMP interface that has now become universal. WIMP stands for Windows, Icons, Mouse and Pull-down menus or alternatively, Windows, Icons, Menus, Pointer – and the term 'user-friendly' was more or less invented to describe this approach.

The Macintosh could do things that the IBM PC could not, such as having more than one application open at once, each in its own 'window', and transferring data between applications.

Unfortunately for Apple, from being the most popular PC in the late 1970s, they rapidly fell behind IBM even after the success of their graphical user interface. What went wrong? The major problem lay in the lack of software packages written especially for the Mac. Apple, unlike IBM, owned both the hardware and the operating system, and refused to license the operating system to any other company, so that while sales of PC 'clones' mushroomed, Apple retained a much smaller niche market.  Software developers concentrated on developing software for PCs running MS-DOS because this was a much larger market, even though the operating system was inferior to Apple's.

## The Windows operating system

Successive generations of the Windows operating system have appeared regularly every two years or so since the early 1990s.

Windows 95 and successive generations up to Windows XP and beyond are operating systems offering multi-tasking, and taking full advantage of the 32-bit architecture of newer PCs.

*Figure 20.2: Windows XP Interface*

Windows 95 and subsequent versions also provide 'Plug and Play' support designed to make it easier to install peripherals such as a new printer. The device merely needs to be plugged in and the user can then select 'Add New Hardware' from Control Panel in the Settings menu to be taken through a few easy steps for the device to be automatically configured with the appropriate driver. The **driver** is the software which acts as a "middle-man" or interface between the operating system and a hardware device such as a screen or printer. This makes it easy to write the operating system software because Microsoft does not have to write code for every device that you could possibly hook up to your computer. The device driver intercepts standard system function calls and then uses its own code to communicate with the hardware device and return any data resulting from the call to the operating system (e.g. "Printer ready", "Out of Paper" etc). The driver will translate formatting information into a form that the device can understand.

# UNIX

UNIX is a general-purpose, multi-user, multi-tasking operating system written in C, which has been around since the early 1970s. Unlike other operating systems, UNIX is available on a wide variety of platforms, which is to say that it can be used on computers from many different manufacturers. This means that users can select hardware from different manufacturers and use the same software on different types of hardware, which is not the case with other operating systems traditionally supplied with the hardware.

# Linux

Linux is an operating system created by Linus Torvalds, an altruistic Finnish programmer. It has been developed by thousands of volunteers, many of whom are regarded as some of the best programmers in the world. It is available entirely free and can be downloaded from the Internet, and for many young programmers the beauty of it is that you can pick it up and start improving it immediately. It is said to be far more bug-free than Windows 2000, which at 35 million lines of code, is the biggest program ever written. As more software manufacturers offer Linux versions of their software, it is just possible that Microsoft Windows' dominance may one day be buried.

# Exercises

1. At present there are many different computer operating systems in existence. If operating systems were standardised, give one different benefit for each of the following:

    (a) the user of computers;

    (b) the manufacturer of computers;

    (c) developers of software for computers.

    Give **one** technical reason why this is not likely to happen. (4)
    *AEB Computing Paper 1 Qu 8 1993*

2. Describe **three** housekeeping utilities normally provided with the operating system for a single-user personal computer. Your description should include a typical task for which each utility is used. (6)
    *NEAB Computing AS Paper 1 Qu 9 1996*

3. When using any applications software package on a network, the user is often unaware that an operating system is working 'behind the scenes', managing system resources. Give **three** of these resources and in each case briefly explain the role of the operating system in its management. (6)
    *NEAB IT02 Qu 4 1997*

4. Most modern PCs make use of a GUI (graphical user interface) and have a WYSIWYG (what you see is what you get) word processing package.

    (a) State **four** characteristics of a GUI. (4)

    (b) Describe **three** advantages to the user of a WYSIWYG word-processing package. (6)
    *AQA ICT2 Qu 4 May 2001*

5. Disk directories record information about the files that are stored on disk. State **three** items of information that, typically, would be recorded. (3)
    *AEB Computing Paper 2 Qu 4  1997*

6. From the experienced user's viewpoint, give **three** functions of an operating system. (3)
    *NEAB IT02 Specimen Paper Qu 5*

# Chapter 21 – Categories of Software

## Categorising software

**Software** is the general term used to describe all the programs which run on a computer. There are three general categories of software: systems software, applications software and general-purpose software. This categorisation is not rigid, however, and some people would say that general-purpose software and applications software can be lumped together. You will soon discover that very little in computing is black and white; whatever you read, someone will soon come up with an apparently contradictory statement on most topics, leaving you to choose your own truth!

## Systems software

In the last chapter we looked at the functions of an operating system, which must be installed on every computer and is independent of any applications that a user may wish to run. The operating system comes under the general heading of **systems software**, as do the utility programs mentioned in the last chapter. Here is a list of some of the different types of systems software.

1. **Operating system**. Already discussed.

2. **Utility programs**. These are programs designed to make life easier for computer users. Utility programs perform common tasks that thousands of computer users need to do at one time or another, such as search for lost files, sort files of data into a particular sequence, copy disk files to magnetic tape for backup purposes and so on.

3. **Programming language compilers/interpreters**. Compilers and interpreters are different types of program used to translate the statements in a programming language such as Pascal, Visual Basic or C into a form that the computer can understand.

4. **Performance monitoring software**. This is used to monitor, analyse and report on the performance of a computer and its components. It can provide information such as the overall utilisation of the processor and number of disk accesses over a given period of time. In a mainframe environment, this can assist management in monitoring the current and future hardware requirements.

5. **Communications software**. In a mainframe environment, communications software is executed on a separate, dedicated processor ('front-end processor') and controls the flow of data to and from remote locations.

## Applications software

Applications software is written to perform specific tasks such as order entry, payroll, stock control or hospital appointments. The software may be designed specifically for one particular company, ('bespoke software') and written especially for them using a programming language or software such as a database management system. Alternatively, the software may be purchased 'off the shelf'.

# General purpose software

All common application packages such as word processing, desktop publishing, spreadsheet, database, computer-aided design (CAD) and presentation graphics packages fall into this category. Most general purpose software is sold as a package, including a CD containing the software and manuals to help you get started and to be used as a reference.

*Figure 21.1: General purpose software*

# Integrated packages and software suites

The main productivity tools used by organisations include word processing, spreadsheets, databases, presentation graphics and communications software to enable users to communicate with each other either locally or across the world in an international company.

**Integrated packages** which combined features from all five of these products were once very popular, because they offered capabilities from all these packages in a single product at a relatively low price, and data could be transferred between applications. However, a single integrated package (e.g. Microsoft Works) has fewer and less sophisticated features than are found in separately-purchased packages.

Today, complete **software suites** such as Microsoft Office or Lotus SmartSuite offer four or more software products packaged together at a much lower price than buying the packages separately. Microsoft Office, for example, includes Word, Excel, Access and a multimedia presentation graphics package called PowerPoint.

## Common user interface

Terminology in the computer world soon becomes fuzzy and MS Office is sometimes referred to as an integrated suite. The advantage of buying such a suite of programs is that the individual applications are completely compatible so that there is no difficulty importing or exporting data from one package to another, if for example you wish to put a spreadsheet in a word processed report.

Another advantage of buying a software suite such as Microsoft Office is that a common user interface is used in each package, giving them all the same 'look and feel'. This means that similar menus such as **File**, **Edit**, **View**, **Insert** and so on appear at the top of the screen whether you are using Word, Excel, Access or another package. If you have learned how to insert a header and footer in Word, you can easily guess how to do it in Excel. The same icons are used for many operations such as opening, saving or printing a file, cutting, pasting and formatting. The same shortcut keys are used for various operations (such as **Ctrl-S** for **Save**) and this makes learning new software an easier task.

If your experience of software is limited to Microsoft products you may be surprised to find how difficult it can be, relatively speaking, to get to grips with a package from another manufacturer that has a completely different interface.

> ➤ **Discussion: How do you make a particular Toolbar appear on the screen in MS Word, Excel or PowerPoint? How do you copy a format from one cell to another in Excel?**

## Generic and specific software

Note that software such as word processing, spreadsheet and database software is sometimes referred to as **generic** software. This simply implies that any of the dozens of spreadsheet packages, for example, can be made to do many different tasks, and is not designed specifically for one type of application. The other type of application software such as a payroll or stock control system mentioned above, or a software package such as a program to help fill in an income tax return, is in contrast **specific** because it is designed to do one particular task.

## Exercises

1.  Describe the difference between applications software and systems software, giving an example of each. (4)

    *NEAB IT02 Qu 2 1996*

2.  All the staff in a small office use the same word-processing, spreadsheet and database packages. These packages all have a common user interface.

    (a)  Give **four** advantages of having a common user interface. (4)

    (b)  State four specific features of a user interface which would benefit from being common between the packages. (4)

    *AQA ICT2 Qu 6 January 2001*

3.  Give **three** points a user should consider before deciding to purchase a software package. (3)

    *NEAB AS Computing Paper 1 Qu 1 1996*

4.  Describe **three** housekeeping utilities normally provided with the operating system for a single-user personal computer. Your description should include a typical task for which each utility is used. (6)

    *NEAB AS Computing Paper 1 Qu 8 1996*

# Chapter 22 – Generic Software

## Generic software

This is a general term sometimes used to describe the application packages that are used to perform operations that are an integral part of day-to-day business operations. The most common ones are word processors, spreadsheets, database management systems and electronic mail. These four applications form the basis of both integrated packages and software suites from many different software manufacturers, and all have many features in common.

## Word processing

A word processing package is a program or set of programs used to enter, edit, format, store and print documents. A document may be anything from a simple memo to a complete book. In addition to data entry and editing facilities, word processors have several important features:

- **Spelling and grammar checker**. Each word in a document can be checked against words held in the package's dictionary, and in some packages misspelt words and grammatically incorrect sentences are underlined.  If the original word is correctly spelt but was highlighted by the spell checker, it can be added to the dictionary.

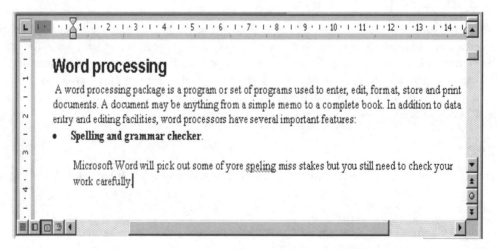

*Figure 22.1: A spelling checker underlines misspelt words*

- **Automatic creation of index and table of contents**. Any word in the text can be marked for inclusion in an index. Headings and subheadings in a given style can be included automatically in a table of contents, which can be updated at any time.

- **Import files**. Tables, photographs, graphics and even video and sound files can be imported from other sources and inserted in a document.

  A sound icon

To play the sound, double-click its icon. (This could be used to insert a verbal message or some music in a document, for example.)

- **Mail Merge**. A document and a list of names and addresses can be merged to produce personalised letters. (see Figure 22.2)

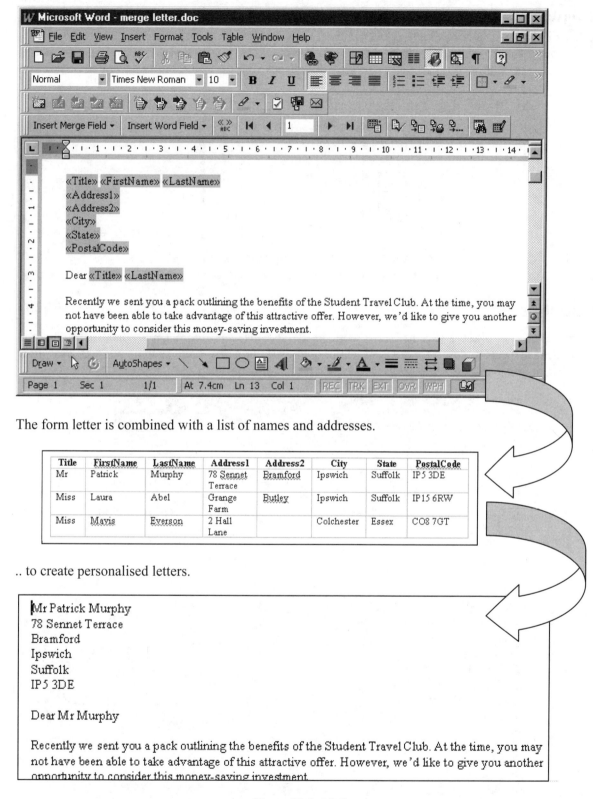

The form letter is combined with a list of names and addresses.

| Title | FirstName | LastName | Address1 | Address2 | City | State | PostalCode |
|-------|-----------|----------|----------|----------|------|-------|------------|
| Mr | Patrick | Murphy | 78 Sennet Terrace | Bramford | Ipswich | Suffolk | IP5 3DE |
| Miss | Laura | Abel | Grange Farm | Butley | Ipswich | Suffolk | IP15 6RW |
| Miss | Mavis | Everson | 2 Hall Lane | | Colchester | Essex | CO8 7GT |

.. to create personalised letters.

Mr Patrick Murphy
78 Sennet Terrace
Bramford
Ipswich
Suffolk
IP5 3DE

Dear Mr Murphy

Recently we sent you a pack outlining the benefits of the Student Travel Club. At the time, you may not have been able to take advantage of this attractive offer. However, we'd like to give you another opportunity to consider this money-saving investment.

*Figure 22.2: Mail merge*

- **Creation of templates** with preset text styles, margins, formatting, letterheading, etc.

- **WYSIWYG** capability. This acronym stands for 'What You See Is What You Get', and refers to the ability to display on screen exactly what you will get when the text is printed. Many word processors have more than one viewing mode so that in page layout view, for example, you can see a page as it will be printed, and in 'normal' view can see and edit text but not see imported pictures or text laid out in columns.

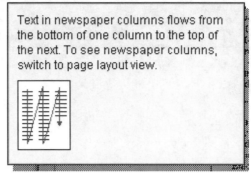

*Figure 22.3: Columns can be viewed in 'Page Layout' view in MS Word*

## Spreadsheets

Spreadsheet packages allow a user to create worksheets (spreadsheets) representing data in column and row form. Spreadsheets are used for any application that uses numerical data, such as budgets, cash flow forecasts, profit and loss statements, student marks or results of experiments.

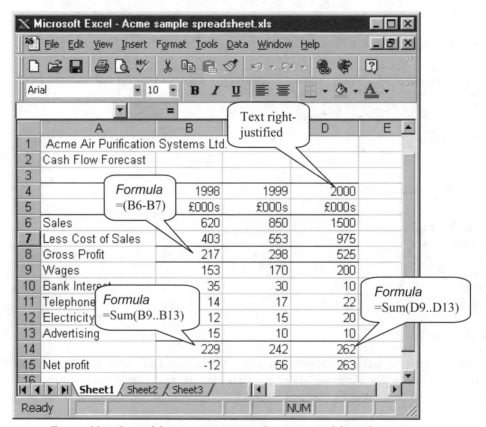

*Figure 22.4: Spreadsheet containing numbers, text and formulae*

# Spreadsheet features

Spreadsheets offer the following facilities:

- Format cells, rows and columns, specifying for example, the alignment of text, number of decimal points, height and width of cell;

- Copy cell contents to other locations, with automatic adjustment of formulae from say B9 to C9, D9 etc.;

- Determine the effect of several different hypothetical changes of data; this facility is termed 'what-if' calculation;

- Insert, move or delete rows and columns;

- Use functions such as SUM, AVERAGE, MAX, MIN in formulae;

- Create a simple database and sort or query the data to produce a report of, say, all females earning over £20,000 for a list of employees;

- Write macros to automate common procedures;

- Create templates – spreadsheets with formats and formulae already entered, into which new figures may be inserted;

- Create 'multi-dimensional' spreadsheets using several sheets, and copy data from one sheet to another;

- Create many different types of charts and graphs (see Figure 22.5).

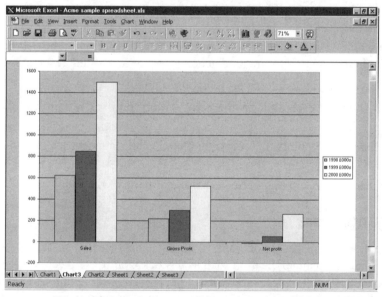

*Figure 22.5: A chart created from spreadsheet figures*

# Databases and Electronic Mail

These two applications are each discussed elsewhere (see chapters 17-19, 6) and are not covered here.

---

> **Discussion: Many integrated suites share common features such as menus, toolbars and shortcut key combinations to perform common tasks. Do you know some of these shortcuts? Do you know how to display toolbars that are not currently on the screen? Do you make use of the 'Help' menu when you are stuck?**

## Presentation Graphics

Presentation graphics software such as PowerPoint is useful for putting together a presentation which can be delivered using a computer attached to a projection device, using transparencies and an ordinary overhead projector or as a self-running presentation in, say, a shopping mall or cinema. The software allows the user to quickly create 'slides' combining text, graphics and pictures and to create animation or sound effects and 'transition' effects between slides.

*Figure 22.6: Creating a PowerPoint presentation*

When creating a presentation it is important to consider how the presentation will be given, and to what type of audience. The following points are good general tips for any slide presentation:

- Start with a title screen saying what the presentation is about.

- Use a consistent style for each slide in the presentation, perhaps a template showing the company logo.

- Don't put more than 4 or 5 points on each slide. People can't concentrate on too much information at once.

- Be sure the font size is large enough to be read from all parts of the room.

## Application generators

An application generator is a piece of software, often database-oriented such as MS Access or FoxPro, which allows a user to develop an application such as a Stock Control or Accounts system without having to do very much programming. The software will automatically generate the code from tables, forms and reports specified by the user. Such software could be extremely useful in, say, a Recruitment department of a large company that wants to keep track of applicants, where they come from, what qualifications they have, and so on in order to plan future recruitment campaigns.

## Report generators

A report generator is a piece of software that allows a business user who may have little knowledge of programming to specify the format and content of a printed report to be composed using values from a database or calculations performed by a computer. In some programming languages, the user designs reports using statements similar to programming language statements. In Access, 'wizards' are used to generate reports without having to write any code.

# Web browsers

Software called a **Web Browser** is used to view information stored on the World Wide Web. The browser interprets the information, displays it on the screen and enables you to move between linked items. Examples of Web browsers include Microsoft Internet Explorer and Netscape.

*Figure 22.7: The Internet Explorer Web Browser*

# Facilities offered by a browser

A web browser is a program that enables a computer to download and view pages from the world-wide web. Browsers can also perform tasks that previously needed special software. A browser will:

- Show a web page for which you have either entered the address or URL (Uniform Resource Locator) or clicked on a 'hot' link;

- Browse back and forward through the most recently viewed pages;

- Allow you to customise the basic options such as the opening page, content censorship, security levels and whether to download the page as text only to speed up transmission;

- 'Bookmark' pages for quick reference later;

- Keep a 'History' list of pages visited within a specified period;

- Save the most recently visited pages for viewing off-line;

- Show animation sequences programmed in Java script;

- Play back sound, video clips and multimedia if the appropriate 'plug-in' software (usually a Visual Basic ActiveX control) is installed, e.g. Shockwave;

- Download files to a local hard disk;

- Allow you to fill in an on-line form and submit it by e-mail;

- Give links to search engines;

- Allow access to some personal e-mail;

- Allow you to have pages 'pushed' at you (Netcasting) rather than having to request them.

## Search engines

A search engine is a piece of software that allows you to search the Internet for information about a given subject. Search engines are often used just to find the web address of a particular company – for example, if you wanted to go to the website of Blockbuster, you could either guess the address and type www.blockbuster.co.uk into the address box, or you could type 'Blockbuster' into a search engine such as Google and it would probably give you a link to the site.

Some search engines such as Ask Jeeves (www.ask.com) use a **natural language interface**.

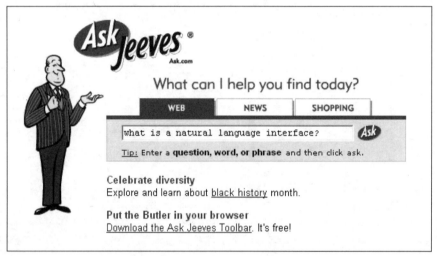

*Figure 22.8: Natural language Interface*

This means that you can type in a question in ordinary English, or 'natural language' and the software will interpret your request. This is attractive in some ways as it means that the user does not have to know the 'correct' way of searching for a topic. However natural language interfaces have several disadvantages:

- Natural language is often ambiguous, with the same word (like 'Match' or 'bug' for example) having many different meanings.

- If words are incorrectly spelt the computer will probably not recognize them – if 'interface' is entered as 'inteface' in the above query, it will not find anything about interfaces.

- Grammar is often ambiguous. Natural language requires a knowledge of how the world works. For example if your friend says to you 'We're having the Jacksons for supper' you will probably correctly interpret this as meaning that the Jacksons will be sharing a meal at your friend's house, rather than a planned cannibalistic evening.

## Working with the Web

The World Wide Web is a concept rather than a 'thing'. It allows people to view information stored on computers all over the world. When you connect your computer to a network, the communications software on each computer has to send and receive information that all of the computers can understand. The network **protocol** is the set of rules that defines the format of messages sent over the network. The World Wide Web standardised on a protocol named TCP/IP.

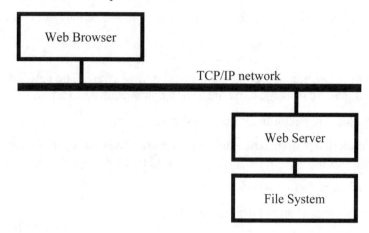

*Figure 22.8: TCP/IP Protocol is a protocol for sending data over the World Wide Web*

What your computer sends within the packaging parameters of a protocol depends on the applications sending and receiving the information – the *application* protocol. When you copy a file to a local server using Windows Explorer, Explorer packages up your file information in a format that the receiving file system understands. Windows than wraps these packages in a *transport* protocol (TCP/IP) for sending over the network.

When you work on the World Wide Web, the browser uses standard application protocols to send and receive information. Two of the most common Web protocols are *Hypertext Transfer Protocol* (HTTP) for transmitting things like Web pages and pictures, and *File Transfer Protocol* (FTP) for uploading and downloading files.

## Exercises

1. A particular word processing package is described as having a WYSIWYG (what you see is what you get) output capability. Give the advantages of using such a package rather than one which does not possess this capability. (3)

   *NEAB IT02 Qu 1 1996*

2. A mail-order book club holds its customer data on a computer file. The club wishes to contact its customers who have not ordered a book for one year or more. Briefly describe the stages involved in the necessary mail merge. (3)

   *NEAB Computing AS Qu 2 1995*

3. What type of software would normally be used for the following tasks?
   (a) Creating a directory, or folder, on a computer (1)
   (b) Writing a book (1)
   (c) Viewing a website (1)
   (d) Querying a set of records (1)
   (e) Keeping financial records (1)

   *AQA ICT2 Qu 2 January 2003*

4. One common business application package is the spreadsheet. Give **two** different reasons why a spreadsheet package is particularly useful as a decision-making tool. (2)

    *AEB Computing Paper 1 1996*

5. An office worker has created a macro which imports data from one spreadsheet file to another and then performs some calculations. However, the macro fails to work as expected when it is used.

    (a) Explain the term "macro" as used in the above description. (2)

    (b) What could the office worker have done to reduce the chance of the macro failing when it was used? (3)

    *NEAB IT02 Qu 3 1999*

6. A small company is purchasing a new computer system and software. The new software includes an operating system, and generic package software which contains an application generator.

    (a) Give **three** tasks that are performed by an *operating system*. (3)

    (b) State **three** characteristics of generic package software. Illustrate your answer with three different examples of the type of packages that could be chosen by the company.

    *(The use of brand names will not gain credit.)* (6)

    (c) State **two** characteristics of an application generator. (2)

    *AQA ICT2 Qu 6 May 2001*

7. The head of a sales team has developed a presentation. It is planned for members of the sales team to deliver this presentation as part of a sales talk to large audiences at various locations throughout the country.

    (a) State **three** advantages to be gained using presentation software as opposed to the use of traditional methods, e.g. OHP. (3)

    (b) State **three** design considerations that should be taken into account when the head of the sales team is developing the presentation. (3)

    *NEAB IT02 Qu 4 1999*

8. An Internet search engine is said to have a natural language interface.

    (a) Explain, using examples, **two** advantages to the user of the natural language interface. (2)

    (b) Explain, using examples, **two** limitations of a natural language interface. (2)

    *AQA ICT2 Qu 7 January 2002*

# Chapter 23 – Capabilities of Software

## Object Linking and Embedding (OLE)

Using OLE, it is possible to share information between programs. For example, if a report is being written in Word which requires the use of a spreadsheet or chart created in Excel, the spreadsheet can be either linked to, or embedded in, the document.

In the Word menu, selecting **Insert**, **Object** and then **Create from file** in the next window brings up the following screen:

*Figure 23.1: Linking a file to another document*

The spreadsheet 'Sample Stats.xls' is then linked into the report.

| Mortimer College | | | | | | |
|---|---|---|---|---|---|---|
| **A Level Statistics 1997-98** | | | | | | |
| Cumulative Percentage of Candidates at each grade | | | | | | |
| | A | B | C | D | E | N | U |
| 1997 | 8.35 | 18.22 | 37.00 | 58.63 | 74.19 | 88.99 | 100.00 |
| 1998 | 9.11 | 24.55 | 53.07 | 73.66 | 92.28 | 98.81 | 100.00 |

*Figure 23.2: This spreadsheet is linked to the original in Excel*

## About linked and embedded objects

The main differences between linked objects and embedded objects are where the data is stored and how it is updated after you place it in the destination file.

*Figure 23.3: The difference between linked and embedded objects*

Use **linked** objects if:

- you want the information to reflect any changes to the original data, or
- file size is a consideration.

With a **linked object**, the original information remains stored in the source file. The destination file displays a representation of the linked information but stores only the location of the original data. The linked information is updated automatically if you change the original data in the source file. For example, if you select a range of cells in a Microsoft Excel workbook and then paste the cells as a linked object in a Word document, the information is updated in Word if you change the information in your workbook.

In contrast, an **embedded object** becomes part of the destination file. Because an embedded object has no links to the source file, the object is not updated if you change the original data. You can still edit a spreadsheet or other object embedded in Word, though, by double-clicking it to open and edit it using Excel.

## The need for portability of data

**Portability** is the ability to run the same program on different types of computer. It can also refer to the ability to transfer a file from one computer to another.

For all sorts of reasons, it's important to be able to transfer data between applications and between computers of the same or different types, perhaps using different operating systems. For example:

- You're writing a report in Word and you want to be able to insert an Excel spreadsheet in the report.
- You're using a desktop publishing system and you want to be able to import some graphics from a drawing package.
- You're doing a research assignment and want to download articles from the Internet on 'Computers and Dolphins'.
- You want to e-mail your friend on a Unix machine in Hull from your PC in Southampton, and send her a scanned photograph she requested.

Files (binary, text or graphical) can be downloaded from the Internet using **ftp** (File Transfer Protocol) – software that can copy files between different types of computer.

# Problems with portability

There are several reasons why files may not be portable.

- A document created using one word processing package (e.g. Word) commonly cannot be read by a different word processing package (e.g. Word Perfect) running on the same computer. Different formatting codes are used by different packages; for example, the information that a word or paragraph is in bold text must be stored along with the actual text, but exactly how this information is coded varies between packages.

  For this reason, most word processing packages allow documents to be stored in 'Text only' format. This strips out all the formatting information and any graphics, leaving only the text, which can be read into a different package and reformatted.

- A document created on one computer using a particular word processor appears differently on the screen of another computer running the same word processing package.

  Some word processors (e.g. Word Perfect) lay out a document based on the printer that is being used. If the document is transferred to another computer, and a different printer specified, the document may appear with a completely different layout, with line breaks and page breaks appearing in different places.

Another reason why a document may appear differently on a different computer is that it may not have the same fonts (typefaces) installed. An alternative font will be substituted, which usually changes the layout.

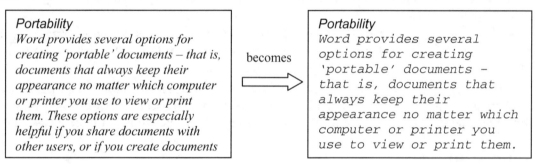

*Figure 23.4: Transferring a document to another computer can change its appearance*

# Upgradability

Software manufacturers commonly bring out upgrades about every two years, to the intense annoyance of many customers who soon find themselves either using out-of-date software or having to pay for the upgrade. Software upgrades frequently cause some or all of the following problems:

- Documents or applications produced by the upgraded software are not 'downwardly compatible'. In other words, a document written in Version 6 can usually be read in Version 7, but not vice versa. Usually, the newer version allows the user to save the file as a 'Version 6 file' so that it can be read by the earlier version.

- The new version is likely to contain new features non-existent in earlier versions, so that data or formatting may be lost if it is converted to the earlier version for another user.

- The upgraded software frequently needs more memory, more disk space and a faster processor to work efficiently, meaning that hardware has to be upgraded.

On the other hand, of course, the march of progress brings its advantages and a new version often brings impressive improvements in ease of use, functionality and speed.

> ➢ **Discussion: A College has several independent local area networks in different open-access rooms, each with its own file server. Periodically the oldest computers are replaced with the most up-to-date hardware available. Why does the College continue to run older versions of software on the new computers?**

## Criteria for selecting a software package

The most important factor in evaluating software is how well the software meets your needs, but there are many other factors to consider as well.

1.    Compatibility with existing hardware. Will the software run on existing equipment?

2.    Compatibility with existing software. Can files from other packages be imported or exported to and from the new package to other packages?

3.    Quality of documentation.

4.    Ease of learning. How good is the on-line help? Are tutorials available?

5.    Ease of use. Is the package easy to use? Are there shortcuts for advanced users?

6.    Technical support. Is this available, and at what cost?

7.    Upgrade policy. Will future upgrades be available at a discount? Can files created in older versions be used without change?

8.    Speed. How long does it take to perform complex but frequently performed operations such as database queries? Some database packages, for example, are very fast with small amounts of data but grind to a halt when presented with several thousand records.

9.    Cost.  This may involve simply the cost of an individual package. If the package is to be used throughout an organisation, the cost of a licensing agreement that specifies how many copies of the software may legally be made, or how many users can use it on a network, has to be investigated.

## Evaluating software

Before selecting a particular software package you could:

• Read reviews of it in a computer magazine. Magazines commonly compare similar software packages on dozens of different criteria;

• Consult other users who have experience of the type of software you are thinking of purchasing;

• Perform benchmark tests (performance tests) to see how fast various packages perform a number of different tasks. Computer magazines often publish the results of benchmark tests.

## Software reliability

As software becomes increasingly complex, it becomes more and more difficult to test. Batch systems, where the data is entered together in a batch, processed and output produced, are relatively easy to test. Test files can be created and expected results of all processing calculated and compared with actual results. If something is wrong, the program can be fixed and the same set of tests run again. Different types of test data are used in a comprehensive test plan.

• Normal, valid data is used to show that it is processed correctly

- Invalid data is used to ensure that this type of data is rejected without crashing the program.

- Extreme data (data at the edges of what is acceptable or treated in a particular way) is used to test that the programming is correct for such values. For example if a program is awarding a grade base on a percentage, and a mark between 61 and 70 is awarded a Grade B, then test data should include marks of 60, 61, 70 and 71 to make sure the grades are correctly calculated. The test data should also include values such as 101, -1 and ABC all of which are invalid, to test validation routines.

With GUI interfaces and on-line systems, however, this type of testing is not possible. It may be impossible to recreate the conditions under which a program crashed. The difficulties arise because:

- There is no single, well-defined flow of events at the user interface;

- It is often impossible to restore a database to the condition it was in before a bug was detected. In a client-server environment, the data may be held on different servers and across networks;

- Rapid, iterative and continuous development techniques mean that software continues to develop and new, weekly versions of systems are released by programmers. Testing simply cannot keep pace with these rapid changes;

- Users often use new software in ways which were not anticipated by the software engineers who wrote the system. When the system finally crashes, ("I was just trying to add a new record and it crashed") it is impossible to retrace the sequence of events that caused the crash;

- Performance testing is difficult to set up. An on-line, multi-user system that works well when tested with 1,000 records and 2 users may fall over when a million records are added and hundreds of users are simultaneously accessing the database.

## Exercises

1. Most word processors provide users with the facility to save a document as 'text only' as well as in the 'usual' format. Explain briefly the difference between the versions of a document stored in each of these two ways giving **one** reason why the 'text only' option is provided. (6)
*NISEAC Computing Paper 1 Qu 6 1995*

2. Given an existing hardware platform, selecting the most appropriate software package for a specific application can be a difficult process.
   (a) Describe the criteria and methods you would use to select the most appropriate software package for a specific application. (16)
   (b) Users may encounter problems when software manufacturers upgrade a software package. With reference to specific examples describe **two** such problems. (4)
*NEAB IT02 Qu 9 Specimen Paper*

3. Software packages need to be thoroughly tested before they are released. An 'address book organiser' package is being given away to promote a new software company.
   (a) Explain why it is important that this piece of software is thoroughly tested. (2)
   (b) The organiser stores telephone numbers that can be used for automatic dialling. Describe, using examples, **three** types of test data that should be used for testing the validity of the telephone numbers stored. (6)
*AQA ICT2 Qu 8 January 2002*

4. Explain briefly what is meant by the term *software portability*. (4)
*NISEAC Computing Paper 1 Qu 4 1994*

# Chapter 24 – Modes of Processing

## Processing methods

There are several different ways in which data can be processed, the main distinction being made between **batch processing** and **pseudo real-time processing**. You will also see or hear the terms **on-line processing**, **interactive processing** and **transaction processing** – unfortunately in computing these terms tend to be used rather loosely and seem to mean different things to different people. All these types of processing involve processing transactions, so what exactly is a transaction?

## Transactions

Transactions are events which need to be recorded in connection with the production, sale and distribution of goods and services.

Many organisations have to keep track of thousands or millions of transactions every day. Each time you withdraw cash from a cashpoint machine, for example, you are performing a transaction that has to be recorded and, at some point in time, used to update the balance in your account. Some banks do not update the balance until late at night when all customers' balances are updated. Other banks use a system which updates the bank balance straight away. That is the basic difference between a batch system and a pseudo real-time system.

Other examples of transactions include:

- Buying an item in a store;
- Paying a gas bill;
- Taking out a library book;
- Applying for a driving licence;
- Enrolling on a college course;
- Applying for a University place;
- Notifying a new employer of your full name, address and bank account details;
- Clocking in and out at work.

> ➤ **Discussion: Which of the above transactions need to be processed straight away, and which can wait for a few hours or even days?  Think of some more examples of transactions.**

## Master files and transaction files

A **master** file is a collection of records holding information about an entity such as a person or good. For example, an employee payroll master file will contain a record for each employee, with dozens of different fields holding an employee's surname, first name, several lines of address, department, date joined, pay rate, tax code, national insurance number and bank account number. These are all fields which will not change very often – maybe once or twice a year. In addition, there will be fields which change regularly – fields such as gross pay to date (since the start of the tax year), tax paid to date, N.I. contributions to date.

A **transaction** file holds information about events occurring in the organisation. Notice that in the case of an employee payroll file, there will be basically two different kinds of transactions. There will be the weekly or fortnightly transaction file containing information about hours worked which will be used to calculate each employee's wages or salary. Every so often there will be other transactions to process – additions, changes and deletions to the file.

* When a new employee is hired, a new record must be added;
* When an employee leaves, their record is (eventually) deleted;
* An employee may change address, bank account, etc.

> ➤ **What fields might be included on a record in a stock file in a supermarket? What different types of transaction will cause data on the master file to be changed?**

## Batch processing

With batch processing, a group of similar transactions are collected together over a period of time and processed in one operation. The transactions may be input to the computer over a period of time (as with cashpoint machine withdrawals) or they may be collected together as pieces of paper (like orders sent by customers to a mail order firm). These documents are then batched as described in the last chapter before being entered into the computer. Either way, the actual processing of the transactions is delayed until a convenient time, which may be later the same day, at night, or once a week, for example.

> ➤ **Discussion: Look again at the examples of transactions given above. What processing needs to be carried out in each of these examples?**

## Stages in batch processing

In a typical, large-scale batch system where data is collected on paper documents (such as applications for renewal of a TV or driver's licence) the following stages are gone through:

1. The paper documents are collected into batches of say 50, checked, control totals and hash totals calculated and written on a batch header document.
2. The data is keyed in off-line (i.e. to a separate computer system used solely for data entry, not the main computer) and validated by a computer program. It is stored on a transaction file.
3. The data is verified by being entered a second time by a different keypunch operator. Any discrepancies are followed up and corrected.
4. The transaction file is transferred to the main computer. This may be a matter of carrying a magnetic tape from one room to another, or it may be transferred electronically between computers.
5. Processing begins at a scheduled time – maybe overnight when the computer is not busy dealing with on-line users. All the processing steps (beginning with step 6) can take place without operator intervention.
6. The transaction file may be sorted into the same sequence as the master file (using a sort utility program) since this may speed up the processing of the data.
7. The master file is updated.
8. Any required reports are produced.

## Interactive processing

In interactive processing, data is entered and processed straight away. Organisations such as insurance companies are often able to make changes to a customer's household insurance, for example, while the customer is on the phone. The insurance clerk simply calls up details of the customer's policy on the screen, and types in any required changes which immediately update the customer's record. A report of the change would be automatically generated and a copy sent to the customer.

Some interactive systems allow queries to be made, but cannot process transactions right away. Examples include:

- Cashpoint machines which allow you to query your balance and withdraw cash but do not update the balance until late at night;

- Point-of-sale terminals which can access a stock file to look up the description and price of an article when the bar-coded label is scanned, but do not alter the quantity in stock when a sale is made. (This is done later in batch mode.)

## Real-time and pseudo real-time processing

Real-time processing occurs when a computer responds instantly to events occurring. The term is normally used in the context of, say, a computer controlling the flight of an aeroplane where on-board computers respond instantly to changes in wind speed, air pressure and so on. In data processing of a more mundane nature (selling tomatoes in Sainsbury's or borrowing a library book) a system where the computer records a transaction and more or less immediately updates the master file is termed 'pseudo real-time' because a delay of a few seconds is quite acceptable, unlike genuine real-time processing.

An example of a pseudo real-time processing system is the British Airways Booking System which is operated by a central computer at Heathrow linked to thousands of British Airways agents in the UK and overseas. A person wanting to book a seat can enquire at any airline office or travel agent about a flight on a particular day, and the booking clerk can call up details on a screen. A booking can be made if a free seat is available, or alternative choices offered. Such systems need to have methods of ensuring that the same seat is not booked simultaneously by two different agents at different terminals. (This would be a function of a *database management system*.)

## Criteria for choice of processing mode

The choice of whether to use a batch processing system or a pseudo real-time system depends on such factors as:

- Whether the information obtained from the system needs to be completely up-to-date at all times.

- The scale of the operation. Batch systems are well suited to very high volumes of data, when it becomes economical to have an off-line key-to-disk system for data entry.

- Cost. A real-time system is generally more expensive because of the more complex backup and recovery procedures required to cope with power failures or breakdowns in hardware.

- Computer usage. The advantage of a batch system is that it can make use of spare computer capacity overnight or at times when the computer would otherwise be idle. Batch processing is often carried out on mainframe computers.

Many applications use a combination of batch and interactive processing.

## Exercises

1.  A chain of estate agents has eighty branches. Daily transactions relating to house sales, purchases and enquiries are processed using a batch system based on a mainframe computer at head-office.

    (a) Outline the flow of data through such a batch processing system. (4)

    (b) The company is considering changing from the batch system to an interactive system. Describe the advantages and disadvantages of moving to an interactive system. (4)

    *NEAB IT02 Qu 3 1996*

2.  A proposal has been put forward by a school's management to introduce a computerised system for recording pupils' attendance. Two different systems are under consideration:

    -   The register books currently in use will be filled in manually as they are now, and these registers will be batch processed.

    -   Pupils will record their own presence directly into the computer system.

    (a) Describe briefly what is meant by **batch processing** in this context. (2)

    (b) Suggest, with a reason, how often the batch processing should take place. (2)

    (c) Suggest and justify a method by which pupils could record their own presence into the system. (3)

    (d) Describe **one** advantage and **one** disadvantage of the proposed batch system over the other proposal. (2)

    *New question*

3.  The management of a company which sells goods to customers by mail order is considering computerising the sales accounts of its customers.

    The system would record details of new orders, issue invoices, and record payments received from customers. In particular the management is considering whether to implement a batch processing system or an on-line transaction processing system.

    (a) State **two** advantages of batch processing and **two** advantages of on-line transaction processing. (4)

    (b) Describe **four** criteria which should be considered when choosing the processing method. (4)

    (c) State **three** validation checks which should be made to ensure that customers' accounts are correctly updated when payments are received. (3)

    (d) Describe **two** steps which should be taken to protect against the consequences of the system failing. Explain and justify how often these steps should be taken. (4)

    *London Computing Paper 1 Qu 9 1996*

4.  A nation-wide chain of retail clothing stores processes its daily sales transactions using a batch system based on a mainframe computer at a central location.

    (a) Outline the flow of data through such a batch processing system. (6)

    (b) The company is considering a change from the batch system to an interactive system. Describe the advantages and disadvantages of moving to an interactive system. (4)

    *NEAB IT02 Qu 9 1999*

# Chapter 25 – Processing Different Types of Data

## Types of data

In this chapter we will look at how computers can process data in the form of numbers, pictures and sound. All these different types of data can be represented in a computer's memory using the binary code – different combinations of 0s and 1s.

## Representing numbers

We have seen that each character has a corresponding code, so that if for example the 'A' key on the keyboard is pressed, the code '01000001' will be sent to the CPU. If the key '1' is pressed, the code '00110001' will be sent to the CPU. To print the number '123', the codes for 1, 2 and 3 would be sent to the printer. (Look back at Figure 14.4 for the table showing the ASCII code representing each character.)

This is fine for input and output, but useless for arithmetic. There is no easy way of adding two numbers held in this way, and furthermore they occupy a great deal of space. Numbers which are to be used in calculations are therefore held in a different format, as **binary numbers**.

Before we look at the binary system, it is helpful to examine how our ordinary decimal or **denary** number system works. Consider for example the number '134'. These three digits represent one hundred, three tens and four ones.

| 100 | 10 | 1 | |
|-----|----|----|----|
| 1 | 3 | 4 | $100 + 30 + 4 = 134$ |

As we move from right to left each digit is worth ten times as much as the previous one. We probably use a **base 10** number system because we have ten fingers, but essentially there is no reason why some other base such as 8 or 16 could not be used.

In the binary system, as we move from right to left each digit is worth twice as much as the previous one. Thus the binary number 10000110 can be set out under column headings as follows:

| 128 | 64 | 32 | 16 | 8 | 4 | 2 | 1 | |
|-----|----|----|----|----|----|----|----|----|
| 1 | 0 | 0 | 0 | 0 | 1 | 1 | 0 | This represents $128 + 4 + 2 = 134$ |

> ➢ **Discussion: Convert the following binary numbers to decimal:**
>   0011        0110        1010        01000001        01000101
> ➢ **Convert the following numbers to binary:**
>   5        7        1        26        68        137
> ➢ **What is the largest binary number that can be held in 8 bits?**

Obviously, using only one byte (8 bits) to hold a number places a severe restriction on the size of number the computer can hold. Therefore two or even four consecutive bytes are commonly used to store numbers.

## Binary arithmetic

One advantage of this method of storing numbers is that arithmetic becomes easy. To see how the 'carry' system works, first count from 1 to 16 in binary. Copy and complete the table below:

| Decimal | Binary | Decimal | Binary | Decimal | Binary |
|---------|--------|---------|--------|---------|--------|
| 0 | 00000 | 6 | | 12 | |
| 1 | 00001 | 7 | | 13 | |
| 2 | 00010 | 8 | | 14 | |
| 3 | | 9 | | 15 | |
| 4 | | 10 | | 16 | |
| 5 | | 11 | | | |

We can now try some binary addition:

```
    00011001
+   01010110
=   01101111
```

> ➤ **Discussion: Convert the above sum to decimal to make sure it is correct.**
>
> ➤ **Add together the binary equivalents of 7 and 9.**

## Real numbers

Numbers with a decimal point are known as **real numbers**. These numbers are represented differently inside the computer, enabling very large and very small numbers to be represented with a high degree of accuracy.

A discussion of how negative numbers and real numbers are held is beyond the scope of this course. The main thing is to have an appreciation of the fact that numbers which are going to be used in calculations have to be defined as such, and not held as 'text', or individual characters.

## Digitised sound

**Sound** such as music or speech can be input via a microphone, CD or electronic keyboard with MIDI (Musical Instrument Digital Interface) to be processed by a computer. Since sound waves are continuously variable or **analogue** in nature, an **analogue to digital converter** is needed to transform the analogue input to a **digital** form, i.e. a binary pattern, so that it can be stored and processed.

The basic piece of hardware required is a **sound card**, which fits into a vacant slot in the PC. Sound starts off as waves of pressure in the air. Before the computer can store this, it must be digitised – turned into numbers. To hear the sound, the computer must turn the digitised sound back to analogue. The sound card does the conversion from analogue to digital and vice versa.

The sampling rate and the resolution of the sound card determines the quality and accuracy of the sound produced. The **sampling rate** tells you how often the sound card takes a digital snapshot of the sound wave – the higher the sampling rate, the greater the accuracy of the sample (see Figure 25.1). 'CD quality' sound requires a sampling rate of about 44,000 samples per second: a 44kHz frequency.

The **resolution** of the sound card determines how accurately the amplitude of the sound can be measured. An 8-bit sound board uses 8 bits of data to measure sound wave amplitude giving 256 ($2^8$) sound levels, whereas a 16-bit sound card using 16 bits can represent 65,536 ($2^{16}$) levels of amplitude.

1 unit  **Time**  2 units          1 unit  **Time**  2 units

*Figure 25.1: Increasing the number of samples in 1 time 'unit' (fraction of a second)*
*means that the sound is more faithfully represented.*

The sound card also has a built-in **synthesiser** for producing music and sound effects.

## MIDI (Musical Instrument Digital Interface)

MIDI is an industry standard applied to electronic musical instruments as well as hardware, cables, connectors and data formats. Adding a MIDI interface to a computer allows it to communicate with, say, a MIDI keyboard, drum pad or guitar.

The MIDI data system stores all the information about each note to be played on the synthesiser, including the pitch, length, dynamics and type of sound. MIDI data in this format is very compact, taking only about $1/20^{th}$ of the space on disk of even the lowest quality recorded sound samples. For example, a minute's worth of MIDI synthesised music occupies about 30Kb of disk space compared with 600Kb of low quality recorded sound.

Floppy disks and CDs containing MIDI music files can be loaded into a PC's memory and played through a sound card or synthesiser. Because the data is stored as 'instructions' rather than recorded sound, you can speed it up or slow it down, change the pitch, turn a keyboard solo into a voice or guitar solo, or alter the balance between several synthesised instruments.

MIDI synthesiser

MIDI interface

*Figure 25.2: A MIDI interface connects a keyboard to a computer*

# Bitmapped graphics

In a bitmapped system for displaying text and graphics on a VDU, the screen is divided up into a grid, and each square on the grid is called a **pixel** (picture element). A low resolution screen may have 320 by 240 pixels, and a high resolution screen may have 1024 by 1024 pixels or more. A monochrome screen will need just one bit in memory to represent each pixel; if the bit is 1, the pixel is on, and if it is 0, the pixel is off. On a colour screen, each pixel may correspond to one byte in memory, giving a possible 256 colours for each pixel. The memory used is additional to the RAM used for programs and data; it is supplied on a graphics 'card' specific to the type of screen.

*If the screen was magnified you would be able to see the individual pixels. The more pixels to the square inch, the higher the resolution and the smoother the image.*

*Figure 25.3: An image on the screen is composed of thousands of pixels*

# Bitmapped versus vector-based graphics

There are two different kinds of graphics; **bitmapped** (also known as pixel-based) and **vector-based** (also known as object-oriented). Paint programs and scanners produce bitmapped images in the form of a collection of pixels, creating images by altering the colours or attributes of each individual pixel, and the amount of memory taken up by the image is dependent on the resolution of the display adapter where the image was first created. As a result, finished bitmap images are difficult to edit when you transfer them from one application to another. If you increase the size of a finished bitmap image, you see unsightly white spaces and jagged edges. If you greatly decrease the size of a finished bitmap image, parts of the image may 'smudge' because of the compression involved. Distortion can occur if you transfer bitmapped images to another computer that has a different display resolution.

(i)                                        (ii)                                        (iii)

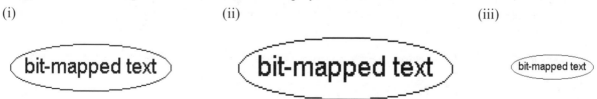

*Figure 25.4 - Bitmapped graphic image created in a PAINT package: (i) original size (ii) expanded (iii) shrunk*

137

Object-oriented graphics, on the other hand, have none of these limitations. The information used to create and represent a drawing is real geometric data, rather than graphic data. For example, a line is defined by its endpoints, length, width, colour, and so on. A CAD program (and object-oriented graphics software such as CorelDRAW!) then uses this information to create a representation of the line on the computer screen. Since this method of storing information has nothing to do with the resolution of a given display adapter, line-art is considered to be **device-independent**. No matter what computer you use to create an object-oriented graphic, you can stretch, scale and resize it flexibly without distortion. Object-oriented graphics also tend to create smaller files than bitmapped images because the computer does not have to store the attributes of each individual pixel.

(i)                                              (ii)                                              (iii)

*Figure 25.5 - An object-oriented graphic created in CorelDRAW!: (i) original size, (ii) expanded, (iii) shrunk.*

Another characteristic of CAD programs is the degree of accuracy that can be attained. Since a CAD program works with real geometric data, you can easily draw lines that meet exactly at a point, or move a line to a precise location, or draw an arc of an exact degree. When you zoom in on a portion of a line, no degradation occurs, and you can get an infinite degree of magnification. (The resolution of the laser printer may, as in this case, make the image appear less than perfectly smooth.) Using bitmapped graphics, by contrast, a line degrades when you zoom in and you see the individual pixels.

## Exercises

1. Give **three** advantages of using vector-based graphics rather than bitmapped graphics for a computer-aided design package. (3)

   *New question*

2. Describe how music can be input and stored in a computer's memory. What additional hardware is required to do this? (5)

   *New question*

3. Graphical images can be stored in a bit mapped format.
   Explain what is meant by the term *bit mapped*. (3)

   *AQA ICT2 Qu 1 June 2000*

# *Chapter 26 – Storage Devices*

## Primary and secondary storage

A computer's main memory (RAM) is known as **primary storage**. In order to execute a program, the program instructions and the data on which it is to operate have to be loaded into main memory. Primary storage, however, is **volatile**; when the computer is switched off, all the contents of memory are lost. This is one good reason to perform frequent saves to disk when working on, for example, a word-processed document.

A more permanent, **non-volatile** form of storage is required by all computer systems to save software and data files. Magnetic tape, magnetic disks, CD-ROM (Compact Disk Read Only Memory), and microfilm are all examples of what is known as **secondary storage**.

## File processing concepts

Data stored on secondary storage is typically stored in **files**, with a file of data being defined as a collection of records. A payroll file, for example, will contain a record for each employee, and a stock file will contain a record for each stock item. The manner in which these files are **processed** depends on whether every record in the file is to be processed one after the other, or whether individual records will be processed in no particular sequence. These two methods of processing are known as sequential and random processing.

**Sequential processing.** Each record in the file is read. If only the 200th record on the file needs altering, the first 199 records must be read anyway, and left as they are. Sequential processing is very fast and efficient for an application such as payroll where every record needs to be processed because every person in the company will be paid.

**Random processing.** Each record on the file has its own address, which can either be calculated from its unique key, or held in a separate index, so the record can be directly accessed. This type of processing is essential if for example you want to look up the price of an item of stock on a file of 20,000 items.

These two types of processing are similar to the different ways in which you would access a particular song on a cassette tape and on a CD. On a tape, you have to wind forward until you find the song you want, whereas on a CD, you just select the track and press the correct button. Note, however, that whereas you can 'process' a CD sequentially (listen to all the tracks from beginning to end) you cannot go directly to a particular song on a tape.

Similarly, some files need to be processed sequentially on some occasions, and randomly on others.

> ➤ **Discussion: Many files need to be processed sequentially on some occasions and randomly on others.**
>
> **When would the following files need to be processed (a) sequentially? (b) randomly?**
>
> **(i) Payroll file     (ii) Electricity billing file          (iii) Library book file**

## Floppy disks and Zip disks

The standard 3½" floppy disk is a thin, flexible plastic disk coated in metal oxide, enclosed in a rigid plastic casing.

- A high density disk has a storage capacity of 1.44 Megabytes.

- It has a write-protect hole with a built-in tab which can be positioned to leave the notch open, which write-protects it so that it cannot be written to. Positioning the tab so that the hole is closed enables the disk for writing.

No hole in this corner indicates a double density disk, capacity 720Kb

Write-protect tab

Recording window with sliding cover

*Figure 26.1: A floppy disk*

- A Zip disk is slightly larger and thicker than a floppy disk, and has its own disk drive. These disks hold 100Mb or 250Mb of data and cost up to £10.00 each.

## How data is stored

A diskette consists of two surfaces, each of which contains typically 80 concentric circles called tracks. Each track is divided into sectors. When you buy a floppy disk it is normally already formatted, which means that the sectors have been defined ready for use. If you reformat a disk that already has data on it, all the data will be erased.

The tracks near the centre store the same amount of data as the outer tracks – the data is recorded more densely near the centre.

Tracks

Sector

*Figure 26.2: Tracks and sectors on a magnetic disk*

## Hard disks for microcomputers

The hard disk used with PCs consists of one or more disk platters permanently sealed inside a casing. Hard disks typically have a capacity of between 20Gb and 40Gb. (1Gb = 1,000Mb.)

Each surface has its own read-write head. The heads are mounted on a single spindle so they all move in and out together.

*Figure 26.3: A microcomputer hard disk drive*

External hard drives which can be plugged into a microcomputer are available as extra storage.

## Hard disks for minis and mainframes

For large-scale applications storing huge amounts of data, several hard disk units will be required. The disks may be either fixed (sealed inside the unit) or removable. Fixed disks are faster, more reliable, and have a greater storage capacity.

As with other types of disk, data is stored on concentric tracks, with tracks being divided into sectors. All the tracks that are accessible from one position of the read-write heads form a **cylinder**; data is recorded cylinder by cylinder to minimise movement of the read-write heads, thereby minimising access time.

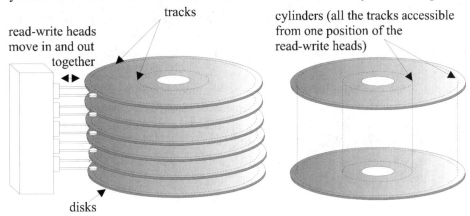

*Figure 26.4: A disk drive*

## Magnetic tape

Data is recorded in 'frames' across the tape, with one frame representing one byte. The frames form tracks along the length of the tape, with 9 tracks being common, giving 8 data tracks and one parity track.

```
                              1 0 1          Track 1
- - - - - - - - - - - - - - - 1 1 1 - - - - - - - - - - - - - - - - - -
                              0 1 1
                              0 0 0
                              1 1 0
                              1 1 0
                              0 0 1
                              0 0 1
- - - - - - - - - - - - - - - 0 0 1 - - - - - - - - - - - - - - - - - -
                              0 0 1         Parity track
```

*Figure 26.5:Tracks on a magnetic tape*

Magnetic tape is a serial medium, meaning that an individual record can only be accessed by starting at the beginning of the tape and reading through every record until the required one is found. Likewise, it is impossible to read a record, amend it in memory, then backspace to the beginning of the block and overwrite the old record. Therefore, updating a magnetic tape file always involves copying the file to a new tape with the amendments made.

## Uses of magnetic tape

Tape is a cheap and convenient medium for backup, and is also used for **archiving** past transactions or other data that may be needed again, such as for example, weather records collected over a number of years.

Cartridge tape drives are in common use for backing up the hard disk of personal computers, being much more convenient than using dozens of floppy disks. Cartridge tapes storing between 20Gb and 200Gb can be bought for £10-£60.

> ➢ **Discussion: Discuss the relative advantages of hard disks, floppy disks and magnetic tape.**

## CD-ROM

CD-ROMs can store around 680Mb of data, equivalent to hundreds of floppy disks. The data may be in text form, or may be in the form of graphics, photographic images, video clips or sound files. Although they do not transfer data as fast as a hard disk drive, their speed is increasing every year and is acceptable for most applications.

As the name suggests, the disks are read-only. When the master disk is created, a laser beam burns tiny holes in the surface of the disk, which (unlike a magnetic disk) has a single spiral track divided into sectors. To read data from the disk, a laser beam is reflected off the surface of the disk, detecting the presence or absence of pits which represent binary digits.

These disks are used typically for distributing software and collections of clip art. Copies of the master CD are pressed in the factory rather than being individually written, which is impossible on a CD-ROM.

## CR-R disks

These CDs can be written to and read but not erased and rewritten, and hold 650Mb-700Mb of data. They cost about £1 each. They are useful for writing large files to, which need to be sent through the post – for example, a manuscript for a book with line art and photographs. The manuscript for this book will be sent to the print company on a CR-R. CD-Rs may also be used for archiving material such as last year's accounts, or scanned images of important documents.

## CD Rewritables

These have a similar capacity to CD-R disks and cost more but can be written to many times. They have similar uses to CD-Rs.

## Case study: Computers in court

In Crown Court cases, every word said in court is taken down by a stenographer and written to a computer, where each sentence is indexed according to its subject matter. When a barrister says to a witness "I believe you told the court yesterday that you had spoken to Mr Smith on 30th April", the relevant statement can be immediately searched for, found and displayed on screens in front of the judge and barristers for both the defence and prosecution. Everyone can then check exactly what was said and it can be proved, for example, that the witness actually said that he spoke to Mrs Smith, not Mr Smith.

**Discussion: What would be a suitable storage device to use for storing the words of those involved in a court case so that they can be used in this way?**

## Exercises

1.  Why do many software manufacturers now prefer to sell their software on CD-ROM rather than on floppy disk? (2)

    *NEAB Computing Paper 1 Qu 1 1997*

2.  Modern personal computers usually include a CD-Rewriter.

    State **two** legal uses for a CD-Rewriter. (2)

    *AQA ICT2 Qu 2 May 2002*

3.  WORM (Write Once Read Many times) is an acronym sometimes used for certain types of data storage.

    Give **one** example of this type of storage and describe a typical use for your example.

    Give **one** feature of WORM type of storage which makes it appropriate for the example you have given. (3)

    *AEB Computing Paper 1 Qu 5 1995*

4.  Although large disk storage devices are now readily available for computer systems, the use of magnetic tape is still widespread.

    Describe **two** distinct uses of magnetic tape and explain its suitability in each case. (4)

    *London Computing Paper 1 Qu 8 1995*

5.  Modern personal computers usually include a floppy disk and a CD-ROM drive.

    (a) List **three** main differences between these two devices. (3)

    (b) (i) Describe **one** example of an application for which floppy disks are used. (2)

    (ii) Describe **one** example of an application where a CD-ROM is used. (2)

    *AQA ICT2 Qu 3 June 2000*

# Chapter 27 – Security of Data

## Issues of privacy

Everyone has a right to privacy – the right not to have details about our lives to be held or circulated without our knowledge. Data of a personal nature are regularly collected by numerous different organisations – for example:

- **Employers** hold personnel records that include data on address, age, qualifications, salary, sick leave, dependents and so on;
- **Stores** hold details on credit card payments, account history, items purchased;
- **Banks** hold details on salary, income and withdrawals, direct debits to various organisations;
- **Insurance companies** hold details of property, cars, accidents, claims and health.

The list is endless, and modern technology has made it possible not only to store vast quantities of data about individuals, but to view it from anywhere in the world, and to correlate data held in different databanks to produce a comprehensive profile of an individual.

## Case study: TRW Information Service

TRW is a company that sells thirty-five million credit reports each year to 24,000 subscribers in the United States. Every month TRW receives data from thousands of companies containing the status of their customer accounts. They then process and organise this data to build up a comprehensive credit history of each person, so that when a customer wants to buy an item on credit from a store who subscribes to the TRW service, they can carry out an immediate credit check.

The downside is that TRW do not carry out any checks on the accuracy of their data. Each year some 350,000 people register formal complaints about errors in TRW reports and about 100,000 of these result in changes to the data held by TRW. But how many errors pass unnoticed, resulting in people being denied credit completely erroneously?

## Threats to information systems

Computer-based information systems are vulnerable to crime and abuse, natural disaster and human error. In this chapter we'll look at some of the ways that an organisation can protect the **integrity** of data (by preventing inaccurate data entry, malicious or accidental alteration), and simple measures that can be taken to protect the **security** of data from theft or destruction.

## Data integrity

This refers to the **correctness** of the data. The data held in a computer system may become incorrect, corrupted or of 'poor quality' in many different ways and at many stages during data processing.

1.  **Errors on input**. Data that is keyed in may be wrongly transcribed. A batch of transaction data could go astray, or be keyed in twice by mistake.

2.  **Errors in operating procedure**. An update program could for example be run twice in error and quantities on a master file would then be updated twice.

3.  **Program errors could lead to corruption of files**. A new system may have errors in it that will not surface for some time, or errors may be introduced during program maintenance.

## Standard clerical procedures

To protect against input and operating procedure errors, standard procedures may be documented and followed for both input and output.

**Input**

- Data entry must be limited to authorised personnel only;
- In large volume data entry, data may be verified (keyed in twice by different operators) to guard against keying errors;
- Data control totals must be used wherever possible to verify the completeness and accuracy of the data, and to guard against duplicate or illegal entry.

**Output**

- All output should be inspected for reasonableness and any inconsistencies investigated;
- Printed output containing sensitive information should be shredded after use.

> ➤ **Discussion: What are 'data control totals'? Give an example of a data control total that could be used by an Examining Board entering marks from students' 'A' Level scripts.**

## Write-protecting disks

A simple measure such as write-protecting disks and tapes so that they cannot be accidentally overwritten can be effective in guarding against operator error. Both disks and tapes have write-protect mechanisms.

When the write-protect notch is open, the disk contents cannot be altered

*Figure 27.1: Write-protecting a floppy disk*

## User IDs and passwords

Each user in an organisation who is permitted to access the company database is issued with a user ID and a password, which will normally give them a certain level of access rights set by the database manager. Common rules issued by companies regarding passwords include the following:

- Passwords must be at least 6 characters;
- Password display must be automatically suppressed on screen or printed output;
- Files containing passwords must be encrypted;
- All users must ensure that their password is kept confidential, not written down, not made up of easily guessed words and is changed regularly, at least every 3 months.

> ➤ **Discussion: Describe several ways by which a password may become known to an unauthorised person.**

# Access rights

Even authorised users do not normally have the right to see all the data held on a company database. In a hospital, for example, receptionists may have the right to view and change some patient details such as name, address and appointments but may not access the patient's medical records. In a stock control system, salesmen may be permitted to view the price, description and quantity in stock of a particular item, but not to change any of the details held.

Access rights to a particular set of data could typically be set to Read-Only, Read/Write, or No Access. This ensures that users within a company can only gain access to data which they are permitted to see, and can only change data on the database if they are authorised to do so.

Likewise, the computer can also be programmed to allow access to particular data only from certain terminals, and only at certain times of day. The terminal in the database administrator's office may be the only terminal from which changes to the structure of a database may be made. An 'access directory' specifying each user's access rights is shown in Figure 27.2.

**Access Profile: User ID 26885**

| Data | Access right | Terminal number | Permitted time | Security level |
|---|---|---|---|---|
| Customer Number | Read only | 04,05 | 0830-1800 | 7 |
| Credit Limit | Read Write | 04 | 0830-1800 | 10 |
| Payment | Read/Write | 04,05 | 1830-1700 | 7 |
| Credit Rating | No Access | | | 12 |

*Figure 27.2: A security access table as part of a database*

# Securing against fraudulent use or malicious damage

Organisations are often exposed to the possibility of fraud, deliberate corruption of data by disgruntled employees or theft of software or data which may fall into the hands of competitors. Measures to counteract these risks include the following:

- Careful vetting of prospective employees.

- Immediate removal of employees who have been sacked or who hand in their resignation, and cancellation of all passwords and authorisations.

- 'Separation of duties'; i.e. trying to ensure that it would take the collusion of two or more employees to be able to defraud the company. The functions of data preparation, computer operations and other jobs should be separate, with no overlap of responsibility.

- Prevention of unauthorised access by employees and others to secure areas such as computer operations rooms, by means of machine readable cards or badges or other types of locks.

- The use of passwords to gain access to the computer system from terminals.

- Educating staff to be aware of possible breaches of security, and to be alert in preventing them or reporting them. This can include politely challenging strangers with a "May I help you?" approach, not leaving output lying around, machines logged on, or doors unlocked.

- Appointing a security manager and using special software which can monitor all terminal activity. Such software can enable the security manager to see, either with or without users' knowledge, everything being typed on any screen in a network. It will also record statistics such as number of logins at each terminal, hours of login time, number of times particular programs or databases were accessed and so on. It will even log the security manager's activities!

## Protection against viruses

Steps can be taken which minimise the risk of suffering damage from viruses. These include:

- Making sure that all purchased software comes in sealed, tamper-proof packaging;

- Not permitting floppy disks containing software or data to be removed from or brought into the office. (This is a sackable offence in some companies);

- Using anti-virus software to check all floppy disks before use. (This is sometimes known as a 'sheep-dip station'.)

## Biometric security measures

Passwords are only effective if people use them properly: if obvious passwords are used, or people tell them to their friends or write them down on a piece of paper blue-tacked to the computer, they are useless. *Biometric* methods of identifying an authorised user include fingerprint recognition techniques, voice recognition and face recognition. One such system uses an infra-red scanner to capture the unique pattern of blood vessels under the skin, and can even differentiate between identical twins by comparing the scan with the one on disk stored for each person.

### Case study: Iris recognition technology

The Nationwide Building Society started customer trials in March 1998 of 'iris recognition technology' – cash machines which are capable of recognising an individual's unique 'eye-print'. Special cameras are installed at the counter of the Swindon Head Office branch and at the cash machine. The camera captures a digital image of a person's iris, and from then on, every time a customer uses the cash machine, the system verifies their iris record within seconds.

However, retina verification can be unreliable, as checking the iris requires a person to look into a device at exactly the same angle each time.

## Communications security

Telecommunications systems are vulnerable to hackers who discover a user ID and password and can gain entry to a database from their own computer. One way of preventing this is to use a callback procedure so that when a remote user logs in, the computer automatically calls them back at a prearranged telephone number to verify their access request before allowing them to log on.

*Data encryption* can also be used to 'scramble' highly sensitive or confidential data before transmission.

## Disaster planning

The cost of lack of planning for computer failure can be ruinous. IBM estimates that 70% of organisations that experience a failure (caused by fire, flood, power failure, malice etc) cease operating within 18 months. The main consequence of a computer failure is loss of business, but other problems include loss of credibility, cashflow interruptions, poorer service to customers and loss of production.

### Case study: Safe as Houses

One summer evening last year, the heart of Tony Pidgeley's computer system was stolen. "Someone walked into the office at 6pm and walked away with the network server. Incredible!" he says.

The consequences could have been catastrophic for Pidgley's construction business. "We would have lost everything – all our accounts and land acquisition programmes," he says.

The firm was saved from disaster by a small cartridge no bigger than a couple of cigarette packets. Inside was a tape containing a backup copy, made the previous evening, of everything on the server's 1Gb hard disk. All that was lost was one day's data input, which was re-keyed in a couple of hours. The firm's PC dealer worked through the night to set up a replacement server, and insurance covered the hardware cost.

The firm's backup is run every evening. It takes most of the night, but this does not matter since it can run unattended. The next day, somebody takes the tape home, in case fire or flood should destroy the entire office. Once a month, a tape is checked to make sure the backup is working properly.

*Source: Paul Bray, The Sunday Times 19 October 1997*

> **Discussion: What are the main points of Tony's backup strategy?**

Many companies have comprehensive emergency plans, and even after suffering severe bomb or fire damage, can be up and running after a day or two. They generally subscribe to disaster recovery services offered by companies specialising in this field. Smaller companies may not need such elaborate backup and recovery procedures, but a backup system is still vital.

## Periodic backups

The most common technique used to ensure that data is not lost is to make **periodic backups**, by copying files regularly and keeping them in a safe place. This scheme has several weaknesses:

- All updates to a file since the last backup may be lost;
- The system may need to be shut down during backup operations;
- Backups of large files can be extremely time-consuming;
- When a failure occurs, recovery from the backup can be even more time-consuming.

A **benefit** of periodic backups is that files which may have become fragmented by additions and deletions can be reorganised to occupy contiguous space, usually resulting in much faster access time.

An important feature of all backup systems is the safe storage of the backup copies: it is usually necessary to store one backup copy in a fire-proof safe in the building, and another copy off-site.

## Backup strategies

The simplest backup strategy for a small business is to install software which automatically copies the contents of the server's hard disk at midnight to a cartridge tape, labeled 'Monday', 'Tuesday', etc. The previous night's tape is taken home each evening by a responsible employee.

However, it is not necessary to copy software programs except when they are changed, so a better solution is to keep data files in separate directories from the software and selectively back up only certain directories.

If this still results in backing up huge quantities of data, it can be reduced by backing up only those files which have changed since the last backup – an 'incremental backup'. Backup devices come with special software that helps you to select which files to copy, when and how.

As an added precaution, an extra backup can be taken at the end of each month, on to one of 12 cartridge tapes labeled 'January', 'February' etc.

## Backup hardware

- For small quantities of data, removable disks are the simplest. A Zip drive is usually an optional extra on a PC. Zip disks similar to floppy disks cost up to £10 each.

- For larger backups, magnetic tape is the preferred medium. A network server for a small company can have a cartridge tape drive which takes small cartridge tapes holding, say, 24Gb of data.

- A rewriteable optical disk drive costs around £280 and holds about 650Mb.

- RAID (Redundant Array of Inexpensive Disks) – see below.

## Backing up on-line databases

When a database is on-line and being constantly updated, precautions have to be taken to ensure that data is not lost in the event of hardware failure such as a disk head crash. Methods used include:

- **Transaction logging.** Information about every updating transaction is recorded on a separate transaction file. A *before-image* and an *after-image* of any record being updated is saved so that if part of the database is destroyed by a disk failure, an up-to-date copy can be created from the backup copy together with the transaction log using a utility program.

- **Using RAID (Redundant Array of Inexpensive Disks).** These devices use a technology which enables data to be written simultaneously to several disks. Three copies of the database may be held, two in the same room and one at a remote location, and all three copies are kept completely up-to-date. Then if one disk fails, the data is still safe on the other two disks.

## Factors in a backup strategy

When a company is planning its backup strategy, there are several factors to be taken into account. For example:

- **Frequency of backups.** Many organisations, such as a school or college, find it sufficient to back up data once or twice a day. On-line databases (for example in a hospital or airline booking system) need to be backed up constantly to prevent any loss of data.

- **Backup medium.** Magnetic tape is cheap, compact and can store large amounts of data, and is used by many organisations to back up data from hard disks every night. Smaller amounts of data may be backed up on removable disks using a Zip drive.

- **Location of backup storage.** The data needs to be held in a secure location in case of fire or burglary. Many organisations have a fireproof safe for the latest backups, with another set of backups being stored off-site.

- **Number of generations to be kept.** A typical strategy is to:
  - keep the daily backups for a week;
  - keep Friday's backup for a month;
  - keep one backup each month for a year;
  - give each tape or disk a serial number and keep a log book, to prevent mix-ups.

- **Responsibility for implementing the backup strategy.** Although the regular backup routine may be performed by a computer operator or an office worker, a senior manager should have overall responsibility for ensuring that all aspects of the backup strategy are properly implemented.

- **Testing of recovery procedures**. At regular intervals the effectiveness of the backup strategy needs to be tested to ensure that the organisation can recover quickly from loss of data. It would be rather tragic to discover that the magnetic tapes that were supposed to store the backup data were in fact blank!

# Recovery procedures

A contingency plan needs to be developed to allow rapid recovery from major disruptions. In addition to file back-up procedures, it is necessary to:

- Identify alternative compatible equipment and security facilities, or implement a service agreement which provides replacement equipment when needed. This may also include putting up temporary office space;

- Have provision for alternative communication links.

# Exercises

1.  An on-line information retrieval system holds confidential personal data.

    (a)  What precautions should be taken to

         (i)   minimise unauthorised access

         (ii)  detect unauthorised access?                                    (4)

    (b)  Why might different users be given different access privileges?       (2)

    (c)  Explain how the data should be protected from corruption.             (4)

                                                          *NEAB IT01 Qu 6 Sample Paper*

2.  The owner of a small newsagents uses a computer to manage her orders and deliveries. Every week she copies the files onto a number of floppy disks and puts the disks into a drawer next to the computer.

    (a)  State three problems that may be caused by this method of backup.     (3)

    (b)  Suggest a more appropriate backup procedure.                          (6)

                                                          *AQA ICT2 Qu 4 June 2000*

3.  An Internet sales company carries out its business with the assistance of a database system running on a network of PCs. The main tasks are the processing of customer orders and the logging of payments. You have been asked to advise the company on backup strategies and to explain their importance.

    (a)  Give **two** reasons why it is essential that the company has a backup strategy.     (2)

    (b)  State **five** factors that should be considered in a backup strategy, illustrating each factor with an example.                                                                  (10)

                                                          *AQA ICT2 Qu 9 January 2001*

4.  All employees of a company have an eight-digit password to access the company's computer network.

    State **three** rules that the employees should follow to ensure the effective use of the password system.                                                                             (3)

                                                          *AQA ICT2 Qu 4 May 2002*

5.  Give two functions that should be incorporated into a software package to prevent accidental deletion/alteration of data.                                                             (2)

                                                          *AQA ICT2 Qu 1 May 2002*

# Chapter 28 – Output Devices

## Printers

Printers come in all shapes and sizes, and the type of printer chosen will depend on several factors such as:

- **volume of output** – for high volumes, a fast, heavy-duty printer is required;

- **quality of print required** – business letters and reports to clients, for example, will require a high quality print, probably on special headed stationery;

- **location of the printer** – if the printer is going to be situated in a busy office, the noise that it makes is an important consideration;

- **requirement for multiple copies** – some printers cannot produce multiple copies;

- **requirements for colour** – does the output need to be in colour?

## Dot matrix printer

A dot matrix printer is an **impact printer**, producing its image by striking the paper through a ribbon. Its print head consists of a number of small pins, varying between 9 and 24 depending on the manufacturer. A 24-pin print head will produce a better quality of print than a 9-pin print head because the dots are closer together.

As the print head moves across the page, one or more pins strike the ribbon and make a dot on the paper. The figure below shows how the letter F is produced.

*Figure 28.1: Dot matrix print head*

In order to produce 'near letter quality' (**NLQ**) print, a line is printed twice, with the print head being shifted along very slightly in the second printing so that the spaces between the dots are filled in. The disadvantage of this technique is that the document then takes approximately twice as long to print. Many dot matrix printers are 'bidirectional', meaning that they can print in either direction, thus eliminating the need to start printing each line from the left hand side of the page.

Dot matrix printers are extremely versatile, with most of them able to print in condensed, standard and enlarged mode, in 'bold' or normal print.

Many dot matrix printers have a graphics mode that enables them to print pictures and graphs by activating individual print head pins separately or in combination to produce any shape or line. With appropriate software any typeface can be produced, and using a special 4-colour ribbon (red, yellow, blue and black), colour output for, say, a graphical presentation can be produced. However the quality of colour is not as good as that produced by other types of colour printer.

One of the main drawbacks of a dot matrix printer is its noise; in an office environment it can be an irritating distraction. Covers can be obtained to cut down the noise, but it is still audible.

## Ink jet printers

Ink jet printers are a popular type of non-impact printer, with prices ranging between £40 and £1500; a popular colour inkjet printer such as Hewlett Packard's DeskJet 3820 costs around £70. They are compact and quiet, and offer resolution almost as good as a laser printer. However, they are slow in operation; on average 5-10 pages per minute are printed, but a complex combination of text and colour can take several minutes for a single sheet.

Inkjet printers such as the HP Deskjet fire a droplet of ink at the page by boiling it in a microscopic tube and letting steam eject the droplet. Heating the ink can damage the colour pigments and matching the ink chemistry to the broad range of papers used in the office is a technical challenge. Large areas of colour can get wet, buckle, and the ink may smear. Printing an ink jet colour page can cost as much as 75p if all colour inks are supplied in a single cartridge; more thrifty printers will use separate red, blue, yellow and black cartridges which can be individually replaced. Although ordinary photocopy paper can be used, special smooth-coated paper may produce a more satisfactory result.

*Figure 28.2: A Canon Bubble Jet Printer*

## Laser printers

Laser printers are becoming increasingly popular, with prices dropping rapidly to under £200 for a printer suitable for desktop publishing applications. Laser printers use a process similar to a photocopying machine, with toner (powdered ink) being transferred to the page and then fused onto it by heat and pressure. A laser printer produces output of very high quality at a typical speed in the region of ten pages per minute, and is virtually silent in operation. The main running expenses are the toner, which costs about £75 for a cartridge lasting for around 5,000 copies, and a maintenance contract which is typically up to £300pa.

A high quality colour laser printer may cost between £3,000 and £7,000.

## Plotters

A plotter is an output device used to produce high quality line drawings such as building plans or electronic circuits. They are generally classified as pen (vector plotters) or penless (raster plotters). The former use pens to draw images using point-to-point data, moving the pen over the paper. Pen plotters are low in price and hold a large share of the plotter market.

Penless plotters include electrostatic plotters, thermal plotters and laser plotters. They are generally used where drawings of high densities are required, for example drawings of machines, printed circuit boards or maps. Colour electrostatic plotters are increasingly being used in, for example, assembly drawings of machines and building plans, making them easier to read and understand.

*Photograph
courtesy of Hewlett
Packard Company*

*Figure 28.3: Hewlett-Packard plotters*

## Visual display unit (VDU)

A VDU has three basic attributes: size, colour and resolution. It has its own fixed amount of RAM associated with it to store the image being displayed on the screen, and the amount of RAM it has will determine the resolution and the maximum number of colours that can be displayed. Note that:

- The resolution is determined by the number of pixels (addressable picture elements) used to represent a full-screen image;

- the number of colours that can be displayed is determined by how many bits are used to represent each pixel. If only one bit is used to represent each pixel, then only two colours can be represented. To display 256 colours, 8 bits per pixel are required, and to display 65,536 (i.e. $2^{16}$) colours, 16 bits (2 bytes) per pixel are needed. It is usually possible to adjust both the resolution and the number of colours - *if a high resolution is selected you won't be able to have as many colours because of the memory limitations of the VDU.*

For example, if a resolution of 800x600 pixels is selected together with 65,536 colours, the amount of video RAM required will be 800x600x2 bytes = 960,000 bytes, i.e. almost 1Mb. If 1Mb is all the video RAM supplied by the manufacturer, the resolution cannot be increased to say, 1000x800 unless the number of bytes used to represent each pixel is reduced, thus limiting the number of colours which can be displayed.

On a PC, the number of colours and the resolution of the screen can be adjusted on the Display option of the Control Panel.

*Figure 28.4: Adjusting the number of colours and resolution of a PC*

# Communicating with the CPU

Data, addresses and control signals are transferred between the various components of a computer by means of **buses**. The name originates from the analogy of carrying many people at once around town in a double-decker, but in this case it is simply a set of wires connecting components. There are two sorts of buses:

- **internal buses** which connect the various registers and internal components of the CPU

- **external buses** which connect the CPU to main memory and to the input-output units.

Input and output units vary enormously in their speed, mode of operation, code conversion requirements and so on, and so cannot be connected directly to the CPU by means of a simple bus. Instead, each device comes with its own **interface unit**, which in turn is connected to the bus.

# Parallel and serial data transmission

Data may be transferred in either **parallel** or **serial** mode. A parallel bus with 8 lines can transfer one byte at a time, whereas a serial bus transfers one bit at a time. A commonly used serial interface is the 25-pin RS232C interface, used for example to connect an external modem to the CPU. A mouse commonly uses a 9-pin serial interface.

*Figure 28.5: Different types of serial interface connectors*

Although only one line is used for transmitting data, other lines are needed for control signals, timing signals, secondary data channels, grounding and so on. Some lines are not used at all.

Transferring data in parallel mode is obviously faster than transferring in serial mode because 8 bits are transferred simultaneously, but parallel connections can only be made over a short distance of two or three metres. Printers and scanners normally use parallel interfaces when the printer is close to the computer. Many printers have both types of connector so that if for example the parallel port on your computer is being used to connect a scanner, you could use the serial port for the printer.

# Buffering

A buffer is an area of memory used for holding data during input or output transfers to and from I-O devices. Because the CPU can process data thousands of times faster than, say, a printer can print it, input and output are handled independently of the main processor. Once an I-O operation is initiated, a special I-O channel takes control of the operation, leaving the CPU free for other tasks.

Information that is to be printed is placed in a print buffer which may be several megabytes long, located either in the computer or the printer, or both. A laser printer, for example, comes with its own memory buffer of say 1 or 2 megabytes.

# Spooling

Spooling is a technique used to speed up communication between devices which operate at differing speeds. Output to a printer, for example, may be spooled (written) to disk, which is a high-speed device. When the printer becomes free, the output will be printed. This technique enables several users on a network to share a single printer without their output getting muddled up. Each user's output is spooled to a different position on the disk, and printed using a queuing system.

# Installing hardware devices such as a printer

When you add a new device such as a printer, scanner, mouse, soundcard or videodisk player to a computer system, you have to install a piece of software called a **device driver** to control the device. For example, when you attach a new printer to a computer, you have to do the following before you can print anything:

- Install the printer-driver file for the printer;
- Select the port you want to assign the printer to.

A printer-driver file is a piece of software that specifies information about the printer, including details about printer features, descriptions of fonts (sizes and styles) and control sequences that the printer uses to produce various formats. When you give an instruction to print, the driver translates the information about fonts, formatting, highlighting etc. into a form that the printer can understand.

# Exercises

1. A printer fails to work or perform as the user expects when a document has been sent to be printed. The user has checked that the on-line light of the printer is illuminated and the printer paper is correctly inserted. Give **two** other possible reasons why the printing process failed. (2)

   *AEB Computing Paper 1 Qu 1 1997*

2. Explain the relationship between the resolution of a screen and the number of colours that it can display. (3)

   *New question*

3. A new printer is supplied with printer driver files. The files are provided both on a floppy disk and on a CD-ROM. The CD-ROM also contains sound files for use with the printer.

   (a) Describe the functions of a printer driver. (2)

   (b) State one reason why the sound files are not provided on a floppy disk. (1)

   (c) Give one possible use of the sound files. (1)

   *AQA ICT2 Qu 3 May 2001*

# Chapter 29 – Network Environments

## Communications networks

A Local Area Network (LAN) is a collection of computers and peripherals confined to one building or site, connected together by a common electrical connection. A LAN can be connected to other LANs, or to a Wide Area Network.

A WAN connects computers or networks over a wide geographical area; for example different sites, towns or continents.

## Advantages and disadvantages of LANs

A network has several advantages over a collection of stand-alone microcomputers:

- It allows the sharing of resources such as disk storage, printers, image scanners, modems and central servers;
- It allows sharing of information held on disk drives accessible by all users;
- It is easier to store application programs on one computer and make them available to all users rather than having copies individually installed on each computer;
- It allows electronic mail to be sent between users;
- It is easier to set up new users and equipment;
- Backups can be controlled by the network manager, and data on a network server backed up automatically every night;
- It allows the connection of different types of computer which can communicate with each other.

The main **disadvantages** of networks are:

- Users become dependent on them: if for example the network file server develops a fault, then many users will be unable to run application programs. (On many sites, a back-up file server can be switched into action if the main server fails);
- If the network stops operating then it may not be possible to access various hardware and software resources;
- The efficiency of a network is very dependent on the skill of the system manager. A badly-managed network may operate less efficiently than stand-alone machines;
- It is difficult to make the system secure from hackers, novices or industrial espionage;
- As traffic increases on the network the performance degrades unless it is properly designed.

## Network topologies

The **topology** of a network is its physical layout — the way in which the computers and other units (commonly referred to as **nodes**) are connected. Common topologies include **star**, **bus** and **ring**, discussed below.

# Star network

Each node in a star network is connected to a central **host computer** which controls the network. This is a common topology for a wide area network in large companies which have a mainframe computer at the Head Office, and computer facilities (perhaps linked together in a LAN) at each branch. It has the advantage that each node is independent of the others so a fault at one branch will not affect the other branches. On the other hand if the main computer goes down, all users are affected.

*Figure 29.1: A star network*

## Advantages of a star network

- If one cable fails, the other stations are not affected;
- Consistent performance even when the network is being heavily used;
- No problems with 'collisions' of data since each station has its own cable to the server;
- Easy to add new stations without disrupting the network.

## Disadvantage of a star network

- May be costly to install because of the length of cable required. The cabling can be a substantial part of the overall cost of installing a network.

# Bus network

This is a typical topology for a LAN, with all the devices on the network sharing a single cable. Information can be transmitted in either direction from any PC to any other. This system works well if the channels are not too heavily loaded. On the other hand if sixteen students sit down at sixteen computers all at once and all try to load software from the network's hard disk, the whole system more or less grinds to a halt!

*Figure 29.2: A bus network*

The **advantages** of a bus system are that it is:

- easy and inexpensive to install as it requires the least amount of cable;
- easy to add more stations without disrupting the network.

The **disadvantages** are that:

- the whole network goes down if the main cable fails at any point;
- cable failure is difficult to isolate;
- network performance degrades under a heavy load.

## Ring network

In a ring network, a series of computers is connected together and there is no central controlling computer. Each computer may communicate with any other computer in the ring, with messages being specifically addressed to the destination computer.

*Figure 29.3: A ring network*

The **advantages** of a ring system are:

- there is no dependence on a central computer or file server, and each node controls transmission to and from itself;
- transmission of messages around the ring is relatively simple, with messages travelling in one direction only;
- very high transmission rates are possible.

The **disadvantage** is:

- if one node in the ring breaks down, transmission between any of the devices in the ring is disrupted.

## Server-based vs peer-to-peer networks

There are two types of local area network. A *server-based* network is generally used when there are more than 3 or 4 computers on the network. A *peer-to-peer* network is suitable for a small company with just a few computers in different offices. Data can be accessed easily from any computer, and documents can be printed on any of the printers connected to any computer.

In *client-server architecture*, different devices on the network are treated as clients or servers. The client devices send requests for service, such as printing or retrieval of data, to specific server devices that perform the requested processing. For example, the client devices might consist of twenty workstations in a room, and the server devices might be a laser printer and a computer dedicated to managing the network (the file server).

*Peer-to-peer* architecture is an alternative to client-server for small computer networks. In peer-to-peer, each workstation can communicate directly with every other workstation on the network without going through a server. Peer-to-peer is most appropriate when the network users mostly do their own work but occasionally need to share data or communicate with each other. One disadvantage of this arrangement is that if the workstation from which a user wishes to retrieve data is switched off, the data cannot be retrieved!

Any sort of network requires maintenance – someone has to be responsible for ensuring that:

- Response time is adequate;
- Hardware is upgraded when necessary;
- The required software is loaded;
- Software is upgraded when necessary and users are kept informed of changes;
- A system of regular backups is adhered to;
- Network security is maintained.

The differences between the client-server and peer-to-peer networks are summarised in the table below:

| Server-based networks | Peer-to-peer networks |
|---|---|
| **Example: Novell's NetWare** | **Example: Microsoft Windows 98** |
| A central backing store is available to all users. | Storage facilities are distributed throughout the network. |
| Software is centrally held and shared. The server distributes the programs and data to the other microcomputers in the network (the 'clients') as they request them. Some processing tasks are performed by the desktop computer; others are handled by the file server. This is termed **client-server** architecture. The use of servers provides the network with more speed and power, but adds expense and complication. | Copies of software may be held on individual machines. Peer-to-peer networks provide basic network services such as software, file and print sharing, and are less expensive and less difficult to administer than those set up with servers. They are most appropriate for smaller businesses that do not need the power and speed of client-server architecture. |
| User IDs, passwords and access levels are controlled by the central computer. | Security is not centrally controlled. |
| Backup facilities are centralised; data and information held centrally are backed up regularly. | Backup is the responsibility of individual computer users. |
| All users are reliant on the service provided by the central facility. If the central computer goes down, all users are affected. | No reliance on a central computer. |
| All communication takes place through the central computer. Computers on the network may be of different types (from different manufacturers) and the central node computer controls the communications protocol. | The individual computers on the network must have software to control communication with other computers of the same or different types on the network. |

*Figure 29.4: Comparison of client-server and peer-to-peer networks*

# Wide area networks

When the devices in a network are close together, for example in the same building, they can be linked by means of cables, and this is what is meant by a Local Area Network. However, when devices are separated by more than a few hundred yards, data has to be sent over a communications link (e.g. telephone line) and extra equipment such as a modem is required.

A wide area network is a collection of computers spread over a wide geographical area, possibly spanning several continents. Communication may be via microwave, satellite link or telephone line, or a combination of these. The use of global networks (including the Internet) has increased enormously over the past few years, owing to:

- Changeover of telephone networks from old-style analogue to high-speed digital technology;
- Reduction in cost of connecting to and using networks;
- Improved compression techniques which allow faster transmission of text and graphics.

# Communications links

In the UK, British Telecom, NTL and other telecom operators provide services and data links. Telephone lines may be either:

- Public lines, on which the cost of sending data depends on the length of time taken;
- Private or leased lines, for which there is a fixed annual fee and the line can be used as often as needed for no extra cost.

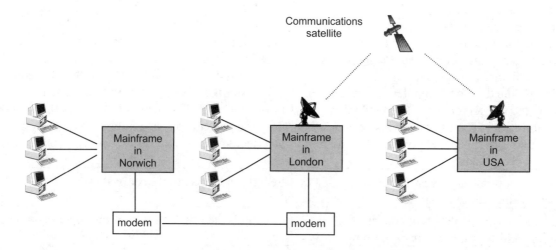

*Figure 29.5: Satellite transmission*

# Communications media

Communication may take place over a combination of different media:

- Twisted pair (copper cable), used in much of the telephone network;
- Coaxial cable – high quality, well insulated cable that can transmit data at higher speeds;
- Fibre optic cable through which pulses of light, rather than electricity, are sent in digital form;
- Microwave – similar to radio waves. Microwave stations cannot be much more than 30 miles apart because of the earth's curvature as microwaves travel in straight lines. Mobile telephones use microwave radio links. Wireless networking is also increasingly adopted for LANs, using systems such as Bluetooth.

- Communications satellite, using one of the hundreds of satellites now in geosynchronous orbit about 22,000 miles above the earth. (Geosynchronous orbit means that they are rotating at the same speed as the earth, and are therefore stationary relative to the earth's surface.)

## ISDN lines

The amount of data that can be sent over a line depends partly on the **bandwidth**, which is the range of frequencies that the line can carry. The greater the bandwidth, the greater the rate at which data can be sent, as several messages can be transmitted simultaneously.

A network that is capable of sending voice, video and computer data is called an **Integrated Services Digital Network (ISDN)**, and this requires a high bandwidth.

## Bridges and gateways

A **bridge** is a connection between two local area networks. Wide area networks may be connected through a system of **gateways**, a gateway being a computer which acts as a point of connection between different networks.

*Figure 29.6: Local area networks connected to a central computer*

# Hardware required for networking

## Network interface cards

**Cabling** is an obvious requirement to connect computers in a network. Each PC must also have a **network interface card** (NIC) installed before it can be linked into a network. The network cable plugs into this card.

## Modems

To communicate over a WAN, each PC must be connected to a **modem**. Telephone lines were originally designed for speech, which is transmitted in analogue or wave form. In order for digital data to be sent over a telephone line, it must first be converted to analogue form and then converted back to digital at the other end. This is achieved by means of a modem (MOdulator/ DEModulator) at either end of the line.

*Figure 29.7: A modem converts digital signals to analogue and vice versa*

# Exercises

1.  A local surgery uses a number of stand-alone computer systems to manage patient records, appointments, staff pay and all financial accounts. The surgery manager is considering changing to a local area network.

    Compare the relative advantages of stand-alone and local area network systems. (6)
    *NEAB IT02 Qu 9 1996*

2.  Two people working on a new piece of software both work from home, and frequently need to send data and files to each other via e-mail. Describe briefly **two** ways in which they could minimise the data transmission charges. (4)
    *New question*

3.  The manager of a small hotel uses a stand-alone computer to administer the booking and billing systems. He is considering setting up a small local area network to replace the stand-alone computer, with work stations in reception, in his office and in the dining room.

    (a)  State **two** different types of network that would be suitable. (2)

    (b)  (i)  Give **two** advantages of this change for the manager. (2)

         (ii)  Give **two** advantages of this change for his customers. (2)

    (c)  A friend suggests that a connection to the Internet would also be an advantage to allow customers to book electronically. Explain the extra factors that need to be considered if the customers are allowed to pay a deposit electronically over the Internet. (4)
    *AQA ICT2 Qu 5 June 2000*

# *Chapter 30 – User Interfaces*

## Introduction

The '**human-computer interface**' is a term used to describe the interaction between a user and a computer; in other words, the method by which the user tells the computer what to do, and the responses which the computer makes.

It's important not to allow the word 'computer' to limit your vision to a PC sitting on an office desk. You also need to think in terms of a person getting cash from a cash machine, a pilot of a jumbo jet checking his instrument panels, the operator of a high-volume heavy-duty photocopier, a scientist monitoring a chemical reaction, a musician composing a symphony using appropriate hardware and software.

> ➢ **Discussion: Name some other tasks for which computers are used, and for which special-purpose interfaces are required.**

## The importance of good interface design

A good interface design can help to ensure that users carry out their tasks:

- **Safely** (in the case of a jumbo jet pilot, for example);
- **Effectively** (users don't find they have recorded two hours of Bulgarian clog dancing instead of the Cup Final);
- **Efficiently** (users do not spend five minutes trying to find the correct way to insert their cash card and type in their PIN and the amount of cash they want, and then leave without remembering to extract their card);
- **Enjoyably** (a primary school pupil using a program to teach multiplication tables).

Well-designed systems can improve the output of employees, improve the quality of life and make the world a safer and more enjoyable place to live in.

> ➢ **Discussion: In the early days of cash machines, it was found that users sometimes forgot to remove their cards after withdrawing their cash. What simple change was made to eliminate this fault?**

## Designing usable systems

In order to design a usable interface, the designer has to take into consideration:

- **Who** will use the system. For example, will the users be computer professionals or members of the general public who may be wary of computers? For an educational program, will the users be young, for example primary school children, or teenagers on an A Level course? Will the system have to cater for both beginners and experienced users?

- **What tasks** the computer is performing. Is the task very repetitive, does the task require skill and knowledge? Do tasks vary greatly from one occasion to the next? A travel agent who spends most of the day making holiday bookings will require a different interface from an office worker who needs to be able to switch between word processing, accounts and accessing the company database.

- **The environment** in which the computer is used. Will the environment be hazardous (in a lifeboat setting out to rescue a stricken vessel), noisy (in a factory full of machinery), or calm and quiet (some offices)?
- **What is techologically feasible** (is it possible to simply dictate a letter to a word processor instead of typing it in?)

## Interface styles

There are a number of common interface styles including:

- Command line interface;
- Menus;
- Natural language;
- Forms and dialogue boxes;
- Graphical user interface (GUI).

## Command-line interface

The command-line interface was the first interactive dialogue style and is still widely used in spite of the availability of menu-driven interfaces. It provides a means of expressing instructions to the computer directly using single characters, whole word commands or abbreviations.

With this type of interface very little help is given to the user, who has to type a command such as, for example, **Format a:** to format a disk. Commands enable a user to quickly and concisely instruct the computer what to do, but they do require the user to have a knowledge of the commands available and the syntax for using them. How for example do you format a double-density disk rather than a high-density disk? *(E.g.: **Format a:/n:9/T:80**)*

> ➤ **Discussion: Identify TWO situations in which a command-driven interface would be appropriate.**

## Menus

There are several different types of menu interface, outlined below.

1. **Full screen menu.** This type of menu is often used as the 'front end' of an application. It stays on screen until the user makes a choice.

*Figure 30.1: Full screen menu*

2. **Pull-down menu.** This type of menu is displayed along the top of the screen, and when the user clicks on an item, a submenu appears. The menu is always present whatever screen the user is looking at in the application.

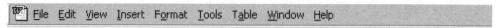

*Figure 30.2: Pull-down menu*

3. **Pop-up menu**. The menu pops up in response to, say, a click of the right mouse button on a particular area of the screen.

*Figure 30.3: Pop-up menu*

## Natural language

It is a very attractive idea to have a computer which can understand natural language – 'plain English' in other words. *'Please, dear computer, format this double-density disk for me and don't give me obscure error messages which I can't understand'* seems an eminently civilised way of communicating with a PC. Unfortunately, the ambiguity of natural language makes it very difficult for a machine to understand. Language is ambiguous in a number of different ways. Firstly, the syntax, or structure of a sentence may not be clear – for example consider the sentences

*James and Henrietta are married.*

*A salesman visited every house in the area.*

*The man hit the dog with the stick.*

Are James and Henrietta married to each other? Was there only one salesman involved in the house-to-house sales operation?

Secondly, many English words have more than one meaning. How many ways can the word 'match' be interpreted?

## Advantages and disadvantages of natural language dialogue

Advantages:

* Most natural form of dialogue for humans – no need for training in a specialised command language;
* Extremely flexible and powerful;
* The user is free to construct his own commands, frame his own questions, etc.

Disadvantages:

- People find it difficult to stick to strictly grammatical English;
- A well-designed 'artificial language' can often say the same thing more concisely than 'natural language';
- A smooth, natural language can easily mislead the naive user into believing the computer is much more intelligent than it actually is.

## Forms and dialogue boxes

When a user is required to enter data such as, for example, sales invoices or customer names and addresses, it is common to have a 'form' displayed on the screen for the user to fill in. The following points should be noted when designing forms of this type:

- The display should be given a title to identify it;
- The form should not be too cluttered – spaces and blanks in a display are important;
- It should give some indication of how many characters can be entered in each field of data;
- The user should be given a chance to go back and correct any field before the data is accepted;
- Items should appear in a logical sequence to assist the user;
- Default values should wherever possible be prewritten onto the form so that a minimum of data entry is required;
- Full exit and 'help' facilities should be provided – for example, users could enter '**?**' in a field if they require more information;
- Lower case in a display is neater and easier to read than upper-case;
- 'Attention-getting' devices such as blinking cursors, high-intensity, highlighted text, underlining etc should not be over-used.

**Dialogue boxes** are a special type of form often associated with the Windows environment; an example shown below is the dialogue box which appears when the instruction to *Print* is given in Word 2000.

*Figure 30.4: Dialogue box*

# The WIMP interface

WIMP stands for Windows, Icons, Mouse and Pull-down menus.

A **window** is an area on the screen through which a particular piece of software or a data file may be viewed. The window may occupy the whole screen, or the user can choose to have several windows on the screen with a different application running in each one. Windows can be moved, sized, stacked one on top of the other, opened and closed. A Windows environment mimics a desktop on which a worker may have several books or pieces of paper spread out for reference.

An **icon** is a small picture representing an item such as a piece of software, a file, storage medium (such as disk or tape) or command. By pointing with a mouse at a particular icon and clicking the mouse button the user can select it.

Microsoft Windows enables the user to run several different software packages such as MS Word (a word processor), MS Excel (a spreadsheet), MS Paint (a graphics package) simultaneously and to move data and graphics from one package to another. Software packages written by other manufacturers, such as Adobe PageMaker, have been written to run under Windows because of the convenience to the user of this easy-to-use environment.

# Advantages of a common user interface

All the software packages mentioned above use a consistent interface and have a similar 'look and feel' so that a user familiar with one package can quickly learn a second. For example, in each package a single click of the mouse button **selects** an item, and a double click **activates** the item. In each package, the methods for opening, closing, sizing and moving windows is identical. The advantages can be summarised as:

- Increased speed of learning;
- Ease of use;
- Confidence building for novice users;
- Increased range of tasks solvable by experienced users;
- A greater range of software accessible to the average user.

# Speech input (voice recognition)

The ultimate in user-friendly interfaces would probably be one in which you could simply tell your computer what to do in ordinary speech. Two distinct types of voice recognition system are emerging; small vocabulary command and control systems and large vocabulary dictation systems.

- **Command and control systems** can be relatively small and cheap because they need only a small, tightly defined vocabulary of technical terms. Such systems are coming rapidly into use as automatic call-handling systems for applications such as bank account enquiries. In PC systems, voice command can be used to bring up files, control printing and so on, effectively replacing the mouse. In some systems the computer is 'trained' by an individual user pronouncing a given vocabulary of words; it then stores a recording of the user's speech pattern for each word or syllable.

- **Large vocabulary dictation systems** can handle whole sentences and extensive vocabularies but need much greater processing power and memory space. These systems use elaborate probability distributions to estimate which word the accoustic pattern it has picked up is most likely to be, partly by looking at other words in the developing sentence and predicting what sort of word (noun or verb, for example) is likely to be used. Various voice recognition packages after suitable 'training' will take dictation at 70 words per minute and get about 97% of them correct. Voice recognition is however still an expensive technology and widespread use is some way off.

> ➤ **Discussion: Name some other situations in which voice input would be appropriate.**

## Speech/sound output

A speech synthesis system works as follows:

Individual words and sounds are spoken into a microphone by a human being and recorded by the system, thereby training it to speak. Output that would normally be printed can then be spoken, so long as the word is contained in its vocabulary. Sometimes words which are not recognised are spelt out.

Such a system has limited use but could for example be used by a bank computer connected by telephone line to customers' homes and offices. The customer could key in his account number using the telephone keypad, and the computer could then access his account and speak out the customer's account balance.

## Exercises

1.  *see case study below*

---

### Case study: Putting patients in the picture

New software has been trialled in doctors' surgeries to enable patients to see a picture of their condition on screen. An attractive interface features drawings of the human body overlaid with 'hotspots'. The cursor can be moved to the part of the body under investigation and clicked to reveal information. If for example the patient has a problem in the knee, the doctor clicks on the appropriate spot and a menu of options is displayed on the screen. Information can then be obtained on medical history, examinations, investigations, diagnosis, referrals and procedures.

The interface was designed to salvage a £19m coding system for the health service, whereby 245,000 medical conditions were given unique computer codes. The system was difficult to use because in order to do a keyboard search for a particular condition, everything including spaces and syntax had to be typed in with 100% accuracy. With the new system a complete list of possible diagnoses and treatments is available at the touch of a button. In addition, patients are much better informed because they can see a picture of the problem.

Three doctors and two programmers have worked on the interface, called Visual Read, for two years in their spare time.

> ➤ **Questions:**
>
> a.  What name would you give to this type of interface? (1)
>
> b.  Describe **one** advantage of the software to   (i) the doctor;
>     (ii) the patient. (2)
>
> c.  Why do you think the NHS spent £19m on a coding system for medical conditions? What use could such a scheme be put to, apart from the one described in the case study? (4)
>
> d.  Describe briefly **two** possible problems with the software that may come to light during testing in surgeries. (2)
>
> e.  The development team consisted of three doctors and two programmers. Identify the likely strengths and weaknesses of such a team. (4)
>
> f.  "If the system works as well as it is supposed to, the doctor will be superfluous." State whether you agree or disagree with this statement, giving **two** reasons to support your answer. (2)

2.  A college uses a range of software packages from different suppliers. Each package has a different user interface. The college is considering changing its software to one supplier and to a common user interface.

    (a)  Give **four** advantages of having a common user interface. (4)

    (b)  Describe **four** specific features of a user interface which would benefit from being common between packages. (4)

    (c)  Discuss the issues involved, apart from user interfaces, in the college changing or upgrading software packages. (8)

    *NEAB IT02 Qu 8 1997*

3.  A railway station has a computer-based timetable enquiry system for use by passengers. Enquiries are entered from a keyboard and displayed on the screen-based form illustrated below.

    Destination:
    Date of Travel:
    Latest arrival time:

    Details of the train times are displayed at the bottom of the screen.

    (a)  The exact format of the input required for this system is not clear. Redesign the form to make it clear. (4)

    (b)  Some users of the enquiry system find it difficult to use. Suggest **three** ways in which it could be made easier to use. (3)

    *London Computing Paper 2 Qu 4 1995*

4.  Briefly describe **three** important features of a well-designed user interface. (6)

    *NISEAC Paper 2 Qu 7 1996*

5.  A different human-machine interface would be needed for each of the following users:

    (i)   a young child in a primary school;

    (ii)  a blind person;

    (iii) a graphic artist.

    For each user describe and justify an appropriate human-machine interface. (9)

    *NEAB Computing Paper 1 Qu 9 1994*

6.  Describe, with the aid of examples, three ways in which the interface between a computer and a human can be designed to provide an effective dialogue. (9)

    *AQA ICT2 Qu 7 January 2003*

# ICT2 – Sample Questions and Answers

1. SupaGoods is a home sales company. Catalogues are left at people's homes. A local agent calls two days later to take orders and collect the catalogues. The agent sends the details of the goods ordered to the Head Office where they are processed. The completed order is returned to the agent who distributes the goods and collects payment.

    (a) Describe two distinct methods of data capture for the agent. State one advantage and one disadvantage of each method. (6)

    (b) The orders are validated at Head Office.

        (i) Explain what is meant by validation. (2)

        (ii) Describe briefly two validation checks that might be carried out on an agent's order. (2)

*NEAB IT02 Qu 5 1998*

*Notes:*

Think carefully what the question is asking – in general it was answered badly in 1998 by the majority of candidates, who misinterpreted what was being asked. Do you get catalogues left on the doorstep? Take a look at the order form inside. What happens – does the householder fill the order form in and hand it to the agent when he returns, or does he stand in the pouring rain typing the order into his laptop as Mrs Bloggs dictates her requirements for a new potato peeler, a set of nylon sieves and a doormat saying 'Beware of the cat'?

What is meant by 'data capture'? Generally it means the method by which the data is entered into the computer system. In the situation described there are basically two possibilities: the agent enters the data himself, either on the doorstep or later that day, and transmits it to Head Office, or he sends the completed forms to Head Office where they are entered by some means. Once you have thought the question through to this point you should be able to describe two different methods of data capture applicable to one or other scenario.

'Validation' is covered in Chapter 16.

*Suggested answer*

    (a) The paper order forms could be collected by the agent and sent to the Head Office where the data could be keyed in using a key-to-disk system. The advantage of this method is that it is economical for high volume data entry and as the data is verified (i.e. entered a second time by a different operator) the chances of data entry errors are much reduced. The disadvantage is that keying in data is very time-consuming.

        Alternatively the forms could be preprinted with the householder's account number and the form designed in such a way that if carefully filled in it can be read using OCR (optical character recognition). The forms would again be transmitted to Head Office and put through an optical character reader, so no manual data entry would be required. The advantage of this method is that it saves time on data entry and transcription errors do not arise. The disadvantage is that if the forms are not carefully and legibly filled in they will be rejected by the optical character reader and have to be manually keyed.

        (You could also describe Optical mark recognition, or barcoding.)

    (b) (i) Validation is the use of computer software to detect data which is missing or unreasonable.

(ii)   Validation checks: Check-digit on the agent's number or customer code. An extra digit calculated from the code is added to the end of the code, making it self-checking.
A presence check could be carried out on several fields such as agent's code, or quantity of an item ordered.
(Could also mention range check or format check on catalogue numbers etc.)

---

2.   A flat file system is used to store orders taken by an electrical retailer. Examples of records from the file are shown below.

| Customer | Address | Order No. | Date of order | Item No. | Description | Price | Phone No. | Sales Staff No. | Sales Person |
|---|---|---|---|---|---|---|---|---|---|
| Paul Smith | 38 Beech Road | 2345 | 4/11/2001 | 456 | Steam Iron | £35.45 | 01234-665577 | 78 | Sue Sneath |
| Anne Chu | 27 Ash Square | 2359 | 4/11/2001 | 764 | Toaster | £19.99 | 01234-897645 | 62 | Bert Jones |
| Anne Chu | 27 Ash Square | 2359 | 4/11/2001 | 798 | Kettle | £19.99 | 01234-897645 | 62 | Bert Jones |
| Sean Page | 19 Elm Lane | 2361 | 5/11/2001 | 461 | Microwave Oven | £125.00 | 01234-567483 | 78 | Mrs Sneath |
| Joan Patel | 16 Oak Close | 2362 | 5/11/2001 | 764 | Toaster New | £15.99 | 01234-192837 | 78 | Sue Sneath |

(a)   Referring to the examples above, describe the problems that have occurred by storing the data in a single flat file.   (6)

(b)   The flat file is to be replaced by a relational database. What structures would be needed in this database to allow for the effective updating and retrieval of data?   (4)

*AQA ICT2 Qu 9 May 2002*

*Notes:*

The problem with storing data in a flat file system (a 'database' consisting of just one table) is that you need to store all the data pertaining to each transaction, and that means a lot of detail is entered over and over again, with endless possibility for errors of data entry.

Looking at the mark scheme for part (a), you probably need to find 3 problems and an example of each.

When designing a relational database the key thing is to identify the entities that you are storing data about. Here, you are storing data about each customer, order, item and sales person. Some orders consist of more than one line so you are in fact storing data about each order line as well as about each order. That makes a total of five entities, so you will need five tables in the relational database.

*Suggested answer:*

(a)   Problems: **Redundant data** has been stored in the flat file, for example Anne Chu's address has been stored twice. When an order consists of more than one item, every detail of the customer, the order and the sales staff has to be entered.

Some **data is inconsistent** – for example item 764 is described once as Toaster, and once as Toaster New, and the price is different in the two records. Similarly, Sales staff number 78 is described once as Mrs Sneath and once as Sue Sneath. Problems will arise when looking up a particular customer because Name is not a suitable key field – there may be two customers with the same name.

There is no way of recording the total order value. Also Quantity of each item seems to have been forgotten. What if someone buys two kettles?

There is no way of recording the details of a member of staff until they have made a sale. Similarly product details cannot be stored until the first item is sold. If they are recorded, they are in a separate, unrelated file which involves entering the same data on several separate files, which means wasting time on data entry and probably making mistakes.

It will be difficult to update a customer's address or a salesperson's name, because these data items occur in so many different records. This would make it virtually impossible to look up a particular customer's address because after a time it would be different in different records, if a customer changed address.

(b) The structures needed in the database are separate tables for each of the entities ORDER, ORDER-LINE, ITEM, CUSTOMER, SALES-STAFF.

The tables need to be structured as follows:

ORDER(<u>Order-No</u>, date, customer-ID, Staff-No)

ORDER-LINE(<u>Order-No, Line-No</u>, Item-No, Item-No, Qty)

ITEM(<u>Item-No</u>, Description, Price)

CUSTOMER(<u>Customer-ID</u>, Name, Address, Phone No) *(Need several address fields)*

SALES-STAFF(<u>Staff-No</u>, Surname, Firstname)

---

3. A spreadsheet package is described as having a macro facility. Describe what is meant by the term 'macro' and suggest a situation in which the use of a macro would be appropriate. (4)

*NEAB IT02 Qu 1 1997*

*Notes:*

It will be much easier to answer this question if you have done some practical work with spreadsheets and created your own macros. Don't just rely on your textbook to pass this exam – practical work, work experience, watching appropriate TV documentaries, reading relevant newspaper articles, noticing how computers are used in different situations or businesses and just plain old common sense are vital ingredients for success!

*Suggested answer:*

A macro is a sequence of instructions stored with the spreadsheet or other application, and activated by a keystroke, clicking a command button or icon, selecting from a menu etc.

A macro would be appropriate to automate a task which has to be frequently or regularly repeated, and which takes several steps to perform, thus helping to provide a customised user environment. For example a macro might be used to display a data entry form, clear any existing data, put today's date at the top and position the cursor ready for the user to start entering data.

---

4. You have installed a new piece of applications software onto a stand-alone PC. You then find that the printer attached to the PC fails to produce what can be seen on screen in that package. Explain clearly why this might happen. (2)

*NEAB IT02 Qu 2 1998*

*Notes:*

There are some fairly obvious reasons why the printer may not print what is on your screen, for example your screen is showing a full colour image and the printer is not a colour printer. Will that answer score you a mark? Hard to say – I would be inclined to throw it in as a third answer just in case the examiner does not like your first two. Something more technical is probably required.

*Suggested answer:*

If you try to send a very long document, the printer may not have sufficient memory to hold the output and it may not print anything at all.

The correct printer driver may not be installed – this is the software that translates the information about fonts, formatting etc into a form that the printer can understand. If you are using an older version of the printer driver with a new version of the software it may not be compatible.

---

5. A computer system can be described as being a "pseudo real-time system".
   (i) State clearly what is meant by pseudo real-time. (2)
   (ii) Give a situation where pseudo real-time is essential, stating a reason why it is needed. (2)

*Notes:*

Be sure you understand the difference between genuine real-time processing (where for example an aircraft must respond instantly to an instruction to gain height) and pseudo real-time where a delay of a few seconds does not matter (for example in displaying your bank balance at a cash machine).

*Suggested answer:*

(i) A pseudo real-time system is one which accepts transactions from outside sources and processes each transaction more or less immediately, before the next transaction is accepted.

(ii) A theatre booking system would require this type of processing so that as soon as a booking is made the file will show that the seats have been sold, to prevent double-booking.

---

6. Articles in the media referring to computer software which fails to work properly are commonplace. Discuss the difficulties facing software companies when testing and implementing complex software, and the measures that software providers could take to minimise these problems. (6)

*NEAB IT02 Qu 8 1996*

*Notes:*

In the second part of the question you should discuss different types of testing that the developer should carry out. 'Alpha' and 'Beta' testing are not directly on the specification but from your general knowledge you may be aware of how software such as a new version of Windows is tested. Chapter 23 describes the difficulties of testing software.

*Suggested answer:*

In a GUI interface, there is no single, well-defined sequence of events and therefore it is difficult to test for every combination of events.

Users often use software in ways which were not predicted by the developers.

Software may work well with a limited volume of test data but it may be difficult to simulate the actual volume of data or users in a working version. Performance testing involving say 1000 users may be impossible to set up.

The pressure to get a new version on the market and the pace of change of the hardware may mean that there is insufficient time for thorough testing.

Software developers can minimise the problems of buggy software by formulating an effective test strategy, using different types of testing such as testing each module, testing the system as a whole, and then involving the users in testing. Software such as Windows is often issued as a 'beta' version or test version, to a group of users who then use it over a period of months and report any difficulties encountered.

---

7. A publishing company administers its business by using a database system running on a network of PCs. The main uses are to process customer orders and to log payments. You have been asked about backup strategies and their importance.

   (a) Give **two** reasons why it is essential that this company has a workable backup strategy. (2)

   (b) State five factors that should be considered in a backup strategy, illustrating each factor with an example. (10)

   (c) Despite all the precautions, some data might still be lost if there was a system failure. Give two reasons why this might be the case. (2)

   *NEAB IT02 Qu 6 1998*

*Notes:*

Avoid giving one word answers which will probably not score full marks. Be sure to justify or explain any points you make. Very many candidates scored only 5 marks, not 10, in part (b) although they probably thought they had gained full marks.

*Suggested answer:*

   (a) The company needs a workable backup strategy (i) to ensure that no data is lost in the event of a catastrophe such as a fire or flood; (ii) to ensure that if errors are made which compromise the integrity of the data, (i.e. the data becomes completely wrong or unreadable) the files can be recreated from the backups.

   (b) **Frequency of backups.** Many organisations, such as a school or college, find it sufficient to back up data once or twice a day. On-line databases (for example in a hospital or airline booking system) need to be backed up constantly to prevent any loss of data.

   **Backup medium.** Magnetic tape is cheap, compact and can store large amounts of data, and is used by many organisations to back up data from hard disks every night. Smaller amounts of data may be backed up on removable disks using a Zip drive.

   **Location of backup storage.** The data needs to be held in a secure location in case of fire or burglary. Many organisations have a fireproof safe for the latest backups, with another set of backups being stored off-site.

   **Number of generations to be kept.** A typical strategy is to:

   keep the daily backups for a week;

   keep Friday's backup for a month;

   keep one backup each month for a year;

   give each tape or disk a serial number and keep a log book, to prevent mix-ups.

   **Responsibility for implementing the backup strategy.** Although the regular backup routine may be performed by a computer operator or an office worker, a senior manager should have overall responsibility for ensuring that all aspects of the backup strategy are properly implemented.

   **Testing of recovery procedures**. At regular intervals the effectiveness of the backup strategy needs to be tested to ensure that the organisation can recover quickly from loss of data.

---

8. (a) Give two differences between a Local Area Network (LAN) and a Wide Area Network (WAN). (2)

   (b) Discuss the relative merits of server based networks and peer to peer networks. (6)

*NEAB IT02 Qu 5 1997*

*Notes:*

A fairly straightforward question if you have done your homework! Refer to Chapter 29. You will get no marks for answers such as 'A server-based system needs a server and a peer to peer system does not', or 'A peer to peer network is cheaper'.

*Suggested Answer:*

(a) A LAN connects computers within the same building or site, whereas a WAN connects computers over a wide geographical area , in different towns or countries. A LAN connects computers via cables but computers on a WAN are connected via modems and a telecommunications link such as a telephone line or satellite link.

(b) A server-based network has a central backing store available to all users whereas on a peer-to-peer network the storage facilities, although available to all users, are distributed among the computers on the network. The central backing store makes it simpler for backups to be done by the systems manager.

On a server based network only one copy of the software needs to be held on the server, which can be used by all users on the network. On a peer to peer network each computer may have its own copy of the software. This means that upgrades have to be installed on all computers instead of on only one.

A peer to peer network is simpler to install and maintain and does not need a systems manager to control and look after it.

---

9. A large college provides a wide range of courses. The college has three options for distributing the information on the courses to potential students.

   For each of the following options describe one advantage and one disadvantage to the college of this method of disseminating information.

   Option 1. Issue a prospectus containing the details of all the courses.

   Option 2. Publish course information on the college website.

   Option 3. Publish a course information booklet that can be downloaded from the college website.

   (12)

*AQA ICT2 Qu 11 January 2002*

*Notes:*

This is a common-sense type of question and you should be able to get good marks if you note the number of marks given for each point you make, and note that 'Describe' requires more than just a brief phrase or sentence like 'Not everyone has Internet access'. Keep in mind always that you are describing the advantages/disadvantages to the *college*, not the *prospective student*. What constitutes an advantage to the college? Presumably the college wants as many suitable applicants as possible, so any method of successfully disseminating information that helps achieve this goal has advantages. Saving a bit of money on printed brochures may be an advantage but it is not the main issue. You have to think up *different* advantages and disadvantages for each point, you won't get any marks for repeating an answer. It would be a good idea to jot down on rough paper what points you will make for each option before you start your answer.

*Suggested answer:*

**Option 1**.

**Advantage**: The college may be able to give a very good impression with a well-produced glossy brochure with lots of photographs of happy students sitting around on the grass in the sunshine, or visibly enjoying practical computer work in a well-equipped classroom. This may attract large numbers of students. Brochures can be sent to schools where they are on display for prospective students, or available to be taken home, without the student actually having to make much effort to find the information.

**Disadvantage**: Course details may sometimes change after the brochure is printed, so the information given will not always be accurate. This will cause difficulties to the college administration.

**Option 2**.

**Advantage**: The website can easily be updated so that course information will be up-to-date. Extra information and photographs can be added at virtually no extra cost, unlike a printed brochure, and the website can have video clips and sound, which gives added interest and information.

**Disadvantage**: Not every prospective student will have access to the Internet. Many students like to leaf through brochures from different colleges and compare various features before making a decision. If no brochure is available they may look elsewhere.

**Option 3**

**Advantage:** The student can print just the sections of the brochure that are relevant to them, and the college is saved the expense of producing a lot of information in a brochure, most of which will not be relevant to any individual student. (You could also say that a student who is looking for a course on say, Computers and Music, could find the site via a search engine. This increases the number of potential students who may apply to the college.)

**Disadvantage**: The brochure will have to be saved in a format (such as .pdf) that can be downloaded by anyone, and this requires the student to have special software (such as Acrobat Reader). If the student does not have the software they will not be able to download the brochure, so they may not bother applying to that college.

# Section 3

## Coursework:

## The Use of Generic Application Software for Task Solution

# Chapter 31 – Tackling a Minor Project

## Syllabus requirements

The AQA Information and Communications Technology specification requires candidates to undertake a project for Module 3. For the project, you are expected to tackle a task-related problem of limited scope, which in general can be implemented using a single piece of generic applications software such as a database, spreadsheet or desktop publishing package. You are, however, encouraged to use other software tools and objects as appropriate to complete the solution.

There are certain expectations from each type of software, for example:

### Word processing software

Remember that the emphasis for the project is on *developing a solution* to a reasonably substantial problem posed by an end-user. You need to select a problem that can be broken down into subtasks, each of which can be implemented using your chosen package. You will need to use a powerful word processing package such as Word 97 or later version that has sufficient advanced facilities to carry out some non-trivial tasks. For example, your project could be to produce all the templates needed for a club or a small business to send out letters and invoices to members or customers. The project might also involve holding a list of names and addresses so that you could send a mail shot to a selected group, for example a reminder notice to people who had not paid their subscriptions or invoices.

Automating the processes using the macro language might be demonstrated using a User Data Entry form, with macros attached on entry and exit. Finally, the project might attempt to fully customise the solution by tailoring the toolbars and drop-down menus.

You can use a word processing package to:

- Create a company 'ident'; that is, a logo and typeface for letter headings, invoices, fax cover sheets, With Compliments slips and business cards which gives the company or club a recognisable identity.

- Create templates for some/all of the above. Templates can be set to be read-only so that data is added to a document based on the template and not stored with the template itself.

- Create an internal data source containing names and addresses, subscriptions due, whether paid, etc.

- Create a mail-merge letter containing fields. You should explore the advanced features of the software that allow you to insert formulas and IF fields.

- Insert FILLIN fields to enable the user to fill in, say, a subscription rate (Family, Adult or Junior) for each member of a club.

- Insert a table into a document that contains formulae – for example, to add up the individual lines in an invoice, add VAT and calculate a total amount due.

The important thing is to be aware that all these things can be done in Word, and then to carefully analyse the user's requirements and use whatever features of the software are required to perform the tasks involved.

A word of warning – a simple mail-merge letter using a single file of data just won't make the grade, and nor will an application to allow a user to print out business cards.

Steer clear of word-processing software except to write up your project documentation, unless you have a good idea from a real user with a genuine need that can be broken down into several subtasks.

## Database software

Databases must be relational and used in a fully relational manner. This implies that your system must contain at least two related tables. Typically, you should choose a project which gives you scope to perform some or all of the following tasks:

- Draw an entity-relationship diagram;
- Normalise your data;
- Design your table structures, giving due consideration to field lengths and types, validation and default values;
- Create relationships which enforce referential integrity;
- Create and tailor forms and subforms to provide a pleasing and easy-to-use interface for the user;
- Perform multi-table queries;
- Perform some processing or calculation on the input data to produce information;
- Display or print reports, perhaps summarising data or displaying data that has been calculated, sorted or processed in some way;
- Write macros and code modules to customise your database;
- Provide a menu of options (a 'switchboard') as a front end to your application;
- Provide the user with on-line help.

Software such as Works is not suitable for a minor project, since it does not have a full range of advanced facilities available.

*Figure 31.1: A sample opening menu for a database project*

## Spreadsheet software

A spreadsheet application must consist of more than a single sheet containing labels, numbers and formulae into which the user types data. It could well involve the use of:

- A template which can only be altered by an authorised user, while other users would load the template, enter their own data and save the spreadsheet as a worksheet rather than altering the original template;
- A separate area of the spreadsheet set aside for data entry, making use of a User Input dialogue box and validation of input data. Data would then be automatically transferred to a different area for processing;
- Pivot tables for management analysis;

- Multiple scenarios of best, likely and worst case;
- Use of Goal Seek and solver;
- Locking sheets (with some cells unprotected) to prevent unwanted modification;
- Outlining and other auditing tools;
- Table lookup functions;
- Cell naming. Rather than having formulas such as =D2*E2, it is more meaningful to have a formula such as =Qty*Unit_Price;
- Macros to control input, processing and output. Auto Open and Close macros;
- A front-end menu to allow the user to select different options;
- Command buttons to perform various tasks;
- Use of control boxes such as list box, check box and option buttons;
- On-line help for the user.

**Desktop publishing**

It is difficult to score good marks using a desktop publishing package. The essence of the project is that it should not be simply a passive document, for example a beautifully produced newsletter or theatre program. It should have some element of interactivity with an end-user – for example, a template which a user can use over and over again with different text and graphics. The project needs to make use of advanced features of the package and must give scope for the full range of activities (Analysis, Design, Testing etc.)

A DTP project needs to be based on a repeatable need and must not be a one-off. This then gives you the scope to provide test data, such as testing out with different texts or different articles.

It is extremely important to:

- Have a real end-user (even if this is your teacher);
- Establish the aims and objectives;
- State why a DTP solution is appropriate;
- Consider the user's requirements very carefully; for example in this case the layout, appearance, colour restrictions, paper size, how many copies will be printed, how it will be folded;
- Establish how the printing will be done and by whom, how the document will be supplied to the printers (i.e. the human printer, not the LaserJet! disk or hard copy?), whether the printer will be scanning in photographs using high resolution equipment, etc.
- Design a test strategy and test plan;
- Evaluate the final solution against the objectives;
- Write technical and user manuals on how to use your template – NOT on how to use desktop publishing software.

**Presentation packages**

In the main, packages such as PowerPoint are unsuitable for a project at this level. There is simply not enough scope for a high-scoring project.

**Authoring packages**

A package such as Authorware can be used to produce an interactive tutorial, and has plenty of scope for advanced features to be used but as the package costs around £800 for a single copy probably very few centres or candidates would have access to such software.

If you have used sound, video or animation in your project and it is hard to show evidence of how it works in the report, you may as a last resort include a video with the project. Do NOT send a disk.

**Internet Web pages**

It is relatively easy to produce a Web page using Microsoft software, and so unless you can develop a functional site on the Internet that records hits and collects e-mail responses or answers to on-line questionnaires, this is likely to score only low marks.

## Planning the time schedule

Once you have decided on a project, one of the first things you should do is draw up a timetable of when each stage is going to be done and completed, so as to ensure it is handed in before the deadline.

There are many different possible schedules. If your teacher has more or less suspended theory classes to allow you to work flat out on your project, it should be possible to complete it within 6 to 8 weeks. This assumes that you will have 3-5 hours per week of class time, and at least as much again outside class. Even if you don't have a computer at home, and the open-access facilities at school or college are limited, do remember that there is a huge amount of work to be done away from the computer. You can:

- plan your schedule;
- interview the user;
- design the application;
- draw data flow diagrams (Context Level 0 and Level 1);
- read books to find out about the advanced features of the software;
- design your test strategy and test plan.

## The project requirements

Your project should include:

- A clear statement of the problem;
- An appropriate specification, reflecting the end-user's requirements of the solution, the desired outcomes and any constraints or limitations on the development of the solution, e.g. human or physical resources.
- Input, processing and output needs matching the requirements specification. The format of this section will vary according to the software solution available. For example, a database solution will need a database design from which to complete the project.
- A test strategy, test plan and test results cross-referenced to the test plan;
- An implementation using a software package;
- An evaluation of how well the final system met the objectives and performance criteria;
- Documentation showing how all the above were achieved;
- A user guide.

In the next few chapters each of these aspects will be tackled in more detail.

# Chapter 32 – Specification and Analysis

## Selecting a project

For the AS Module 3 project it is acceptable for your teacher to identify a problem for computerisation and act as the end-user. However you are very strongly encouraged to find your own project since this is much more likely to give you the opportunity to show your capabilities in a clearly original way. It's very important that the project is not teacher-led, with the whole class ending up with more or less identical solutions. Even if you find a particularly good way of overcoming some problem encountered in a class project, you're not likely to get any credit if the rest of the class has copied your techniques.

Try and find an application that you have personal knowledge of, or that you can investigate further. Parents can be a good source of ideas, or perhaps you belong to a club of some kind that could use a computerised membership system. The lab technician might like a computerised stock control system, or the school librarian may have an idea for computerising some aspect of the library. Do not be too ambitious – don't try and redo Tesco's stock control or the payroll system for British Gas. It is perfectly acceptable to ask the end-user for their priorities, be selective and model just a small slice of the user's problem.

## Investigating the user's requirements

Analysis involves finding out:

- How the current system works;
- What the problems are with the current system, including any client dissatisfaction;
- What the user's requirements are for a new system;
- What constraints there are on hardware, software, time-scale.

In order to do this, you need to prepare a list of questions and interview the user. Ask to see any (source) documents that are currently used, and if possible include a copy of them in an Appendix.

## Establishing the objectives

It is a good idea to write a clear statement of the objectives, both **qualitative** and **quantitative**. An example of a qualitative objective is:

"It should be easy for the user to locate a particular customer invoice".

An example of a quantitative objective is:

"It should be possible to locate any customer invoice in under 30 seconds".

Having a clear list of objectives will not only make the design of the system more straightforward, it will also enable you to evaluate the implementation by comparing its performance point-by-point with the objectives.

# Writing up the specification

A possible framework for the specification is given below:

---

**1.    Introduction**

    1.1    Background
*Describe and name the user and/or type of organisation (club, library, garage, etc) the project is to be written for and give some background information about the organisation.*

    1.2    Statement of the problem
*Give an overview of the problem that you intend to solve.*

**2.    Investigation**

    2.1    The current system

*Include a summary of the main points of an interview if appropriate. Identify the data flows and tasks being performed, and summarise these in a data flow diagram.*

    2.2    Problems with the current system

**3.    Requirements of the new system**

    3.1    General objectives

    3.2    Specific objectives – quantitative

    3.3    Specific objectives – qualitative

**4.    Constraints**

    4.1    Hardware
*Describe the hardware that is available both for development and at the end-user's organisation, or wherever the system is to be implemented.*

    4.2    Software
*Name the software you have available to use (including the version number) and briefly describe its main capabilities.*

    4.3    User's I.T. skills and knowledge
*Give some indication of the level of the end-user's I.T. skills, and what possible effects this could have on the design.*

---

Do vary this format according to the demands of your own particular project – don't try and force it into a format which does not fit. This is only a starting point from which you can branch out.

# Chapter 33 – Design

## Design tasks

Designing a system involves the following tasks:

- Identifying the required output from the system;
- Identifying the input data;
- Specifying the processing that needs to be carried out;
- Devising a test strategy and test plan;
- Planning a schedule of activities to ensure that the project is finished by the deadline – and sticking to it!

As this is likely to be the first substantial project you have attempted, it may be very difficult for you to produce a complete design before you start the implementation, especially if you are learning about the software as you go along. The AQA Exam Board recognizes this and does not expect you to produce complete design documentation. Rather, you should make what notes you can on design before starting the implementation, and as you implement the project and discover better ways of doing things, or extra features that you can incorporate, document these. Keep a project log and make notes as you proceed through the project.

## Database design (for a database project)

Identify the entities involved and the relationships between the entities and draw an entity-relationship diagram. A database project should involve at least three related tables. A sample entity-relationship diagram is shown below. The meaning of the 'crow's feet' pointing in the direction that they do below is:

   One customer places many orders  (a one-to-many relationship)

   One order consists of many line items (a one-to-many relationship)

*Figure 33.1: An entity-relationship diagram*

## Data descriptions

For each item of data you should specify:

- Name;
- Data type (integer, real, text etc);
- Length (if text);
- Default value (if any);
- Validation.

For a database project, you can use a form with headings similar to those shown below for each table in the database.

**TABLE NAME:**

| Attribute name | Data type | Length | Default value | Description, validation, comments |
|---|---|---|---|---|
|  |  |  |  |  |
|  |  |  |  |  |

*Figure 33.2: Suggested headings for a table layout form in a database project*

For a spreadsheet project, you should specify the purpose and contents of each sheet:

**SHEET NAME:**

| Row/Column heading | Data description and format | Comment | Example |
|---|---|---|---|
| Book code | Unique 6 character code | Acts as a link between sheets "Book" and "Sales" | AC0073, CM0021 |
| Total sales | The total month's sales of a book |  | =sum (d5..d11) |

*Figure 33.3: Designing a spreadsheet*

# Input

In a database project you may well design your screens with the help of 'wizards'. Try to maintain a consistent style and position for headings and buttons – for example buttons on each screen which return a user to the Main Menu or Switchboard should all be placed in the same position in every form.

For each sheet in a spreadsheet project show:

- General layout;
- Which cells will be locked or protected;
- Links to other sheets;
- Fonts, shading etc.

# Output

List the reports or other output (e.g. mailing labels, information available on screen). You should design each report or screen on paper, listing the data items that will appear. It does not have to be done on squared paper with every character shown, but you should give thought to whether a report is to be tabular or not, whether labels are to be printed 2 or 3 across the page, and so on. You can always change the design if you later find you have made some mistakes – such changes can be documented and justified as part of your report.

# Menu design

If your system has a menu structure, draw a chart showing how various submenus relate to each other. An example is shown below.

*Figure 33.4: A sample menu structure chart*

# Test plan

The test plan may be included here or in the Testing section. It will be discussed in the next chapter.

# Writing up the design and implementation

A possible framework for the design and implementation documentation is given below:

---

**1. Database/Spreadsheet design**

    1.1    Entity-relationship diagram (for a database)

    1.2    Data descriptions

**2. Input**

*Design of input forms and screens. (These may develop as the project progresses, and you can show what improvements you have made to original designs)*

**3. Output**

*Design of reports and other output.*

**4. Menu design**

**5. Test plan**

**6. Project log**

*A log describing progress and improvements made to the implementation and further tests that were made.*

---

# Chapter 34 – Implementation and Testing

## Organisation is the key

You will almost certainly be learning more about the software as you go along. There are many things you can do to ensure a successful implementation.

1. Buy a binder to hold everything to do with your project, divided into sections so that you can quickly find what you are looking for. A floppy plastic binder of the type that holds papers securely through punched holes is most suitable.

2. Have your design documentation in front of you and follow it; if you find it needs to be adjusted, remember to do so, and make a note of why this was necessary.

3. Have at least two spare floppy disks and make a backup after every session at the computer. Having 2 backup disks means that you can leave the most recent backup alone and overwrite the previous 'generation'. It is impossible to be too conscientious about backups; sooner or later you will lose the current version, quite possibly through no fault of your own – but blaming the dog, Microsoft or the school network won't bring your project back!

4. Keep a diary and leave 15 minutes at the end of every class to write up what you did and what problems you encountered. This will help you at the beginning of the next class.

5. Test each form, report, macro etc. thoroughly as you go, and make a note of these tests for your test plan.

6. Buy a good book on the software you are using, and spend time actually READING it. Try out the exercises and improve your knowledge of the advanced features of the software.

# The implementation

The implementation is the actual software solution that you create, using whichever package you have chosen to use. It is very tempting to proceed straight to the implementation stage without doing any design work first, but try not to do this. *Write down* the menu structure, *design* the data structures/fields/tables, the input and the output screens or reports. *Construct a list* of subtasks. Then you will be able to see what parts of your project you need help with. It is very hard for a teacher to help students who have nothing written down and have only the vaguest idea of what they are trying to achieve.

If you are using the computer facilities at school or college, there is a lot of work you can do at home. You can:

• Read software guides to learn how to overcome any problems you have encountered;

• Refine your design;

• Create sets of test data;

• Draw up a test plan;

• Work on your documentation;

• Plan how you are going to make the best use of your next practical session.

If you are using computer facilities at home, then all these tasks can be done during practical sessions. If you can plan your time effectively, you will be able to complete the project in the time allowed.

# Testing objectives

The objectives of testing are to prove that:

• All parts of the system work correctly, no matter what data is input;

• All parts of the system as originally specified are present.

In drawing up a test plan, you should bear in mind the following rules proposed by Glen Myers in his book 'The Art of Software Testing'.

1. **Testing is a process of executing a program with the intent of finding an error.**
2. **A good test case is one that has a high probability of finding an as yet undiscovered error.**
3. **A successful test is one that uncovers an as yet undiscovered error.**

In other words, it is not sufficient to think up a few tests which you are fairly sure will not make your program crash or give a wrong result; you must use tests and test data which have been carefully thought out to test all parts of the program.

# Steps in software testing

**1. Module testing**

As you complete each module of your program, it needs to be thoroughly tested. Even if you can't test every combination of paths, you can test the important paths, the extreme cases, valid and invalid data, and so on. For the purposes of your project, you should aim to demonstrate that you have tested systematically and that your testing is **reasonably** exhaustive. A maximum of 20 to 30 pages of actual test runs which cover major processes and show a variety of test data (i.e. extreme, correct, incorrect) is quite sufficient.

**2.     System (or integrated) testing**

When all the modules have been written and the whole system put together, system testing can begin.

At this stage, you should ideally test your system with a realistic volume of data. If the system is designed to hold details of 5000 stock items, and you have never tested it with more than 8, there is no way of knowing how it will perform after installation unless you test it. Obviously, you will not have the time to enter 5000 different records, but it would be reasonable to enter about 20 items of data.

## Drawing up a test plan

For the module testing, draw up a test plan of preferably no more than two or three pages which shows that you have chosen your test data carefully, tested each module, and know what the results ought to be. A suggested table for a test plan is given below.

| Test No | Test Data | Purpose | Expected Result | Comment /Verified |
|---------|-----------|---------|-----------------|-------------------|
| 1 | Enter incorrect password 'ABC' | Test password | Only password 'ABF' accepted | |
| 2 | Enter Customer ID abc | Test invalid digits | Not accepted | |
| 3 | Enter new customer with ID 456, 'Jones K.' | Test 'Add new customer' function | Jones added to database | |

*Figure 34.1: A suggested format for a test plan*

Sometimes it is impossible to show evidence that a test works correctly; in those cases, have your supervisor carry out the test and authenticate the result in the 'Comments/Verified' column. You could also use this column to reference the page number on which your test evidence is shown, or to make notes to yourself of any tests that did not work correctly.

## Selecting tests for the test plan

Try to choose tests that test the more complex aspects of your system, such as calculations, command buttons that perform updating or open up a form with data already in it, and so on. Masses of tests for really trivial validations that are performed automatically by Access (such as a date in the correct format) are fairly pointless.

If, for example, you are testing a mail-merge, it is not necessary to include all the printouts as evidence. A better test would be to see whether your system can insert a new name into the list and then just print out one more letter, rather than printing the whole lot again.

You may well have to amend or add to your initial test plan as the program develops, but you will find it very helpful to have a written plan at all stages, even if you keep adjusting it.

Similarly, if you design your system tests **before** you start coding, you will be forced to think about how this phase will be carried out, what will have to be done to make system testing possible, and how to ensure that it will be successful. The earlier you can foresee any problems, the easier they will be to solve.

## Presenting the test results

Your test results should be presented in an Appendix, and cross-referenced to your test plan. They will normally take the form of test runs, screen dumps and file dumps. You may need to explain exactly what data was input. Use a highlighter pen to emphasise the key point about a screenshot, and annotate the output by hand to show what the test proves. Be selective, and consider it a challenge to make it as easy as possible for a reader to confirm that test results were as expected. As a general rule, include the absolute minimum essential to get the point across.

**Test runs and screenshots with no annotation and no cross-referencing to the test plan are virtually useless!**

*Figure 34.2: Presenting the test results*

# *Chapter 35 – Documentation*

## Introduction

The report that you hand in at the end of your project contains all the evidence of the work you have done over the past few months. No matter how careful your analysis, how appropriate the design, how clever the macros or modules and how thorough the testing; if the written evidence is not there to prove it, you will not achieve a good mark.

**It will take longer than you expect to complete the documentation.** It will pay you to write the documentation in parallel with the other stages of the project and not leave it all to the end. Then, when you have finished the implementation and testing, you will be able to go through it all, proof reading, adding a table of contents, page numbers, and appendices.

Remember that the project is going to be seen by a reader who may have no knowledge of the background to the project. Try to be highly aware of the reader when writing the documentation.

## Should the documentation be word-processed?

The short answer is YES. It should also be thoroughly spell-checked, both using the spell-checking facility provided by the word processor, and by reading it through slowly and carefully.

> They're know miss steaks in my project report cause I used special soft wear witch checked my spelling. However it cannot correct arrows inn punctuation and it will not fined words witch are miss used but spelled rite. An it wont catch the sentence fragments witch you have forgotten to.

*Figure 35.1: Don't rely too heavily on your spell-checker*

## Word-processing skills

There are some crucial word-processing skills which you need to acquire in order to present a really professional-looking final report. This document must do justice to the effort you have so far put into your project; it is all that the examiner will see, and even if you feel you have perhaps not achieved as much as you could have, a well-presented report will help.

Use the Help system to learn new skills, including:

- **Setting styles for the various level of headings and text in your document.** (All the tips below apply to MS Word.) The 'Normal' template comes with built-in styles for Heading 1, Heading 2, Heading 3 and Normal text. You may like to alter the font, size, style and justification of these, or set up new styles of your own.

- **Creating a Table of Contents.** If you have used styles consistently throughout your document, you can create a Table of Contents automatically. Put your cursor where you want the Table of Contents to appear, select Insert, Index and Tables from the menu bar and then select Table of Contents. It can be updated at any time by selecting it and pressing F9.

- **Inserting headers and footers.** The project title and the page number can be placed in either a header or footer. Select  View, Header and Footer from the menu bar.

- **Inserting a page break whenever you want one.** Press Ctrl-Enter.

- **Using numbered points and bullet points.** Use the tools on the toolbar.

- **Creating tab stops.** Never use the space bar to indent; nothing will line up when you print the document. Learn to use the tab stops on the ruler line, and the Tab key (above Caps Lock on the keyboard) to tab.

- **Inserting tables.** Use the Table menu.

- **Inserting screenshots.** When you want to take a screenshot to include in your User Manual, for example, press Alt-Print Screen to copy the current window to the clipboard. Then switch to your Word document and use Edit, Paste.  A better way is to use a screen capture utility program to copy your screens to a file, from where they can be linked to your document using Insert, Picture, From File. Screen capture utilities are available as shareware.

## Putting it all together

Your project documentation should be neatly bound in such a manner that it can be read without a major unbinding job. A ring binder is too large and heavy to be conveniently posted, so investigate the shelves of W.H.Smith or any stationery shop to find something suitable.

**Do not put each page (or several pages together) in a plastic sleeve; it makes the project report heavy, expensive to post, and inconvenient for marking.**

## The title page

The title page should include the title of the project, your name and centre, school or college.  It could also include the date you submitted the project and your candidate number, if appropriate.

## Table of contents

This is a must.  Include in it the sections and numbered subsections, together with page numbers.  Every page in your project should be numbered for easy reference; you can add page numbers by hand at the end to pages of test data, for example.

## Specification

A suggested framework for the Specification section is given at the end of Chapter 32.  You need to make a clear statement of the problem to be solved, with background information.

## Design and Implementation

Headings for the design section are given in Chapter 33.  Your design may change as you learn more about the software you are using, and your documentation needs to reflect this, through the Project Log. Your test strategy should be included in this section. You must aim to show that you have worked out what tests need to be performed and what results you expect. If you number the tests, it will make it easier to cross-reference them to the actual test runs.

# Testing

Testing is a vitally important part of the project. The test data and test plan should all be included in this section. The Testing Section should also contain a test plan analysis to show that it does test all parts of the system. Test runs may be included in an Appendix. **The test runs should be cross-referenced clearly to the test plan**, and be presented in such a way that the reader can see at once what a specific page of output is designed to show. Devising appropriate tests, organising and cross-referencing screen dumps and printed output can take a great deal of time and ingenuity. There is no point including several pages of output with no explanation of what test it relates to or how the output proves that a certain section of the program is working correctly. Make hand-written annotations on the output and use highlighter pen to show significant results.

There is a great temptation to skimp on this section of the project; the feeling is "Right! I've finished the programming and I'm pretty sure it all works. Here's a disk – you try it...". Unfortunately the devising and implementation of the test plan is your job, not the examiner's!

You will also be awarded marks in this section for macro code, if your project has involved writing macros, SQL or other code as part of the customisation of a software package. The listing should be a genuine printout rather than a word-processed document, and should be clearly annotated by hand wherever this helps to explain what is happening. It needs to be made easily understandable, for example by:

- using meaningful variable names;
- stating the purpose of each variable unless it is self-explanatory;
- using comments to state the purpose of each procedure;
- using comments where necessary to explain the logic of a particular section;
- grouping procedures in a logical order so that it is easy to find your way around a long program;
- using indentation to clarify the extent of loops and condition statements;
- using blank lines between procedures to separate them.

**System-generated code such as that produced by wizards or recorded macros should be clearly labelled as such.**

# User manual

This section is aimed entirely at a non-technical user and should use ordinary English rather than 'computer-speak'. For example, do not say 'Boot up the system' when 'Switch on the computer' will achieve the same result.

Presentation is all-important here. Use whatever facilities your word processor has to enhance the appearance of the document, spell-check it carefully and read it through to make sure it flows well and makes sense. It should be a 'stand-alone' document and could even be bound separately from the rest of the project.

Your user manual should include:

- a table of contents;
- an introduction, stating what the system is about and who it is for;
- examples of actual screen displays such as menus, data input screens and output screens;
- samples of printed output;
- an explanation of what each option on a menu does;

- any special instructions on how to input data – for example the format of a date field, or the range of accepted values in an amount field;

- an explanation of any manual procedures such as batching or recording data manually;

- error messages that may be displayed and what to do in that event;

- error recovery procedures – for example what to do if you realise you have made a wrong data entry, or the power goes off in the middle of an update;

- perhaps a hot-line help number.

If you have used a package, explain how to use the system you have created, rather than explaining how to use the software package in general terms. It is a good idea to test out your user manual on the user or a colleague to see if they can follow your instructions without any extra help from you.

## Evaluation

The evaluation is an important part of the project accounting for some 10% of the total mark. It should be clearly related to the list of specific objectives written in the Analysis section. The more clearly you have stated the objectives, the easier it will be to evaluate how well your system achieved them.

If the project has been written for a real user, it is a good idea to include the user's comments in this section, perhaps in the form of a letter written on official headed paper and signed by the user. If any suggestions have been made for amendment or improvement, include these as well, whether or not you have managed to incorporate the suggestions. Add your own suggestions for improvement and possibilities for future development. Do take note that a fake letter from your best friend or a glowing letter from an uncritical parent stating how marvellous your system is, flying in the face of all the evidence, is not likely to gain you any marks.

Be honest about the shortcomings of the project; if it is not complete, maybe this is because it was over-ambitious and you should say so. You will not, however, score many marks for criticising the hardware, software, staff or lack of time. One of the skills to be learned in writing a project is to finish it on time in spite of all the difficulties you may encounter!

*Honesty pays* – if the project has some apparent failures, turn these into successes and gain credit showing what was learnt, documenting what was being attempted, what the outcome was and what difficulties were experienced. Your teacher can authenticate hardware and software difficulties that were beyond your control.

# Appendix A

**AQA Specification Summary**

**Information and Communications Technology**

# Scheme of Assessment – Advanced Subsidiary Level (AS)

The Scheme of Assessment has a modular structure. The AS Level award comprises three compulsory assessment units.

**AS Assessment Units**

| | | |
|---|---|---|
| **Unit 1** | **Written Paper** | **1 ½ hours** |
| *30% of the total AS Level marks* | | |
| **Unit 2** | **Written Paper** | **1 ½ hours** |
| *30% of the total AS Level marks* | | |
| **Unit 3** | **Coursework** | |
| *40% of the total AS Level marks* | *60 marks* | |

# AS Module 1 – Information: Nature, Role and Context

|  | Topic | Amplification | See Chapter |
|---|---|---|---|
| 1.1 | **Knowledge, information and data** | Understand the distinction between knowledge, information and data. Information has context and its meaning is determined by the context.<br><br>Understand the nature of data: recorded facts, events or transactions.<br><br>Understand the different ways in which data can arise; (direct capture or as a by-product of another operation).<br><br>Describe the effect of the quality of the data source on the information produced.<br><br>Understand the need to encode information as data.<br>Understand the problems associated with the coding of value judgements. | 8 |
| 1.2 | **Value and importance of information** | Understand that information is a commodity and as such can have a monetary value, the level of which depends on its accuracy, its potential use and its particular intended use.<br>Describe the overheads involved in ensuring that information is up-to-date and of use to an organisation/individual. | 9 |
| 1.3 | **Control of information** | Describe the legal rights and obligations on holders of personal data to permit access. Understand that the sale of entitlement to access to data may mean paying for a more convenient form of access, the right of which already exists. Understand that files on individuals and on organisations that are non-disclosable have commercial value. | 11 |
| 1.4 | **Capabilities and limitations of information and communication technology** | Understand that ICT systems offer fast repetitive processing, vast storage capability and the facility to search and combine data in many different ways which would otherwise be impossible. | 9 |
|  |  | Understand that the response speed of technology within ICT systems facilitates the use of feedback, e.g. maintenance of optimum stock levels, electronic fund/money management systems. | 9 |
|  |  | Understand that there are limitations in the use of ICT systems and in the information they produce. Factors could include hardware, software and communications limitations in addition to inappropriate data models and data control mechanisms. | 9 |
| 1.5 | **The social impact of information and communication technology** | Explain the benefits and drawbacks of the use of information and communication technology in manufacturing, industry, commerce, medicine, the home and education and teleworking. | 1, 2, 3, 4, 5, 7 |

| | Topic | Amplification | See Chapter |
|---|---|---|---|
| 1.6 | **Role of communication systems** | Explain the use of global communications between single or multiple sources and recipients, including public networks e.g. INTERNET. Describe the hardware, software and services required to access the Internet | 6 |
| | | Describe the facilities offered and the relative merits of: telephone, fax, e-mail, teleconferencing, viewdata, teletext, remote databases and other relevant communication systems. | 6 |
| | | Explain the use of the Internet for a range of activities including communication, information searching and information publication. | 6 |
| | | Candidates should be aware of the recent developments in the area of communication systems. | 6 |
| 1.7 | **Information and the professional** | Recall the personal qualities and general characteristics necessary for a person working effectively within the ICT industry and as part of an ICT team. | 1 |
| 1.8 | **Information systems malpractice & crime** | Explain the consequences of malpractice and crime on information systems. | 10 |
| | | Describe the possible weak points within information technology systems. Describe the measures that can be taken to protect information technology systems against internal and external threats. | 11 |
| | | Describe the particular issues surrounding access to, and use of the Internet; censorship, security, ethics. | |
| 1.9 | **The legal framework** | This section applies to current British legislation and its relationship to the Council of Europe Convention directives. | 11 |
| | **Software and data misuse** | Describe the provisions of the Computer Misuse Act. | 10 |
| | | Describe the principles of software copyright and licensing agreements. | |
| | **Data protection legislation** | Recall the nature, purpose and provisions of the current data protection legislation of the Public Register. | 12 |
| | | Recall the type of data covered and various exemptions from the legislation. | |
| | | Recall the definitions of processing and consent to process. | |
| | | Explain how the requirements of the legislation impact on data collection and use. | |
| | | Describe the obligations of data users under the legislation. | |
| | | Recall the rights of individuals under the legislation. | |
| | | Recall the role of the Registrar in encouraging good practice, acting as Ombudsman and enforcing legislation. | |
| 1.10 | **Health and Safety** | Describe the provisions of the current health and safety legislation in relation to the use of information systems. | 13 |
| | | Recognise that health and safety guidelines cover the design and introduction of new software. | |

# AS Module 2 – Information: Management and Manipulation

|  | Topic | Amplification | See Chapter |
|---|---|---|---|
| 2.1 | **Data capture** | Describe methods of data capture and identify appropriate contexts for their use. Understand the concept of data encoding. | 15 |
| 2.2 | **Verification and validation** | Understand the distinction between accuracy of information and validity of data. | 16 |
|  |  | Explain possible sources and types of error in data capture, transcription, transmission and processing. Describe methods of preventing and reducing such methods. |  |
|  |  | Describe appropriate validation techniques for various types of data process, from data capture to report generation. |  |
| 2.3 | **Organisation of data for effective retrieval** | Describe the nature and purpose of a relational database and how it works. | 17 19 |
|  |  | Understand that data needs to be organised in a database to allow for effective updating and retrieval. Understand how data can be retrieved to produce meaningful information. |  |
|  |  | Recall the relevant advantages of relational databases over flat file information storage and retrieval systems. | 18 |
|  |  | Select and justify appropriate file and database structures for particular applications. |  |
| 2.4 | **Software; nature, capabilities and limitations** | Describe the need for interfacing with peripherals storage devices, input and output devices and display devices; describe the need for printer and other peripheral drivers. | 28 |
|  | **Nature and types of software** | Describe the distinction between systems software and applications software; the purposes of operating systems. | 20, 21 |
|  |  | Describe the nature of package software, generic and specific, and of bespoke software. Describe the general characteristics of generic packages and the integration of objects and facilities for processing data protocols and standards. | 22, 23 22 |
|  |  | Describe the functionality offered by software which provides access to the Internet. |  |
|  | **Capabilities of software** | Describe the desirable features of packages that would be appropriate to particular users and activities such as: links to other packages; search facilities; macro capabilities; application generators; editing capabilities; ability to change or extend data and record structures; short access times; data portability and upgrade paths | 23 |
|  | **Upgradability** | Explain the technical and human implications of package change/upgrade. | 23 |

| | Topic | Amplification | See Chapter |
|---|---|---|---|
| | **Reliability** | Explain the difficulties of thoroughly testing complex software. | 23 |
| 2.5 | **Manipulation and/or processing** | Describe the different modes of operation; batch, interactive, transaction, real-time and identify appropriate contexts for their use. | 24 |
| | | Describe the characteristics of processing data in the form of text, pictures, numbers and sound. | 25 |
| 2.6 | **Dissemination/ distribution** | Describe the need for suitable output formats and orderings to communicate the results of data interrogation and undertake report generation. | 19, 22 |
| 2.7 | **Hardware; nature, capabilities and limitations** | Describe the broad characteristics, capabilities and limitations of current input devices, storage devices, communications devices, processing devices and output devices and identify appropriate contexts for their use. | 14, 15, 26, 28 |
| 2.8 | **Security of data** | Understand the importance of and the mechanisms for maintaining data security.  Describe the distinction between security and privacy. | 27 |
| | | Understand simple processes that protect the integrity of data against malicious or accidental alteration; standard clerical procedures, passwords, levels of permitted access, write protect mechanisms, backup procedures, restoration and recovery procedures. | |
| | **Backup systems** | Understand the need for regular and systematic backup and procedures for recovery. | 27 |
| 2.9 | **Network environments** | Describe the characteristics and relative advantages of network and stand-alone environments. | 29 |
| | | Describe the difference between a Local Area Network (LAN)and a Wide Area Network (WAN). Describe the required elements of network environments including hardware, software, communications and topology. | |
| 2.10 | **Human/ Computer interface** | Understand the need to facilitate an effective dialogue between humans and machines. | 30 |
| | | Explain the need to design systems which are appropriate to users at all levels and in different environments; the impact of clarity of structure and layout. | |
| | | Describe how the user-interface can be designed for effective communication with the user. | |
| | | Describe the advantages of common user interfaces between different generic application packages. | |
| | | Describe the advantages and limitations of a natural language interface. | |

# AS Module 3 – Coursework

## The Use of Generic Application Software for Task Solution

For the AS Module 3 candidates will be required to undertake a project.

For this project the candidate will be expected to tackle a task-related problem which will have a limited scope and will be a self-contained problem. The solution is very likely to be based on the facilities of one piece of generic software but the candidate is encouraged to use other software tools and objects as appropriate to complete the solution.

It is not within the spirit of this syllabus for a candidate to use a stand-alone general purpose programming language.

The problems could be set by the candidate's teacher who will then act as the end-user or by a real end-user. To help with authentication of the candidate's work, if the same problem is given to more than one candidate, it must be tailored individually by the candidate to allow for differentiated outcomes.

To gain high marks the candidate will be expected to provide a detailed solution specification. This solution should reflect the use of advanced generic and package specific skills. It is desirable that a project log be included so that the candidate can show their approach to the solution and the development of the solution with regard to the use of alternative techniques and tools.

## Assessment Criteria

### Assessment of project work

It is necessary to provide a structure for the assessment of project work so that all teachers are, in general, following a common procedure. Such a procedure will assist with the standardisation of assessment from centre to centre. Each project is therefore to be assessed in accordance with the criteria set out below. In assessing candidates, centres must ensure that comparable standards are observed between different teaching groups. Each centre must produce a single order of merit for the centre as a whole.

### Criteria for the assessment of Unit 3

The following categories are to be used in the assessment of the project. The criteria for marking these categories are listed below. The project is marked out of a total of 60.

| | |
|---|---|
| Specification | 13 marks |
| Implementation | 20 marks |
| User Testing | 12 marks |
| Evaluation | 6 marks |
| User Documentation | 9 marks |
| **Total** | **60 marks** |

# Specification (13 marks)

| | |
|---|---|
| **11-13** | A detailed requirements specification has been produced for the identified problem, which matches the needs of the stated end-user(s). |
| | The input, processing and output needs, which match the requirements specification, are clearly stated. |
| | Effective designs have been completed which would enable an independent third party to implement the solution. |
| | An appropriate test strategy has been determined.  An effective test and full testing plan has been devised.  The testing plan includes the test data and expected outcomes and directly relates to the requirements specification. |
| **8-10** | A detailed requirements specification has been produced for the identified problem, which matches the needs of the stated end-user(s). |
| | The input, processing and output needs, which match the requirements specification, are stated. |
| | Designs have been completed but lack detail so as not to allow an independent third part implementation of the solution or, are inefficient in relation to the problem stated. |
| | A test strategy has been determined and testing plan have been devised but are limited in scope or do not relate to the requirements specification stated. |
| **4-7** | A requirements specification has been produced for the identified problem but does not fully match the needs of the stated end-user(s) or lacks detail and clarity. |
| | The input, processing and output needs are stated but do not fully match the requirements' specification or are not sufficiently clear. |
| | Design work has been attempted but is incomplete and does not reflect an efficient solution to the problem stated. |
| | A test strategy has been determined but is either incomplete or does not relate to the requirements specification stated.  The testing plan is either vague or missing. |
| **1-3** | The requirements specification is vague or missing. |
| | The input, processing and output needs are only vaguely considered or are absent. |
| | There is little or no design effort. |
| | The test strategy and testing plan are vague or missing. |
| **0** | The candidate has produced no work. |

# Implementation (20 marks)

| | |
|---|---|
| **16-20** | An effective solution has been developed which is operable in the proposed environment by the intended end-user.<br><br>Appropriate data capture and validation procedures, data organisation methods, output contents and formats and user interface(s) have been used.<br><br>Generic and package specific skills have been fully employed in an effective and appropriate manner.<br><br>The selection of the chosen hardware and software facilities has been fully justified in relation to the solution developed. |
| **11-15** | A solution has been developed which is operable in the proposed environment by the intended end-user but has some inefficiencies.<br><br>There is evidence of the use of some appropriate data capture and validation procedures, data organisation methods, output contents and formats and user interface(s).<br><br>Generic and package specific skills have been fully employed but not always in an effective and appropriate manner.<br><br>The selection of some of the chosen hardware and software facilities has been justified in relation to the solution developed. |
| **6-10** | A partial solution has been developed, but those aspects completed are useable by the intended end-user.<br><br>There is some evidence of the use of some data capture and validation procedures, data organisation methods, output contents and formats and user interface(s).<br><br>Generic and package specific skills have been employed but not always in an effective and appropriate manner.<br><br>The selection of some of the chosen hardware and software facilities has been only vaguely justified in relation to the solution developed. |
| **1-5** | A solution has been developed which is very limited and is not practically operable in the proposed environment by the intended end-user.<br><br>Few, if any, data capture and validation procedures, data organisation methods, output contents and formats and user interface(s) have been used.<br><br>The generic and package specific skills used are simplistic and/or were not always applied appropriately.<br><br>The selection of the chosen hardware and software facilities are not justified in relation to the solution developed. |
| **0** | The candidate has not implemented the system. |

# Testing (12 marks)

| 9-12 | The test strategy and test plan previously devised have now been followed in a systematic manner using typical, erroneous and extreme (boundary) data. |
| --- | --- |
| | The results of testing are fully documented with outputs cross-referenced to the original plan. |
| | Corrective action taken due to test results is clearly documented. |
| 5-8 | The test strategy and plan devised have been followed in a systematic manner but using only normal data. |
| | The results of testing are partially documented with some evidence of outputs cross-referenced to the original plan. |
| | There is some evidence of corrective action taken in response to test results. |
| 1-4 | The test strategy and plan devised have been followed in a limited manner using only normal data. |
| | There is little or no documentation of the results of testing. |
| | There is little or no indication of corrective action required due to test results. |
| 0 | There is no evidence of testing. |

# Evaluation (6 marks)

| 4-6 | The effectiveness of the solution in meeting the detailed requirements specification has been fully assessed with the candidate showing full awareness of the criteria for a successful information technology solution. |
| --- | --- |
| | The limitations of the solution have been clearly identified. |
| 1-3 | The effectiveness of the solution in meeting the original requirements specifications has only been partly assessed with the candidate showing only partial awareness of the criteria for a successful information technology solution. |
| | The limitations of the solution are vague or have been omitted. |
| 0 | There is no evidence of evaluation. |

# User Documentation (9 marks)

| 7-9 | There is extensive user documentation for the solution which covers all relevant aspects including normal operation and common problems and is appropriate to the needs of the end-user. |
| --- | --- |
| 4-6 | A user guide is included, which describes the functionality of the solution and is appropriate to the needs of the end-user. |
| 1-3 | A limited user guide is included which describes only the basic functionality of the solution. |
| 0 | There is no evidence of user documentation. |

# Appendix B

**Book List**

# *Book List*

The following books have been invaluable in the preparation of this text and are a useful source of information for staff and students. All prices are approximate, as obviously they tend to increase over time.

## General texts

Laudon, Kenneth et al. **Information Technology and Society** (1994) International Thomson Publishing. ISBN 0-534-19512-1 £21.95

*An excellent American textbook which deserves to be on the library shelf of every school and college offering A Level I.T. Too long and detailed to be used as a student text but a wonderful reference book. Weighing in at 3lbs, too heavy for the average student's schoolbag.*

Parsons J and Oja D  **Computer Concepts (3$^{rd}$ edition)** (1998) Course Technology ISBN 0 7600 5500 9 £20.95

*Another useful American text, beautifully illustrated. A good reference book covering a large part of the syllabus in a rather roundabout way.*

Stern, Nancy and Stern, Robert  **Computing in the Information Age** (1996) John Wiley and Sons Inc. ISBN 0-471-11061-2  £20.00

*An excellent American text, beautifully illustrated. A good reference book covering a large part of the syllabus in a rather roundabout way. Includes a CD-ROM.*

## Books for specific topics

Barrett, Neil **Digital Crime** (1997) Kogan Page Limited ISBN 0-7494-2097-9 £12

*Written by an ex-hacker with a rather poor grasp of English grammar, but who is nevertheless extremely knowledgeable on all aspects of computer crime and the law. An interesting read.*

Bawa, Joanna **The Computer User's Health Handbook** (1994) Souvenir Press ISBN 0-285-63207-8 £10.99

*Well-written, informative reference book covering all aspects of Health and Safety for computer users. A good chapter on user interfaces.*

Cavoukian, Ann **Who Knows** (1997) McGraw Hill ISBN 0-07-063320-7 £18

*A good book on privacy issues in the computer age.*

Evans, Alastair **Data Protection Policies and Practice** (1987) Institute of Personnel Management ISBN 0 85292 385 6 £10

*A very thorough treatment of the Data Protection Act and all its implications, with guidelines for security policies as implemented in various organisations such as B.P. and Kodak.*

Kallman E.A. and Grillo J.P. **Ethical Decision-making and Information Technology** (1993) McGraw-Hill ISBN 0-07-033884-1 £14.95

*A fascinating book on ethics in computing, with 18 case studies illustrating all manner of ethical dilemmas, excellent for class use. A good book to order for the library.*

Whitehorn, Mark and Marklyn, Bill **Inside Relational Databases** (1998) Springer ISBN 3 540 76092 X £19.50

*Excellent book on database theory with examples in Access. Highly recommended.*

# Index

*Also from Payne-Gallway:*

## Successful ICT Projects in Word (2nd edition)

*by P.M.Heathcote*
February 2000        208pp        ISBN 1 903112 25 7

It gives ideas for suitable projects and explains how to complete each phase from Analysis and Design through to Implementation, Testing and Evaluation. AQA Project Guidelines and a mark scheme are included in an Appendix. This text, updated for the 2001 syllabus and Office 2000, covers the essential features of Word from basic editing and formatting right through to advanced features such as templates, macros, customised toolbars and menus. It is suitable for students on a number of courses such as 'A' Level or AVCE ICT, HNC and HND in Business Information Technology and Access to HE.

## Successful ICT Projects in Excel (3rd edition)

*by P.M. Heathcote*
May 2002        208pp        ISBN 1 903112 71 0

Excel is a powerful and versatile spreadsheet program which is eminently suitable for project work at every level from AVCE to degree work. This book is also invaluable for staff development, and caters for users of Excel 2002, 2000 or 97.

A sample project demonstrates how to lay out a complete project report, and the AQA project mark scheme is also included. The template for the sample project as well as a sample chapter entitled 'Project Ideas' are available on the web site www.payne-gallway.co.uk

## Successful ICT Projects in Access (3rd edition)

*by P.M. Heathcote*
August 2002        224pp        ISBN 1 903112 73 7

This book will help students to complete a project in MS Access, using version 2002, 2000 or 97. It covers database design, creating tables, forms and subforms, queries, importing and exporting data to other packages, analysing and processing data, reports, macros and some Visual Basic for Applications. It includes advice on choice of projects and a sample project.

It is suitable for students on a wide range of courses such as 'A' Level or AVCE ICT, HNC and HND in Business Information Technology and Access to HE.

## Successful ICT Projects in FrontPage (2nd edition)

*by R.S.U. Heathcote*
June 2002        208pp        ISBN 1 903112 68 0

This book will help students on an 'A' Level, GNVQ or similar course to design and implement a web site using MS FrontPage 2002 or 2000. It assumes no previous knowledge of FrontPage and takes the reader from the basics such as entering, editing and formatting text and images on a Web page through to advanced features such as writing scripts, gathering data from forms, and making use of active components. A wide range of examples is used to illustrate the different facilities of FrontPage, and a sample project shows students how to tackle and document each stage of project work.